FAITH
AND
MONEY

A PRACTICAL
THEOLOGY

Chad E. Cunningham

with Howard Dayton

FIRST EDITION

ISBN 978-1-56427-178-1

September 2007 edition

FOREWORD

Over the past three decades I have been teaching and writing on biblical stewardship principles—not merely fund-raising techniques but how money impacts faith in our Lord Jesus Christ. It has become apparent that while strides have been made in educating certain segments of the population regarding biblical stewardship, a void remains in teaching future generations.

The need for the next generation of students to have academically appropriate and student-friendly materials that focus on the connection between faith and money is clear. The Faith and Money: A Practical Theology textbook/curriculum fills that gap through a theologically sound, integrative, and balanced approach amid a myriad of extreme positions.

Since Chad Cunningham arrived on Biola University's campus three years ago to teach biblical principles of stewardship, we have developed a great relationship, and I have come to respect him. Chad's pioneering leadership, teaching and scholarship on our campus is filling this void of stewardship education for generations to come. This textbook/curriculum is a big step in spreading the impact.

Crown Financial Ministries uniquely speaks into the subject of faith and money with continued credibility beyond Larry Burkett through Howard Dayton and Chad Cunningham. I believe Larry is pleased to see this new emphasis of reaching students with a biblical understanding of being a steward.

Your heart and mind will be engaged through this material in such a way that your actions will reflect greater devotion and growth in Christ.

WESLEY K. WILLMER

ACKNOWLEDGEMENTS

My prayer is that God receives the glory for this course. It grew out of the *Biblical Financial Study* for small groups written by Howard Dayton, CEO of Crown Financial Ministries, and incorporates material from it.

I thank my wife, Stephanie, for her wise insight and encouragement through the writing process. Many thanks to Crown Financial Ministries Senior Vice Presidents Chuck Bentley and James Massa for giving me freedom from other responsibilities to develop this curriculum.

To Dr. Dennis Dirks, Dean of Talbot School of Theology, and the entire faculty I owe a debt of gratitude for welcoming me and Crown Financial Ministries into their midst and encouraging me throughout this endeavor. Specifically, I thank Dr. Mick Boresma, and Dr. Klaus Issler for their personal encouragement. I thank Dr. Wes Willmer, Vice President of Advancement, BIOLA University, for his commitment to stewardship education in universities and for his helpful counsel, affirmation, and encouragement. I appreciate my friend and fellow laborer John Krutsinger for his encouragement and help with Scripture references. I thank Russell Stevens, who co-labors with me to reach students with God's life-changing message of True Financial Freedom, for his encouragement and willingness to review the materials. I also thank Drs. Sid and Donna Ward for their insights as educators on the early manuscript.

Dr. Shelly Cunningham's (no relation) peer review of the curriculum helped ensure quality and educational suitability.

And last but certainly not least, I thank Steve Gardner for his editorial skills and gentle spirit as he helped me make the content more readable.

I (Chad) dedicate this book to my father, Lyle Cunningham, who constantly models perseverance under incredible circumstances and who gave up so much to be there for me. Your example and encouragement have enabled me to persevere.

CHAD CUNNINGHAM 2006

PREFACE

The purpose of this book is to explore the theological and practical aspects of faith and money from a Christian perspective and to integrate them into life.

The *Faith and Money: A Practical Theology* curriculum is offered in two versions, each with its own syllabus in the accompanying Study Guide. Version A is an undergrad 15-week traditional three-credit-hour university course. Version B is a seminary level three-credit-hour course in a two-week intensive class setting.

Whether you are using this book for academic credit or for personal growth, we pray that the Holy Spirit will use God's Word to conform you to the image of Christ.

HOW TO USE THIS BOOK

We recommend using sections four and five as study tools while reading this book. The appendixes contain charts that will help visual learners grasp the concepts more quickly.

Those who use this course in a non-credit setting can choose from among several levels of involvement. From lowest to highest:

Simply read the text and glean helpful principles and concepts.

Second, combine reading and interacting with the "Think About It" sections at the end of each chapter. Follow along with the appendixes in Part IV Study Tools.

Third, read and follow along with the weekly readings, projects, and Bible study as laid out in one of the course syllabi in Part V: Curriculum and Study Guide. One of the most practical projects you could incorporate is a personal journal. Throughout the text there will be opportunities for you to stop to think, read passages and respond. You can write your thoughts in the margins of the book or in a separate journal notebook.

Fourth, in addition to the above, we recommend the nine chapter articles listed in the "supplemental readings" section of either syllabus. You can also review the selected bibliography for additional helpful resources.

TABLE OF CONTENTS

PART I

Introduction and Foundations

OVERVIEW

Chapter one asks and answers the question: Why is faith and money an important topic to study? Chapter two considers the impact of money on life. Chapter three defines a steward and offers a proper perspective on faith and money. Chapter four presents a broad theological construct for wealth along with practical implications. Chapter five explores the impact materialism has on spirituality. Section one concludes with Chapter six, an exposition of 1 Timothy 6:3-10 as a foundational passage for the remainder of the study.

CHAPTER ONE

Conceptualizing: Why Is Money Important?

Core Concepts

- What are the five key reasons set forth in the text for studying faith and money?

- Explain the money dichotomy of Aristotle and Thomas Aquinas and its influence on modern thinking.

- List the four reasons why money is important to God.

Overview

This chapter focuses on reasons to study money in relation to our faith, some implications for future church leadership, and the importance of the subject to God.

MONEY, MONEY, MONEY

Get Rich or Die Tryin' is a recent Hollywood film depiction of what people will do in the pursuit of wealth and power. Although most people would avoid openly voicing the sentiment reflected in the movie title, they feel its cultural pressure. From *The Apprentice*, to *Survivor*, to *Fear Factor*, to casinos, sports betting, and the lottery, many people passionately pursue riches. Greed is neither rare nor new; we can trace it all the way back to the fall (Genesis 3-4).

Where does godliness fit into our consumptive lifestyle—arguably the most affluent in history? To grow in relationship with God as we engage and transform culture rather than embrace it, we need to understand what God says about money.

What we do with money reflects the values of our heart. Unexamined assumptions sometimes obscure the discrepancy between how we use money and biblical teachings about significance, idolatry, happiness, greed, honesty, hard work, and covetousness. If we believe Scripture reveals God's will for our lives, we will eagerly study how biblical truth intersects with our use of money and possessions.

Jesus said, *"Where your treasure is, there your heart will be also"* (Matthew 6:21-24). Identifying our treasure is a heart issue: one that determines whether our loyalty resides in what we possess or in the One who has saved us from darkness. Although this is only one of many teachings by Jesus on money and possessions, it alone is sufficient to prove the importance of money to the soul.

Time and space require us to limit the scope of our study in this course. Social justice and business-related finance are examples of topics we will not undertake. Our goal is to help you personally integrate faith and money from a biblical perspective.

Pride, ignorance, or lack of training?

Have you ever wondered how the vision God has given you for your life or ministry will be funded? Have you ever thought that money might be a spiritual issue? Did you know that there are churches in America whose income exceeds their budgets without pressuring or manipulating their congregations? Are you convinced that finding significance and happiness in our culture of affluence is possible without the pursuit of wealth? Many people have resolved these issues and achieved true financial freedom; many more have not.

Some pastors avoid the discussion of money for fear of offending or alienating others.[1] There is indication from the Reluctant Steward[2] study that some avoid it out of fear that their own financial mismanagement will be exposed. The lack of seminary training on a theology of money is another likely cause for weak emphasis from the pulpit. Even personal pride, which resists correction and accountability, probably plays a role.

The war is waged in subtle but profound assumptions we have absorbed from our culture—assumptions the Bible clearly corrects if we have the eyes to see it. Who is the true owner? Who is in control? Who retains the responsibility to provide for our needs? Who gives people the strength and abilities to earn money? Can we make eternally wise decisions about our treasures without basing them on God's perspective?

Unfortunately, many people separate the topics of money and business from anything related to their spiritual life or service within their church.[3] This dichotomy seems to be rooted in the teachings of several key thinkers in church history. In general, the influence of Aristotle and Thomas Aquinas's dualism is felt in how wealth is perceived. They segregated the physical world, including wealth and any other worldly things, from the spiritual world. This resulted in people thinking that spirituality was distinct from, and at odds with, the practical issues of life. When the attainment of spiritual union with God is seen as a denunciation of all things physical, wealth may be treated with disdain. In this archetype, life becomes a struggle to mortify all desire of wealth and avoid any attachments to it. This antagonistic extreme becomes anti-Christian as it condemns money rather than the love of it.[4] Instead of avoiding the subject of money as either irrelevant or evil, Jesus clearly understood that our spiritual and moral development require a proper understanding of it.

It is ironic that while some in the church condemn money as evil, others coerce and manipulate their congregations as if money were their god—the answer to everything. This duplicity makes the mere mention of money a very sensitive issue for churches.

A majority of pastors take a more reasoned approach as they gingerly suggest the practice of tithing. What we need is the recognition that God is just as concerned with our management of the other 90 percent of our income—and that he provides instructions for us to be successful in that stewardship.

Those who have been taught the principles of giving and financial faithfulness often assume that everyone has the benefit of their knowledge. They are shocked when confronted with current statistics from George Barna's research.[5] Mainline believers give, as a percentage of gross income, less than three percent! The giving of evangelical believers hovers around four percent. However important the issue of giving is, being a faithful steward involves more than that single facet.

When we avoid dealing with finances to focus on "real" biblical issues, we overlook the Bible's emphasis on the subject. There may be *no subject more substantive in the sanctification process than that of how we handle money and possessions.*[6] It is possible to understand theological concepts and have biblical knowledge but have little or no growth in the Christian life, especially in the area of personally applying scriptural principles related to money.[7] A key to unlocking a deeper personal relationship with Christ is applying what He teaches us about financial faithfulness. Our bank statements become one the most reliable indicators of our true devotion.

We study Scripture not merely to learn theological concepts but to apply them to life in the process of conforming to the image of Christ. Accordingly, what you get out of this course will be determined by how you apply the knowledge you acquire in it. The Apostle James says, *"But prove yourselves doers of the word, and not merely hearers who delude themselves. For if anyone is a hearer of the word and not a doer, he is like a man who looks at his natural face in a mirror; for once he has looked at himself and gone away, he has immediately forgotten what kind of person he was. But one who looks intently at the perfect law, the law of liberty, and **abides** by it, not having become a forgetful hearer but an **effectual doer**, this man will be blessed in what he does"* (James 1:22-25, NAS, emphasis mine).

Our life impact hinges on this personal character issue: What we say and what we do must coincide. That is integrity.

In every time and culture, believers have had to confront the difficulty of living as Christians in societies where money was a means of selfish gain, power, and manipulation. Tragically, there is often little practical difference between the lifestyles of believers and non-believers. The challenge for believers is to learn how to live for Christ within our culture of affluence.[8] This course is designed to equip you for that challenge.

Statistical data

Consider the future of today's students. A recent survey noted that young adults (ages 18-24) scored higher than any other age group for potential money abuse and debt. Most current college students possess a minimum of four credit cards and hold a balance on those cards of over $3,000. Additionally, most graduating college students will enter the work force carrying an average debt baggage of nearly $18,900 in student loans.[9] This generation is so deeply in debt that giving to the cause of Christ will most likely take a back seat to their debt repayment plans. Have I just described you or someone you know? If God has a significant plan for your life to impact the world for Christ—and we know He does—how will you serve Him if you are enslaved to debt?

The future of our church leadership

Consider the plight of many seminary students and pastors. The Christian Stewardship Association estimates that over 90 percent of pastors are not equipped to teach on money issues. A study of seminary students conducted by Auburn Theological Seminary[10] revealed that seminary students graduate with an average debt exceeding eight percent of their gross income—a staggering ratio. As young pastors accept debt as necessary and normal, they undercut their ability to become change agents.

The implications are profound. Although other professionals graduate with the anticipation of significant incomes, how will young pastors, with relatively modest incomes, repay these loans? Most of their debt repayment takes 10 to 15 years, with interest charges that add thousands of dollars.

Because of their personal and school debt, many pastors feel compelled to look for higher paying jobs, abandoning the ones to which they had felt called by God. If our pastors are increasingly willing to burden themselves financially, how will they equip their congregations to be free to serve, give, and live for Christ?

IMPORTANCE OF MONEY AND FAITH TO GOD

Money in Scripture

Money issues are extremely important to God. The sheer volume of His communication to us on the subject is proof of His concern. The Bible contains over 2.350 verses related to money and possessions. Sixteen out of the 49 parables and approximately one out of every six verses in the Gospels relate to money! This alone should tell us that God correlates the issues of money and our spiritual development. He provides us with a blueprint for handling this potentially dangerous issue of our spiritual lives.

Spiritual development

How we handle money is a direct reflection of our spiritual walk with Christ. Jesus Himself said that we cannot serve both God and mammon. The question becomes, who is lord of our hearts? Randy Alcorn pushes this idea further saying, "Just as Jesus gauged Zacchaeus' true spiritual condition by his willingness to part with his money, He gauged this rich young ruler's true spiritual condition by his unwillingness to part with his money. Jesus sees our heart and soul, and He knows us just as well as He knew those two men. The principle is timeless: There is a powerful relationship between our true spiritual condition and our attitudes and actions concerning money and possessions."[11]

As you consider those two men, an important question for you to answer is, "How would you have responded?"

Our attitudes about money affect every area of our lives, including our relationships to God, ourselves, family, the body of Christ, and our culture. Our challenge is to understand how God would have us think and behave in a way that is consistent with His will in our fallen world.

> ### *Think about it*
> - *What in your background hinders you from handling money from a biblical perspective?*
> - *Pride, ignorance, and lack of training are mentioned as reasons for not considering the topic of faith and money. With which do you identify most and why?*
> - *Page 12 contains this statement: "What we do with money reflects the values of our heart." Take some time now to assess how your use of money reflects the values of your heart. Journal your discoveries. What changes should you ask God to help you make? List them.*
> - *Our emotions play a significant role in how we use money. What emotions do you experience with regard to earning, spending, saving, giving and borrowing? List them. Can you identify any emotional issues that might need adjustment? If so, add them to your prayer list.*
> - *Without looking at the rest of this text or the concordance in your Bible, list every verse you remember that deals with money or possessions. Write them out as well as you can, even if you remember only a phrase. Come back to this question as you progress through the rest of the text.*

CHAPTER TWO

Impact of Money on Life

Core Concepts

- According to the author, what are the six areas of life impacted by money?

- List the seven statistics that provide insight into believers and money.

Overview

This chapter focuses on areas of our lives impacted by money and some sobering statistics regarding money and faith.

AREAS OF LIFE IMPACTED BY MONEY

Our relationship with God

Although the bulk of this curriculum presents biblical principles for the management of money and possessions, the heart of it rests on the issue of trust. We will confront Scriptures that give us a more accurate picture of who God is. We will also get a clearer picture of what He wants for us—and from us. That requires us to make a decision. Do we trust Him?

Without a deepening of trust, there can be no growth in a relationship. When something happens that substantially increases our level of trust, we gain security and intimacy.

God pleads with us to trust Him. Proverbs 3:5-10 says, "*Trust in the Lord with all your heart and lean not on your own understanding; in all your ways acknowledge him, and he will make your paths straight. Do not be wise in your own eyes; fear the Lord and shun evil. This will bring health to your body and nourishment to your bones. Honor the Lord with your wealth, with the firstfruits of all your crops; then your barns will be filled to overflowing, and your vats will brim over with new wine.*"

Not only does God ask us to trust Him, He tests us every day in little ways, changing one element or another so that the test never seems quite the same. Sometimes He moves away slightly, not to become distant or lose intimacy with us but so that we can become closer than ever as our trust deepens.

One of the most important moments in the life of believers occurs when they first realize their lack of trust—when it dawns on them that their glib response to the question of trust is partly a false assumption. Since conversion, they have always assumed that they trusted God. With their finances, however, the natural tendency of fallen humanity is to rely on themselves rather than God. If they do not understand His ownership, they will not really trust His control or promise of provision.

When believers say they trust God but stop short of obeying Him, their trust is in critical condition. The second chapter of James hammers the inseparability of faith and deeds. Verse 17 provides a summary statement: "*Faith by itself, if it is not accompanied by action, is dead.*"

Giving is an example of an action prompted by trust. Why might we choose not to give? The simple answer is fear—fear that we will not be able to afford it, that God is not in control or that He will not provide. Every increase in trust is accompanied by an increase in security and intimacy.

Our recognition of true self-worth

a. *Identity in Christ:* Understanding Christ's atoning work and our identity in Him enables us to live as stewards. Only as we recognize that everything has been reconciled in and through Christ can we understand true contentment in His sustaining power (Colossians 1:19-20). Money can hinder a proper understanding of who we are and what produces true value (Luke 12:13-34, 16:1-15; James 4:1-4).

Money can be a false god. The Old Testament provides numerous examples of God's people replacing Him with idols. Hosea describes them as idol worshippers, exchanging trust in the true God for hope in graven images and the pleasures of hedonism. The book of Exodus reveals the people of Israel making a golden calf and worshipping it. We, too, can fall into serving false gods—money and possessions—by measuring our worth in terms of possessions or earning power.

Our true worth must be found in the only true God. In Christ, we are reconciled to Him and have eternal life. When we live in obedience to Him, we may find some significance in what we earn, possess, or do, but it does not provide our identity or worth.

b. *Filling the heart's void:* We all struggle with this issue at some level, hoping that either more money or new purchases will fill a chronic emptiness. But more money does not result in less trouble; it often increases it. More money means more possessions over which to worry.[1] And the emotional rush that accompanies a new purchase is a temporary pleasure that soon degrades to the status quo or even makes things worse if the purchase is unwise. Christ's offer of an abundant life includes the contentment necessary to fill a hole that will never be satisfied by more stuff.

c. *Slaves to someone else:* Misuse of money and credit cripples the fulfillment of God's purpose in our lives, making us slaves to creditors rather than to God. We find ourselves buying things we do not need, with money we do not have, to impress people we don't even like.[2] Only God can give us a perspective that values the enduring, the eternal, over the glitter of fool's gold that will soon be consumed in His furnace. Since He calls us to be His slaves with a destiny of ultimate glory, we guard our affections, refusing to become slaves of anything less.

Our relationship with family

Consider how money impacts our response to family in the way we make decisions and spend our time.

a. *Decisions*: How does our thinking about money influence career decisions? The lure of a higher salary may obscure the relational consequences when families move thousands of miles away from their extended family. This is not to imply that salary is unimportant but to acknowledge that it frequently usurps the role of primary determinant.

The story of Joseph provides a great picture of God enhancing the career of a faithful servant. When we understand, as Joseph did, that God is in control of our personal and financial well being, we make decisions based on values that transcend money alone.

b. *Time*: Too much time at work means the family always loses. Paraphrasing Pastor Andy Stanley in his book, *Choosing to Cheat*, success in business is more often the result of opportunity—being at the right place at the right time or because of a vital connection—that the volume of hours invested. The opposite, however, is true with the family unit; it takes more time, not mere opportunity, to make it successful. When we are too focused on making money or spending more time at work to pay the bills, everyone pays.

Our relationship with our spouse

Topping the list of problems in most marriages is the challenge of finances. Often cited as a leading cause in divorce, money disputes produce more than smoke. Sparks burst into flames, and people get hurt.

a. *Communication*: Many couples enter marriage with some counseling, but few of them receive any help in financial matters. They are naively unaware that money is likely to become the greatest potential communication barrier in their marriage.

People enter marriage with certain presuppositions about how to get and spend their resources. Each partner has a set of "normals," expectations for how things get done, what is important, etc., derived from previous family experience. Accompanying these normals is the assumption that everyone else's normals are the same. Unfortunately, most couples are comprised of individuals with very different normals. Effective communication enables them to adjust to each other's values in a way that creates a new unified normal. In the absence of such communication, financial issues can become explosive. Or they can smolder, sometimes for years, before erupting like Mount St. Helens. Any financial problem—overspending, manipulative spending, debt abuse, inattention—increases with lack of communication and threatens marital harmony.

b. *Respect:* Both spouses need a voice in money decisions. When one is left out, whether intentionally or not, respect is lost. Speaking to men, Ephesians 5:25 reminds us to love our wives as Christ loved the church. One of the most tangible ways for men to love their wives is to involve them in financial decisions. Valuing their insights can prevent the financial disasters that would otherwise accompany the elevated increased risk tolerance of many men. Productive discussions build mutual respect and prepare both partners to handle emergencies—including the unexpected death of a spouse. Working together on the spending plan also helps to ensure that it is both fair and realistic. This is a very practical part of love.

Ephesians 5:33 directs wives to respect their husbands. They do this by shopping responsibly, treating credit with care and, if they handle the books, by including their husbands in financial decisions.

Our relationship with our children

As a dad, I am sobered to see how often our children reflect our character and repeat our behavior. They learn from our actions, including our spending and borrowing patterns. Paraphrasing Howard Hendricks, without vision there is no success. Vision without a plan is useless. Without successors, there is no success.[3] Parents have a responsibility to create an environment of success for their children, teaching them how to earn, give, save, and wisely spend the resources God gives them. This course lays the foundation for understanding God's blueprint for your finances, starting you on that multigenerational journey.

Our relationship with the church body

a. *Service:* Service to the body of Christ is either enhanced or hindered by our use of money and possessions. Indebtedness limits our availability. When we increase our work hours to pay off debt, we lose both time and energy to use our gifts in service.

b. *Giving:* Randy Alcorn has put it well, saying, "God does not increase your salary to raise your standard of living. He increases your salary to raise your standard of giving." When we abuse money, the body of Christ suffers. When a raise comes, our first thoughts of what we can buy with it often dwarf our thoughts of how much more we can give.

Our relationship with our culture

a. *Set apart:* To be in and not of. What does it mean for us to be in our culture but not of it? It means our ability to be a part of our culture without its values and goals rubbing off on us. It means thinking differently and living a different lifestyle. Unfortunately, there is little difference in the lifestyle and spending patterns of the non-believer and the believer.[4] Instead of being set apart from the culture, the church has become so familiar with it, so identified with it, that it's hard to tell one from the other. God did not call us to conformity with the world system; He has set us apart (Psalm 4:3) as His unique possession (Exodus 19:5; Deuteronomy 26:18; Titus 2:14; 1 Peter 2:9).

b. *Transformed minds:* Romans 12:1-2 reminds us not to conform any longer to the pattern of this world but to be transformed by the renewing of our minds. Our perspective, our thinking about money and possessions, comes to us naturally through our culture and must be transformed by the Word of God. As our lifestyle diverges from the cultural norm, people notice. Some will follow our lead; others may ridicule, but the world is searching for authentic leaders with integrity. We have an opportunity to influence our culture for Christ in the area of money and possessions.

c. *Passing through:* This world is not our home. We are sojourners with the anticipation of eternal life and blessing in heaven (Philippians 3:20; 1 Peter 1:17; 2:11). Since we are passing through, we should not act as though this world is all that matters—as though what we possess gives us true happiness. The eternal, though invisible, is real. Our present sojourn is the opportunity to influence the eternal through our management of God-given resources.

d. *Suppressing evil in the world:* As we teach truth, we oppose the work of Satan, including the abuse of money and power that results in exploitation and suffering. Although we will always have the poor with us, we must never minimize their plight or settle into comfort with their discomfort.

In summary, how we handle money directly influences our fellowship with the Lord. Jesus equates it with the quality of our spiritual life. In Luke 16:11, He says, *"Therefore if you have not been faithful in the use of worldly[5] wealth, who will entrust the true riches to you?"* (NAS) If we handle our money according to the principles of Scripture, we grow closer to Christ, gaining the true riches of intimacy with Him. However, if we are unfaithful with money, our fellowship with Him suffers. This is illustrated in the parable of the talents. The master congratulates the servant who managed money faithfully: *"Well done, good and faithful servant! You have been faithful with a few things; I will put you in charge of many things. Come and share your master's happiness!*"[6] As we handle money God's way, we have an opportunity to enter into the joy of a more intimate relationship with our Lord.

The reason our fellowship with the Lord is so affected by how we handle money stems from the power of money to compete with Christ for the lordship of our lives. Jesus tells us we must choose to serve only one of these two masters. "*No one can serve two masters. Either he will hate the one and love the other, or he will be devoted to the one and despise the other. You cannot serve both God and Money.*"[7] The choice to serve God rather than money does not mean we do not have or use money. The issue is whether the desire for money reather than the desire to obey God controls our lives.

WHERE WE ARE NOW: STATISTICAL EFFECTS

Consider the financial realities of today's culture. Some of the entries on this list are pervasive, touching most of the people you know.

1. *High debt:* Consumer debt is at the highest rate in our nation's history, especially among students. The average college student graduates with over $3,000 in credit card debt and an average of $18,900 in student loans. From 1982 to 2002, revolving debt has risen from over $70 billion to over $764 billion, which does not include home mortgages.[8]

2. *Low savings:* The past quarter century has seen personal savings drop to record lows.[9]

3. *Low giving:* Charitable giving on an average percentage basis is the lowest in our nation's history.

4. *Money abuse*: An entitlement generation raised on millions of TV commercials has embraced the attitude of "deserving before earning." From shoplifting to identity theft and credit card fraud, abuse is on the rise.

5. *Lack of training:* Students enter adulthood with little or no training for handling money, credit cards, etc.[10] Less than five percent of educational institutions have programs to promote financial understanding.[11]

6. *Bankruptcy:* A dramatic rise in bankruptcies has forced a recent change in bankruptcy laws. Bankruptcy is at an all time high for young people, with the quickest growing segment of filers between the ages of 18 and 35.

7. *Gambling:* Gambling has become socially accepted "entertainment." Under the guise of "entertainment" and "educational help," gambling is now legal in nearly every state. Online gambling is one of the leading issues facing students in higher education today. In the state of Mississippi, people spend more on gambling than on groceries!

Choosing to serve God rather than money means handling money faithfully by grace through the power of the Spirit (cf. Galatians 5:16-21).

> **Think about it**
> - *List several reasons why people might want to move directly into the practical discussion of money management without taking time to consider how their identity in Christ relates to every money issue.*
> - *How has money influenced your family both positively and negatively?*

CHAPTER THREE
Starting off Right: The Godly Steward

Core concepts

- How does the author define a godly steward?

- List the three major historical views that have shaped our culture's thinking on money and faith.

Overview

This chapter focuses on proper definitions and approach to Scripture, a brief survey of three historical views on money, and some thought-provoking quotes about faith and money.

HISTORICAL PERSPECTIVE TO CONTEXTUALIZE OUR STUDY

In this section, we will survey some historical issues surrounding faith and money,[1] providing perspective upon which to think more clearly about how we behave in the 21st Century. Although we could devote an entire course to the history of money and thought, we will confine ourselves here to two goals. First, we will examine how money has affected cultures throughout history. Second, we will discover that the financial issues we most commonly face are essentially the same ones that confronted earlier civilizations—rich versus poor, land and ownership, profits and greed, power and money, etc. Exposure to key thinkers and their perspectives can help us avoid their mistakes.

Historical background

We will look briefly at the Greek, Roman, and Jewish views on money and possessions—three cultures that have greatly influenced our modern conceptions.

a. *Greek view on money and possessions:* One of the quickest ways to survey these historical views is to look at a comparative chart of notable thinkers of each period. This enables us at a glance to see the themes they had in common and in what areas they were distinct. Let's look at the summary chart for the Greek view on money and possessions.

Chart 1

Greek Thought	Common Themes	Unique idea	Discrepancies
Plato	Limits on wealth; supported a class system.	Common property; class system; wealth corrupts	Speaks against wealth but is rich himself
Aristotle	Limits on wealth; supported a class system	Private property; family has no place in society	Speaks against wealth but is rich himself
Plutarch	Limits on wealth	Condemns lending with interest	Speaks against wealth but is rich himself
Zeno	Limits on wealth	Distinction between things good/bad	Speaks against wealth but is rich himself

b. *Roman view on money and possessions*: "What difference does it make how much you have? What you do not have amounts to much more."— **Seneca** (4 B.C.- 65 A.D.)

One important theme that stands out in our scan of financial philosophies is the disconnect between statements and actual practice. This dichotomy between what we say we do and what we actually do remains a challenge for us as well.

Three phrases that capture the essence of the Roman philosophy of ownership and wealth are striking: *jus utendi* (use); *jus fruendi* (enjoy); *jus abutendi* (abuse). The Romans maintained that owners had the right to use, enjoy, and abuse their property if they chose to. The Bible affirms private property (Deuteronomy 19:14; 21:16), but it does not allow abuse and deception. The reason becomes clear as we recognize God as the primary owner of everything and ourselves as His managers. If the Romans are right and ownership necessarily includes the right to abuse, then that right resides with God, not us. Fortunately, abuse is not in the character of God.

Chart 2

Roman Thought	Common Themes	Unique Idea	Discrepancies
Cicero	Private property rights: state preserves	Equality of goods=virtue of state; people have right to pursue wealth without hurting others; happiness based on virtue	Wealthy: owned 14 farms/estates
Cato	Private property rights: sacred	Valued the farming class; people have a right to own	Wealthy; valued farming but he preferred to live in the city
Seneca	Private property rights	Seeking wealth is bad: causes anxiety and slavery; speaks against the sorrows of wealth	Wealthy, but spoke against wealth

c. *Jewish view on money and possessions:* The greatest variation among the financial philosophies concerns land ownership and use. God's creation of all things clearly established His ownership of all things, and multiple Scriptures reaffirm that ownership. The Mosaic Covenant reveals God's laws for temporal ownership, use, and sale of land. The Old Testament record, however, reveals that even though the ideals may have been held in high esteem, they were commonly disregarded in actual practice. The concept of allowing the land to lie dormant in the seventh year seems generally unused by the Hebrew people.

Note that I have changed the column headings in Chart 3. Rather than attributing themes and ideas to individuals, I have chosen to allow the unity of Scripture to speak for God's ideal and then to contrast it with human discrepancies.

Chart 3

Areas of Distinction	Ideal	Discrepancies
Land ownership and use	Land is God's; to be managed well; not to be abused.	Sometimes the Hebrews did not follow good management (cf. Leviticus 26:35).
Sabbath rest for land; Jubilee concept of ownership reversion	Encouraged; was a part of system.	Not implemented consistently.
Poor	Valued and should be taken care of; strategies to help poor integrated into God's economic system for Israel.	The poor were often neglected and sometimes even abused (cf. Amos 2:6-8).

We sometimes think of the past as a simpler place to live, assuming that earlier cultures lacked our sophistication and its associated problems. That notion is both naïve and mistaken; the central dilemmas facing humanity are universal. But even if our modern era were the most difficult one in which to live, we cannot remove ourselves from it. God has placed us here for a purpose: to live in our time and culture in a way that glorifies Him and reflects the person of Christ. So how do we learn from the past in order to influence our present and future? Two responses are in order. First, we must recognize the futility of desiring to go back to a different place or time. Second, we must recognize that it is possible to live for Christ in our culture of affluence through faithfulness and a biblical understanding of wealth.

Deliberately choosing to live in poverty is not a scriptural virtue. It can be an easy way out of influencing our culture through responsible management of God's resources. It can also lead to self-righteousness. Equally problematic is the pursuit of riches for selfish gain. The balanced approach to money requires being faithful with whatever God entrusts to us wherever He has placed us.

STARTING OFF RIGHT

What is a steward? What does a steward look like? Meaningful discussions require correct definitions. Unfortunately, the term "stewardship" has become synonymous with "giving" or "fund-raising," thus limiting its impact and depth. Although giving is an essential element of our faithfulness to God as stewards, being a steward involves much more. One of our goals in this course is to provide a proper under-standing of the term "steward."

The Greek root word for steward is *oikonomos*. It contains the idea of one who is entrusted to oversee or manage something. As God's stewards, we are entrust-ed to manage all of His resources with faithfulness, including the gospel, creation, our relationships, our finances, our talent, and our time.

If we look at stewardship merely in the limited sense of giving, we will draw wrong conclusions. Consider theologian Scott Rodin's definition of stewardship.

In order to assure that we make the right start, we must immediately change our language. For too long, attempts to undergird Christian tithing and fund-raising with some sort of theology have employed the term *stewardship*. The problem that should be immediately apparent is that this focus indicates a clas-sic false start. Steward*ship* is the practice, the work, the vocation of the steward. It is the "how-to," the ethical imperatives of the call to be a steward. The very term indicates that we can move past the whole discussion of what it means to *be a steward* and focus on the practice of steward*ship*. This is a false start...in this false start the church is really only following the world. We are a society in search of quick solutions. We want solutions on the how-to level rather than the more fundamental *"who"* level. Tell us *how* to lose weight, not that *we must change* who we are—that is, our habits, our lifestyle and our attitudes. That is the work our society holds in disdain...we want to fix things. We want formu-las that tell us what to do but never mention who we must *become* in order to accomplish what we want...the dichotomy between questions of what we should do—Christian ethics—and who we are—Christian Theology—has a long and sad history in the church. For too long we have divided our theology and ethics in our formal studies and in our more topical writings. In seminary we have separate disciplines and faculties for 'systematic theology' and 'practi-cal theology'—as if systematic theology is not practical and practical theology has no systematic basis. Both disciplines suffer if the study of the practice of Christian ministry is not built on sound theological basis....Our call, then, is to build the right theology of the steward upon which we can develop a credible ethic of stewardship. That is the order we must discipline ourselves to maintain if we are to make a right start.[2]

Dr. Rodin is right on the mark. How quickly we turn to the "how-to" without focusing on "being" and understanding the underlying theology that should form the foundation for our lives. To *be* a steward is my role on this planet—managing the things

God entrusts to me during my stay here. Steward*ship* is what I do with those things.

> **Definition**
> *The following definition of a steward will serve as the basis for our study:*
> *A good steward is a disciple of Jesus Christ who faithfully manages all of God's unique provisions according to God's instructions.*

This definition assumes the process of a transformed mind that allows the Spirit to reflect Christ's values in the steward's lifestyle.

Steward/disciple

As we seek to redefine what being a steward means, Scott Rodin brings further breadth to the term.

> It is the life of discipleship in which obedience, sacrifice, taking up our cross and bearing each other's burdens is wholly redefined by the God who has redeemed us and called us to worship. At the same time joy, fulfillment, peace and contentment are redefined as well. A theology of the steward is a theology of worship as a joyful response to the God who is for us in Jesus Christ. A steward is a new creation in Christ. A steward is a joyous servant in the kingdom of God. A steward is a child of the King. A steward has a mission and a purpose in life. A steward is one who knows God in real, personal and certain terms, and who knows that this God is for us. These are the foundations upon which a theology of the steward must be built. A theology of the steward begins with the understanding that we have certain knowledge that our God is the triune God who created us for relationship, who is gracious toward us even in the face of sin and its devastation, who has redeemed us, and who Jesus Christ calls unto Himself for a fruitful life of fulfillment and joy. This God has established His kingdom on earth and has called us as His people to live in this kingdom, exhibit its ethics, to be a light on a hill, an alternative to the lostness and brokenness of the world around us. We are, by definition, Kingdom people. The world would try, through distortion and confusion, to pull us back into its own kingdom. As it does, we lose our way as stewards and, consequently, our purpose and our joy in life.[3]

Our focus is to allow Scripture to guide our development of a theology of God's stewards. This theological grid then serves as our filter to live for Christ in a practical way within our culture of affluence.

Interpretation and truth

Our primary source of truth for this course is the Bible. How we approach understanding the Bible affects our ability to apply it correctly. We hope to establish several principles acceptable to most, if not all, evangelical Christians, allowing each theological persuasion to emphasize its perspective on the application of materials.

1. High view of Scripture

We agree that God's Word is our primary source of truth for all of life. Crown Financial Ministries recognizes that the Bible is the believer's authority in the area of money and provides the grid through which we are to walk in obedience to Christ. Where the Bible speaks clearly, we speak with clarity. When issues are complex and Scriptures seem unclear, we will attempt to use Scripture to interpret Scripture, adding logical thinking to conclusions where a direct Scripture is not available.

2. Inspiration and inerrancy

Our study approaches Scripture as "God breathed" and understands it at face value within its proper context. Our study of biblical principles revealed by God about money will be in topical form. The Bible (Old Testament and New Testament) is the Word of God coming through the inspiration of the Holy Spirit upon human authors, using their unique personalities, cultural context and background. This inspiration is the supernatural empowerment of the Holy Spirit guiding the writers in whose original texts we have the inerrant, infallible, living Word (cf. Mark 12:26, 36; 13:11; Luke 24:27, 44; John 5:39; Acts 1:16; 17:2–3; 18:28; 26:22–23; 28:23; Romans 15:4; 1 Corinthians 2:13; 10:11; 2 Timothy 3:16; 2 Peter. 1:21). The goal of our study will always be to drive us to servant-led application rather than mere intellectual assent. "The Word of God was not written to satisfy our curiosity; it was written to change our lives."[4]

3. Bible as our trainer

The Bible says in 2 Timothy 3:16-17, "*All Scripture is inspired by God and profitable for teaching, for reproof, for correction, for training in righteousness; so that the man of God may be adequate, equipped for every good work*" (NAS).

This course utilizes Scripture to:

1. *Teach* God's children His blueprint for handling His money.
2. *Reprove* us for our wrong actions related to money.
3. *Correct* our thinking and our materialistic tendencies.
4. *Train* us to respond with good works as God's stewards.

Quotations to enrich our study

1. Prefatory quotations

As we continue laying the foundation of our study of money and ministry, it is helpful to hear the wisdom of those who have preceded us.

"Before the Lord made man upon the earth He prepared for him a world of useful and pleasant things for his sustenance and delight. In the Genesis account of the creation these are called simply 'things.' They were made for man's use, but they were meant always to be external to the man and subservient to him. In the deep heart of the man was a shrine where none but God was worthy to come. Within him was God; without, a thousand gifts which God had showered upon him. But sin has introduced complications and has made those very gifts of God a potential source of ruin to the soul. Our woes began when God was forced out of His central shrine and things were allowed to enter. Within the human heart things have taken over. Men have now by nature no peace within their hearts, for God is crowned there no longer, but there in the moral dusk stubborn and aggressive usurpers fight among themselves for first place on the throne. This is not a mere metaphor, but an accurate analysis of our real spiritual trouble. There is within the human heart a tough, fibrous root of fallen life whose nature is to possess, always to possess. It covets things with a deep and fierce passion. The pronouns *my* and *mine* look innocent enough in print, but their constant and universal use is significant. They express the real nature of the old Adamic man better than a thousand volumes of theology could do. They are verbal symptoms of our deep disease. The roots of our hearts have grown down into things and we dare not pull up one rootlet lest we die. Things have become necessary to us, a development never originally intended. God's gifts now take the place of God, and the whole course of nature is upset by the monstrous substitution."—**A.W. Tozer**

"If a person gets his attitude toward money straight, it will help straighten out almost every other area in his life."—**Billy Graham**

"Give me five minutes with a person's checkbook, and I will tell you where their heart is."—**Billy Graham**

"The principal hindrance to the advancement of the kingdom of God is greed. It is the chief obstacle to heaven-sent revival. It seems that when the back of greed is broken, the human spirit soars into regions of unselfishness. I believe that it is safe to say there can be no continuous revival without 'hilarious' giving. And I fear no contradiction: wherever there is 'hilarious' giving there will soon be revival!"—**O.S. Hawkins**

"Take it from me. I went down the road of 'be all you can be, realize your dreams,' and I'm telling you that fame and fortune are not what they're cracked up to be. We live in a society that seems to value only physical things, only ephemeral things. People will do anything to get on these reality shows and talent contests on TV. We're obsessed."—**Madonna**

"I've just been a machine for making money. I seem to have spent my life in a golden tunnel looking for the outlet that would lead to happiness. But the

tunnel kept going on. After my death there will be nothing left."
—**Aristotle Onassis**

"One of the reasons churches in North America have trouble guiding people about money is that the church's economy is built on consumerism. If churches see themselves as suppliers of religious goods and services and their congregants as consumers, then offerings are 'payment.'"—**Doug Pagitt**

"If anyone does not refrain from the love of money, he will be defiled by idolatry and so be judged as if he were one of the heathen."—**Polycarp**[5]

"Proportion thy charity to the strength of thine estate, lest God proportion thine estate to the weakness of thy charity. Let the lips of the poor be the trumpet of thy gift, lest in seeking applause, thou lose thy reward. Nothing is more pleasing to God than an open hand and a closed mouth."
—**Francis Quarles**

"Earn as much as you can. Save as much as you can. Invest as much as you can. Give as much as you can."—**John Wesley**

"I judge all things only by the price they shall gain in eternity."—**John Wesley**

"Do all the good you can, by all the means you can, in all the ways you can, in all the places you can, at all the times you can, to all the people you can, as long as ever you can."—**John Wesley**

"Money never stays with me. It would burn me if it did. I throw it out of my hands as soon as possible, lest it should find its way into my heart."
—**John Wesley**

"I do not believe one can settle how much we ought to give. I am afraid the only safe rule is to give more than we can spare. In other words, if our expenditure on comforts, luxuries, amusements, etc., is up to the standard common among those with the same income as our own, we are probably giving away too little. If our charities do not at all pinch or hamper us, I should say they are too small. There ought to be things we should like to do and cannot do because our charitable expenditures exclude them."—**C.S. Lewis**

"It may be said with truth that the Christian world has never at any previous time so earnestly directed its thoughts to the claims and uses of money as it is doing now. A great necessity is laid upon it by the condition of the world and of the Church, which is without parallel in the past. It may be said further, that, never before have men been so desirous as now to learn what God teaches and commands in the book of eternal truth, with regard to this subject. It requires a study of only a limited number of texts, out of the multitude in the Bible which relate to money, to lead almost any thinking person to the conclusion that no one of us comprehends and measures the true nature of money, and its office and importance in the Kingdom of God on earth. Such an examination convicts the Church in modern ages of failure to employ it in acts of worship and service according as God has ordained. It reveals the source of an immeasurable loss to Christians of spiritual strength, of heavenly joy, of comfort amidst earthly troubles, and of hope in death. It brings to light one of the greatest causes of the vast and abounding iniquity and crime in the world. It shows why glorious and everlasting rewards are promised for the faithful use of money, and why eternal penalties are attached to its abuse. The subject so vast, its relationship so extensive, its applications so important, that we are precluded, for the ends of a manual...of the great principles, and of prominent facts necessary to illustrate them, which are plainly related to the particular Divine ordinances respecting the pecuniary gifts of New Testament believers."—**William Speer**

Much of life revolves around the use of money. The Lord talked so much about money because He knew that much of our lives would center on its use. During your normal week, how much time do you spend earning money in your job, making decisions on how to spend money, thinking about where to save and invest money, or praying about your giving? Fortunately, God has prepared us by giving us His road map for living.

Think about it!
- *What was the most compelling thought in this chapter for you? Why?*
- *Which quotation struck you as most thought provoking? Why?*

CHAPTER FOUR

Wealth Reloaded: A Christian View of Wealth

Core Concepts

- Describe what the word "wealth" signifies.

- What does the term "wealth" represent?

- In the Old Testament, what dual perspective about wealth is taught?

- List three Old Testament people who were wealthy and loved by God.

- What are three Old Testament law assumptions of inherent value related to wealth?

- Describe two things God expects of those to whom He entrusts wealth.

Overview

This chapter provides a broad theological construct of the Christian view of wealth. It enables us to explore the relationship between money and godliness and focus on specific passages without losing the broader biblically informed theology.

CHRISTIAN VIEW OF WEALTH[1]

The word commonly used for "wealth" in the OT is *hayil* (Gen. 34:29), and in the NT *euporia* (Acts 19:25). But the term *wealth* actually comes from an Anglo-Saxon word meaning a general state of well-being. When ascribed to an individual, the word *wealth* signifies the well-being resulting from outward, opposed to inward causes such as health or contentment. Whether pertaining to an individual or a community, the term *wealth* represents the evaluation of things according to distinct priorities.[2] Someone possesses wealth, then, if he possesses an abundance of something prioritized as valuable.

A significant portion of Scripture, in both the Old and New Testaments, focuses on the right and wrong use of wealth. The difference usually involves priorities—the value placed on possessions versus spiritual well-being.

Old Testament

"Wealth" would characterize Adam's first estate, which was pronounced good and over which he was given dominion (Genesis 1:26). This dominion was the original stewardship, which continued through the fall (Genesis 9:1-3) but has been corrupted through sin. Many of the patriarchs were wealthy as a token of blessing from God (Genesis 24:35; 26:13; 30:43).

Abraham was a very wealthy patriarch who owned gold, silver, and livestock. Lot, too, was extremely wealthy. Job is an example of a person who honored God first in great wealth, then in catastrophic loss, and then again in increased wealth. Boaz, in the book of Ruth, is the model of a wealthy man who generously observed the laws of gleaning and served as an example of a kinsman redeemer. There is no indication that God questioned the legitimacy of the personal wealth of any of these individuals.[3] Solomon, having asked first for wisdom, was granted incredible prosperity by God (1 Kings 3-4).[4] Yet in spite of—or because of—Solomon's wealth, foreign allegiances, and very large harem, he was drawn into idolatry in the latter part of his life (1 Kings 10-11).

Despite the dangers of wealth, the Old Testament generally portrays it as a blessing from God and poverty as a curse. Old Testament law assumes the right to private property, field boundaries, and inheritance rights (Deuteronomy 19:14; 21:16). Along with the promise of the land and abundance for obedience (Numbers 13:27; 14:8; Deuteronomy 6:3), the law simultaneously provided safeguards against theft and covetousness (Exodus 20:15, 17; 22:1-15), and forbade usury (Exodus 22:25; Deuteronomy 23:19-20) and the hoarding of manna (Exodus 16:16-18). This latter prohibition can be argued to have some application to hoarding wealth (cf. Exodus 16:16–18, 2 Corinthians 8:15).[5] Tithes and offerings were also to be given to God (Deuteronomy 14:22-29). Additionally, provisions were prescribed for the poor and aliens in their land (Leviticus 19:9-10; Deuteronomy 15:4-11; 23: 24-25; 24:19-22).

Moving into the Psalms and Proverbs, we see a balanced approach to wealth and poverty—the recognition that wealth is not better than poverty if it is unaccompanied by higher values. Consider these passages: Psalm 112; Proverbs 12:11; 15:16-17; 16:8. This view is affirmed throughout the Bible, an insight that enables us to resist extreme teachings on either end of the wealth-poverty continuum.

New Testament

The Gospels indicate that most of the disciples were from the middle class, with Matthew being the exception. Joseph of Arimathea is called rich (Matthew 27:57). An essential theme of Jesus' teaching on wealth is that "mammon" or material resources compete with God for our loyalty (Matthew 6:19-24; Luke 16:1-13). That is why, in Matthew 19:23-24 he said, *"I tell you the truth, it is hard for a rich man to enter the kingdom of heaven. Again I tell you, it is easier for a camel to go through the eye of a needle than for a rich man to enter the kingdom of God."*

In 2 Timothy 3:1-5, Paul condemns not money but "lovers of money" and expands on Jesus' teaching of a competition of loyalties by adding "lovers of pleasure rather than lovers of God." It is wealth's potential to bring pleasure that makes it attractive. Any attempt to find fulfillment—pleasure, power, wealth, fame, etc.—outside of God's design for us is idolatry and violates the first commandment (cf. Jeremiah 2:1-13; 10).

The proper use of money was another crucial element in Jesus' teaching on discipleship. The deceitfulness of wealth, highlighted in Mark 4:19, can result in the errant notion that building wealth on earth is better than living with an eternal perspective (Mark 8:36). The individual who accumulated wealth without thought for

God or the poor was condemned in Luke 12:16-21 and 16:19-31, and most harshly in Matthew 25:31-46 as a depiction of what it will be like in the end times.

The early church took Jesus' teaching on wealth very seriously. Many of them sold private property and shared resources to meet the needs of others (Acts 11:29). Paul reminds believers that "the love of money [not money itself] is a root of all kinds of evil" (1 Timothy 6:10; cf. 2 Timothy 3:2). He emphasized giving to support ministry leadership (1 Timothy 5:17) and the destitute (Galatians 2:10), and he taught that giving should be in proportion to one's income (2 Corinthians 8:12-15; cf. 1 Corinthians 16:2b). The Apostle James, as he is showing the emptiness of faith without corresponding deeds, uses an example that demonstrates the unacceptability of ignoring the needy around us (James 2:14-17).

CONCLUSIONS

Wealth is not evil. It can be used for evil or for good depending on the heart of its possessor. It is never worthy of our trust because it can and will be lost. The Bible elevates several values above wealth: fear of the Lord, wisdom, knowledge, understanding, integrity, a humble spirit, righteousness, and peace.

God entrusts wealth to some individuals for their management. He expects them to increase its value (Matthew 25:14-30) and to use it for His (the true owner's) purposes.

Our worldview determines our attitudes regarding wealth. The dualism of Aristotle and Thomas Aquinas has influenced our conception of wealth.[6] An extreme separation of physical and spiritual has led some to divorce spirituality from the practical issues of life. When the attainment of spiritual union with God (our highest purpose) is seen primarily as a renunciation of pleasure and all things physical, wealth is viewed with disdain. Life that is merely a struggle to mortify all desire of wealth and avoid any attachments to it can lead to an antagonistic perspective that is negative, harsh, and may ultimately be anti-Christian.[7]

Wealth, even when given by God, is not to dominate our life. Its limitations are seen in such passages as Psalm 49:6-7, and its transitory character observed in Job 21 and Jeremiah 12. Wealth may even jeopardize one's salvation as it did with the rich young man in Matthew 19. The Bible directs many warnings toward the rich (1 Timothy 6:17; James 5: 1-3). It also teaches us that the wealthy are subject to specific sins: trusting too much in self (Proverbs 18:11); conceit (Proverbs 28:11); haughtiness (1 Timothy 6:17); and selfishness (Luke 12:19).

Although wealth is not evil, our natural depravity makes its accumulation potentially dangerous. Covetousness is always evil, as are domination, exploitation, and other illegitimate uses of wealth. Often, but not always, the Bible depicts wealth as a sign of blessing from God. God expects his people to manage wealth faithfully in light of New Testament instruction. The uncertainties of life dictate that no commodity (or wealth) will hold its value under all contingencies. And our greatest certainty regarding life is that it is fleeting and unworthy to be compared with eternity. For these reasons, Christ cautions us not to lay up treasures in such an uncertain place but to trust Him for the safekeeping of treasures that can never diminish.

CHAPTER FIVE
Materialism and Spirituality

Core Concepts

• What portion of the definition of materialism is emphasized in this curriculum?

• List the seven lies that Satan promotes about money in the world.

• List the seven biblical truths that counter worldly thinking about money.

• List the eight components of the destructive nature of materialism.

> **Overview**
> *Our view of God and stuff significantly affects how we understand the relationship between faith and money. The last chapter provided a theology of wealth. Now we look at the impact of materialism as we work to renew our thinking and behavior to make them Christ-like rather than a Christianized version of our old baggage. One goal of this section is to contrast false impressions with God's Word to gain discernment into how God provides answers to our inner needs.*

TERMINOLOGY

Although the term *spirituality*[1] can mean many things, my use of it here incorporates five components.

1. Spirituality is not detachment from the "good" created world of God.
2. God's revelation is the final authority on His will for our lives; human wisdom is not to supersede it.
3. Christ, as the God-man, is at the center of our spirituality; believers in Christ enjoy union with Him.
4. Christians accept and live for the triune God—Father, Jesus the Son, and Holy Spirit—three in one.
5. Christian spirituality is God's grace in a process that begins at conversion and progresses toward Christ-likeness. It entails community (Ephesians 4:15-16) by which character is deepened through the fellowship of God's people, prayer (1 Thessalonians 5:17), an eternal focus (Genesis 50:19-20, Romans 8:28), and living by the Spirit (Galatians 5:16-23).

MATERIALISM AND THE INFLUENCE OF CULTURE

Our materialistic culture imprints on us its false impressions about value, worth, eternity, and true happiness. These false impressions affect our attitude toward God and, consequently, our relationship to Him and the resources He graciously gives us. Modern media and advertising desensitize us to the difference between needs and wants, further eroding prudent spending and borrowing patterns.

Materialism's maze

1 John 2:15-17 sets the stage for our discussion. Use these verses to answer the questions that follow, and fill in the chart at right.

"Do not love the world nor the things in the world. If anyone loves the world, the love of the Father is not in him. For all that is in the world, the lust of the flesh and the lust of the eyes and the boastful pride of life, is not from the Father, but is from the world. The world is passing away, and also its lusts; but the one who does the will of God lives forever" (NAS).

The components (Chart 5.1)[2]

	Lust of the Flesh	Lust of the Eyes	Pride of Life
Definition	Selfishness	Envy	Pride
Key Word	I will	I want	I am
Genesis 3:6	"saw that the fruit of the tree was good for food" v. 3	"and pleasing to the eye" v. 8, 9	"and desirable for gaining wisdom" v. 6
Jesus' Temptation Matthew 4	"tell these stones to become bread" v. 3	"showed him all the kingdoms of the world…all this I will give you" v. 8, 9	"Throw yourself down" v. 6
Motivation	Pleasure	Possessions	Deceit to gain
Leading to	Overindulgence	False values	Status building
Resulting in	Obsession	Disillusionment	Hypocrisy
Attitude	Me first	Poor me	Look at me
Question	Who is in control?	Where is your treasure?	Who am I trying to impress?
Solution	Recognize God's ownership Phil. 2:3-4	Seek kingdom treasure Matt. 6:33	Set your sights on God's glory

Perhaps the greatest battle waged on the church today is the battle for the wallet—allegiance to God or money. Although we live in the most affluent society in history, the church sometimes struggles on the edge of impotence. The lost in our culture rarely look to the church for help.

- Why is this true?
- Are pastors viewed as cultural leaders in the 21st century? Why or why not?
- How do we explain the secularization of our nation?
- Is our culture exposed to too few authentic believers and too many idol worshipers?
- Are Christians motivated any differently than the general population or are they driven by the same patterns of consumption?

Secular writer Don Aslett observes that our culture is suffocating from too much stuff. The headline in a recent news article says, "Their distinctive faith aside, evangelicals are acting more and more like the rest of us."[3] Such commentary should shake us deeply.

Independent research reveals little difference in the financial lifestyle of believers and unbelievers.[4] We have become acculturated to the point of irrelevance, salt that has lost its saltiness. Our relentless pursuit of a dizzying array of toys and pleasures beyond our means has removed our focus from the eternal and placed it squarely on the modern equivalent of the trinkets for which Manhattan was traded.

Many Christians are leveraged beyond comprehension as they chase the dream of a rich lifestyle. What would happen to believers if another great depression hit? With an average of less than a month's worth of wages in savings, it is easy to conclude that many would be destitute. The recent ad by *LendingTree.com* typifies our society—believers and unbelievers alike—in its commercial with a man standing next to a barbecue grill beside his new swimming pool, pointing to his new house and new car. He smiles happily to the camera, saying, "How can I afford all this? I'm in debt up to my ears. Somebody please help me!"

Consider the status of marriages today. What is the main cause of marital conflict leading to divorce? Although infidelity is an important issue, it yields top spot on the list to financial conflict, which claims 56 percent of divorces.[5] If we were to get money issues right, particularly the underlying attitudes of selfishness and pride, think of how many lives—especially children—would be spared the devastation of their world collapsing around them.

Consider the leading reason people who feel called to enter ministry as a vocation fail to follow through. Financial issues—particularly debt—become chains that limit their options. Look around at your classmates. Many mission organizations say that a significant portion of potential missionaries fail to go the mission field because of the indebtedness incurred while in school. It is sobering to think that we who should be shaping our culture would instead become victims to it and disqualify ourselves. That is one of Paul's implications in 1 Corinthians 9:25-27 when he says, *"Everyone who competes in the games goes into strict training. They do it to get a crown that will not last; but we do it to get a crown that will last forever. Therefore I do not run like a man running aimlessly; I do not fight like a man beating the air. No, I beat my body and make it my slave so that after I have preached to others, I myself will not be disqualified for the prize."*

Spending and borrowing patterns established early in life—particularly credit cards and student-loan debt—can hinder our ability to listen to the Spirit's call. Remember, money and possessions are the primary rivals with Christ for the throne of our heart.

When God called us to Himself, He called us to be free. He bought our souls at the price of His own Son's life, making us His bondservants on this side of heaven.[6] However, there is a profound disconnect between whom we say we serve and whom we actually serve when it comes to money. Few of us would admit to being materialists, but our spending patterns say otherwise. We live as if the only things that matter are the things we acquire—the clothes we wear, the cars we drive, the parade of gadgets we buy to make our lives easier. And when the car no longer satisfies us, we routinely borrow the money to get a new one, rarely stopping to think that borrowing is a presumption on the future. Not only do we increase our debt, we often lose an opportunity to experience God's creative means of provision through His people.

Debt is really a surface issue, a symptom. The disease is selfishness, and it afflicts many of us. Our intent in this discussion is not to condemn anyone's financial situation but to speak truth that enables us to escape bondage. As the Holy Spirit guides us into all truth, the truth sets us free. This is why we rely so heavily on God's Word, which *"is inspired by God and profitable for teaching, for reproof, for correction, for training in righteousness"* (2 Timothy 3:16 NAS).

Our challenge is that many believers do not realize the relevance of Scripture. The chart below contrasts two opposing perspectives regarding money. Evaluate your perspective as you study the chart.

Contrasting views (Chart 5.2), (cf. Philippians 2:12-18; Colossians 2:8; 1 Corinthians 2:6-16)

test

Worldly perspective (Satan says)	Biblical perspective (God says)
Pay at the last minute.	Don't withhold payment when you have it (Proverbs 3:27-28).
Charge it; spend more than you earn.	Owe nothing to anyone (Romans 13:8).
The money is mine; I earned it!	All you have is from God (1 Chronicles 29:11, 12). *God's ownership*
You need this product to feel worthy.	In Christ you have been made complete (Colossians 2:10).
It's just entertainment; roll the dice!	Wealth comes from work, not luck (Proverbs 28:20; 1 Timothy 6:9).
Wealth is the ultimate goal.	Wealth is vanity (Ecclesiastes 2:11).
Do whatever it takes to get ahead.	Be honest in everything; be faithful (1 Corinthians 4:2)

Overcoming materialism requires us to recognize how desensitized we have become to its destructive deception in our culture. This section defines materialism and examines how it degrades our spiritual development.

MATERIALISM DEFINED

The *American Heritage College Dictionary* defines materialism as: 1) The theory that physical matter is the only reality and that everything can be explained in terms of matter and physical phenomena. 2) The theory or doctrine that physical well-being and worldly possessions constitute the greatest good and highest value in life. 3) A great or excessive regard for worldly concerns.

Since every Christian must summarily dismiss the first definition, we will focus on the latter two in our discussion of materialism and spirituality. Materialism is a temporal worldview that excludes the eternal and assumes that all meaning and values exist only in this material world. Spirituality to the materialist is a figment of man's imagination.

Destructive nature of materialism

Minimizes the spiritual life[7]

Materialism promotes self-sufficiency, and our Christian culture goes along. The spiritual life, however, depends on God's sufficiency and cultivates interdependence within the body of Christ. We recognize along with John the Baptist that *"He [Jesus] must increase, but I must decrease"* (John 3:30 NAS). The spiritual life is not about self-discovery; it's about Christ-discovery.[8]

As the primary rival with Christ for the throne of our hearts, money has a magic-like attraction that tends to pull us away from the lordship of Christ. Since He has stated clearly that we cannot serve both God *and* money, we must learn to be on guard against the love of money in the same way as Paul warned Timothy to *"flee the evil desires of youth"* (2 Timothy 2:22). In Joshua 7, Achan's failure and punishment demonstrate God's seriousness about the sins of covetousness, dishonesty and greed. Ananias and Sapphira in Acts 5 teach us a similar lesson and underscore the torment that comes not only to the offender but to the body of Christ as well.

Hinders our prayer lives

Materialism also hinders our prayer lives. When self-reliance becomes our habit, we pray less. Instead of turning to God during a tough financial time, we turn to VISA™ or MasterCard.™ This corrodes our need to stay close to God as Jehovah Jireh—the God who provides. The central question we must ask ourselves regarding materialism and spirituality is this: Do we trust God's loving care and provision enough to yield control and seek Him first?

Misdirects us from our purpose in Christ

What is our purpose in life? What is our purpose while attending seminary? It is always doxological: to glorify God by loving His Son with all our hearts and to follow His leading in fulfilling the Great Commission. When possessions rise in our priorities, they begin to direct our purpose rather than being instruments over which we are effective stewards. We spend too much time comparing, shopping, evaluating, using, accommodating, repairing, storing, and eventually discarding. The same risk accompanies a preoccupation with economic ease and security. Any thing or person on which we focus an inordinate amount of attention threatens God's priority and our purpose in life.

Undermines the family unit

The materialistic world system stands in complete opposition to the self-sacrificing focus of the marriage covenant established by God, seen perfectly in Christ's sacrificial love for the Church. The financial issues that contribute to so many divorces include lack of communication, deliberate secrecy, mismanagement that leads to debt stress, power plays, poor work ethic, overwork, too little money, and too much money. The issues are rarely limited to amounts—they are about control. Failing to recognize and accept God's control is a direct and necessary result of materialism.

Underestimates the liabilities of wealth

Materialism depends on the naïve assumption that money automatically makes our lives easier and less complicated. Properly managed, money can have that effect, but it is hardly automatic. Many people with enormous amounts of money are obsessed with retaining it. As it increasingly becomes their god and they realize its instability, anxiety over the complexity and multitude of risks overtakes them. Putting too much faith in its power to enhance their lives, they fail to realize that life consists of much more than money and possessions (Luke 12:13-34).

Increases anxiety and unhappiness

Many people believe that more money translates into greater happiness. To the contrary, people in our society are twice as rich as people were in 1956, and a little less happy.[9] The dismal stories of most lottery winners should serve as a warning that the mere infusion of money is likely to end in disillusionment and less happiness as friends and relatives become objects of suspicion.

Leads to ultimate futility

In Ecclesiastes 2:2-10, King Solomon decries the ultimate futility of materialism. Having had it all and tried it all, He concludes in chapter 12 that living for this life always leads to futility. Nothing solves the equation for meaning and fulfillment short of God's eternal perspective. Life on this fallen planet is tough, even with God, but Solomon demonstrates that when happiness is tied to earning power, accomplishments, or possessions, it cannot be sustained.

Breeds pride

Jesus uses the parable of the rich farmer in Luke 12: 13-21 to teach us another danger of materialism: the pride of life. Review this passage and identify three ways the rich farmer allowed materialism to breed this pride.

The rich farmer's security and pride lay in his accomplishments, without regard to God's will or purpose for him. "*...Soul, you have many goods laid up for many years to come; take your ease, eat, drink and be merry*" (Luke 12:19 NAS). He thought only of his own comforts and mistakenly thought they were due solely to his own effort. God came in, shook up his perspective, and revealed that his materialism had left him spiritually bankrupt. What he had failed to take into account is that the spiritual, not the material, is what endures.

We would be wise to examine ourselves and honestly answer two questions. 1) What pride infects my money (including retirement plan) and possessions? 2) How is it hindering my ability to be rich toward God and His plan for me?

Think about it.

- *What do you possess (or long for) that consumes more time, energy or money than it should?*

- *What possession or enjoyment do you feel you cannot live without?*

- *How much stuff would you buy if you were blind?*

CHAPTER SIX
Needs, Wants and Contentment

Core concepts

- How does the author describe contentment in relation to needs and wants?

- What does the apostle Paul say about the love of money in 1 Timothy 3:6-10?

- How should the godly steward view needs and wants?

Overview

The distinction between needs and wants is a theme throughout this course. This chapter begins with a brief treatment of that question and then moves into an exegesis of 1 Timothy 6:3-10 to shed light on the subject of contentment and the temptations that accompany the desire for wealth.

NEEDS, WANTS AND CONTENTMENT

Every culture with an expanding economy has probably suffered confusion between wants and needs. The rapid pace of new technology and the profusion of powerful advertising images in our time have deepened the problem. Obsolescence has changed from a practical reality to a mere perception, making our perfectly functional mobile phone no longer acceptable if it doesn't take pictures, play music, offer the latest games, or download internet files. From clothes to cars, functionality now plays only a minor role in our decision to upgrade or replace.

How do we distinguish between a need and a want? A recent ad for an SUV says, "Not more than you need, just more than you are used to." Think about that for a moment. What is it saying? It deliberately and cleverly blurs the distinction between what we really want and what we really need. Consider what God says about needs and wants.

> For we have brought nothing into the world, so we cannot take anything out of it either. If we have food and covering, with these we shall be content. But those who want to get rich fall into temptation and a snare and many foolish and *harmful desires* which plunge men into ruin and destruction. For the love of money is a root of all sorts of evil, and some by *longing* for it have wandered away from the faith and pierced themselves with many griefs. But flee from these things, you man of God, and pursue righteousness, godliness, faith, love, perseverance, and gentleness. Fight the good fight of faith; take hold of the eternal life to which you were called, and you made the good confession in the presence of many witnesses (1 Timothy 6:7-13 NAS; italics mine).

FALSEHOOD AND THE PLACE OF MONEY IN THE CHRISTIAN LIFE

One of the key New Testament passages on faith and money is found in 1 Timothy 6:3-10. Digging deeper into the argument, background, meaning and significance of this key passage should provide much needed clarity on the questions of needs, wants and desire for more money and stuff.

Exegetical idea of 1 Timothy 6:3-10

In light of the Apostle Paul's two concerns of false teachers and Christian conduct within the church, he seeks to encourage Timothy by linking the errant motives of false teachers for financial gain to their errant doctrine. He then establishes for Timothy a true, Christ-honoring doctrine for teaching and conduct regarding material possessions.

Argument

False teachers promote beliefs that conflict with the teaching of Jesus and godliness. Attitudes of the false teachers reveal their ignorance, promoting confusion, conflict and complacency.[1] False teachers, characterized by warped thinking, desire to profit financially from religion.

Right doctrine and actions lead to true wealth when accompanied by a heart of contentment. Having brought nothing into this world at birth, nothing can be taken from it into the next life. Physical nourishment and shelter should provide sufficient basis for contentment. The desire for wealth subjects people to the risk of traps and destruction.

Context

While in prison, the Apostle Paul wrote this first letter to Timothy, who had been left to minister at the Church in Ephesus.[2] This church appears to be adapting to the culture around it, settling into the moral code and lifestyle of Graeco-Roman society. Some have described Ephesus as the greatest commercial center in Asia,[3] and it, along with the Ephesian Church, was dominated by the middle-class.[4] This congregation also had affluent members, as is evident from [Paul's] comments on slaves and masters and on proper attitudes for wealthy Christians.[5] Timothy's ministry, like Titus's, was increasingly endangered by a judaizing-gnostic counter-mission that included church leaders and probably former co-workers.[6] Paul wrote to warn Timothy of these dangerous false teachers.

Commentary

We begin our study of 1Timothy 6:3-10 by observing its link to verse two. Here, Paul introduces our section by saying, "Teach and preach these principles."

This phrase applies to previous sections as well as what is to follow.[7]

A.   A charge to false teachers (vv. 3-5)

v. 3   *If anyone advocates a different doctrine, and does not agree with sound words, those of our Lord Jesus Christ, and with doctrine conforming to godliness,*

The key verse of 1 Timothy is back in the first chapter, where Paul says, "instruct certain men not to teach strange doctrines" (1 Timothy 1:3b). Paul's warning, as it relates to this section, deals with the financial motivation for false teaching as well as the proper understanding of money and possessions and the risks of pursuing wealth. 1 Timothy 6:3 introduces an "if/then" clause. The "if" shows the condition (errant doctrine) that leads to the results (errant behavior) in verses 4-5. Godliness (Greek *eusebia*) is, in Paul's mind, both a set of beliefs equivalent to sound teaching, *and* proper conduct: godliness describes a life totally consecrated to God, with right teaching and right practice bound together.[8] The primary issue of verse three is the meaning of "healthy words of our Lord Jesus Christ."[9] Some say they are the actual words of Christ,[10] and others agree that the phrase means "healthy words concerning Jesus."[11] The most probable explanation: that Paul regarded his own words as though Christ were speaking through him.[12]

v. 4   *he is conceited and understands nothing; but he has a morbid interest in controversial questions and disputes about words, out of which arise envy, strife, abusive language, evil suspicions,*

Here is the "then" statement that completes the "if" proposition in verse three. This is the "fruit" of the person who advocates errant or different doctrine: conceit, lack of understanding and interest in dark controversies. The word conceited in this sentence needs clarification. For example, (Gk *tetuphotai*) can mean either "to be conceited" or "to be foolish" and presents some difficulty in the Pastoral Epistles.[13] Because "is conceited" is contextually emphasized (cf. 3:6), and fits with 2 Timothy 3:4, and Paul has used this phrase elsewhere (cf. 1 Corinthians 8:1), it is likely to mean that the conceited one believes he has the answer from his own intellect.[14] The conceited person's state of knowing nothing starts with a rejection of Jesus Christ (that which is healthy) and develops an appetite for superfluous issues and arguments (that which is unhealthy). Mental error often leads to moral consequence.[15]

v. 5   *and constant friction between men of depraved mind and deprived of the truth, who suppose that godliness is a means of gain.*

False teachers, characterized by warped thinking, try to subvert religion into a profitable enterprise—similar to the moneychangers whose tables Jesus upset in the temple. These false teachers have no interest in godliness itself, only in their ability to enrich themselves at its expense.[16] The word "mind" in the next phrase refers to a person's inner disposition, the moral and intellectual capacity to make a decision.[17] Their mind, depraved as it was, led to the assumption that appearing to do spiritual things would make them wealthy. This is the true motivation of false teachers. In this case, charging for their teaching is perhaps what Paul was alluding to.[18] The word "profit," occurring here and in the next verse refers to financial gain. The issue is not about religious leaders making money *per se*. Paul previously mentions that those who serve in leadership are due double honor and should be paid well (cf. 1 Tim 5:17). He is not saying that making money is bad. He *is* saying that the false teachers' underlying motivation was to make an illicit profit from their teaching.[19] They were not motivated by Christ-honoring edification but by pride and selfishness. In contrast, Paul says in 1 Timothy 1:5 *"But the goal of our godly instruction is motivated by love from a pure heart and a good conscience and a sincere faith"* (emphasis mine).

B.   A charge to the typical Christian concerning wealth (vv. 6-10)

v. 6   *But godliness actually is a means of great gain when accompanied by contentment.*

To think that godliness could be a means to gain (5b) sounds outlandish. But the way Paul undermines the statement is to confirm it rather than contradict it.[20] Paul says, godliness (*eusebeia*) is "gain" (*porismos*), even great gain (6a) assuming what is meant is spiritual gain, not financial, with the accompaniment of contentment.[21] Echos of Paul's previous statement "godliness has value for all things (4:8), brings blessing for this life and the next" can be heard in this play on words.[22] Paul also enlarges the discussion of greed in this section. His definition of contentment is crucial. The Greek word for contentment (*autarkeia*) is one that was often used by the Stoics to denote inner self-sufficiency, the ability of a man to be sufficient on his own, independent of circumstances. Christian contentment—also independent of external circumstances—does not rest in one's own self-sufficiency but on sufficiency in Christ.[23] Paul further defines contentment in verses 7-8 as a willingness to be satisfied with food and clothing (which includes shelter). Paul discusses contentment also in 2 Corinthians 9:8 as "sufficient" or "adequate." But New Testament scholar J.N.D. Kelly offers a more helpful explanation saying, "but the deeper, more characteristically Christian meaning which it has here is illustrated in Philippians 4:11 where he claims, 'I have learned to be content whatever my situation (abundance or need).'"[24]

Godliness that is profitable does not depend on circumstances or, specifically, wealth and possessions. Nor does godly contentment depend on inner strength apart from Christ.[25]

v. 7   *For we have brought nothing into the world, so we cannot take anything out of it either.*

This verse reminds us that the things of this world are unavailable in eternity. We know the reason why from other passages: everything on this planet is corruptible and decaying (cf. Matthew 6:19-21; 1 Peter 3:10). But most people want to live forever,[26] a truth conveyed in Job 1:21 and Ecclesiastes 5. This desire for eternity should frame how we view possessions.

This verse is an awkward phrase in the Greek.[27] The conjunction (*hoti*) can be translated several ways, as *and*, *so*, *since* or *because*. Some have sought to insert "it is plain" or "it is true" before hoti.[28] The question is how the second clause relates to the first. Several explanations are interesting, with Mounce[29] preferring "and" while Kelly prefers "since." Regardless of which is used, *and*, *since*, *because* or *so*, Paul's point regarding the temporal nature of our world is clear: we cannot take our stuff with us.

v. 8   *If we have food and covering, with these we shall be content.*

This passage is powerful, especially for an affluent church. All believers are emphasized here: "we shall be content" can be either a simple future action or a present action. Either way it carries the force of a command. "We should be content with food and covering" is a more probable reading and the one that seems best.[30]

Jesus reminds us in Matthew 6:25 not to worry about the basic necessities of life because life is much more than what we eat, drink or wear. In the following verses, He assures us that God can be trusted to provide those things. So Jesus tells us that God will provide them, and Paul tells us that with them we should be content.

With regard to *food and covering* (the Greek *skepasmata* specifically), some question has arisen as to whether covering means just clothes or could include shelter. Kelly believes dictionary usage generally precludes shelter.[31] Mounce disagrees, saying it is common to have the two words that refer to clothing and shelter together,[32] thus depicting the minimum **not** the maximum that is compatible with contentment.[33] There is clarity with such a perspective because Paul has already portrayed God as the "good Creator, whose gifts we are to receive with thanksgiving (4:13ff), and he will soon add that God 'richly provides us with everything for our enjoyment (6:17).'"[34] Therefore it is affirmed that the couplet of food and covering should be extended to include shelter as a logical essential for life on earth.[35]

v. 9 *But those who want to get rich fall into temptation and a snare and many foolish and harmful desires which plunge men into ruin and destruction.*

"But" distinctly contrasts those contented with what they have against the dissatisfied, who in their desire for riches (Greek *bulesthai* "those who have set their hearts on being rich") succumb to the pull of stupid and destructive passions. The inordinate focus on money—the love of money—is clearly the issue in verse 9.[36] Paul has generalized his comments beyond the false teachers to "anyone wanting to be rich," indicating that all people must be cautious about this temptation.[37] Note that it is not the rich whom Paul rebukes in this passage; nor does he condemn their wealth and possessions; his warning is for those whose *focus* is getting rich.[38] The passion that places wealth and possessions above all else is exceptionally dangerous.[39] Indeed, "it is difficult to decide which is more dangerous—the love of money in a materialistic society or the Christian's rationalization for joining in the chase."[40] The flow of Paul's words presents a natural progression: desire leads to a special temptation; that temptation then leads to the devil's snare of further foolish and harmful desires ending in ruin and destruction. I call this a special temptation because it seems to affect only those who choose to pursue riches. According to Mounce, the text does not say that temptation is "Satan's snare" *per se,* but the Greek word *pagis* "snare" is used two other times in the Pastoral Epistles (cf. 1 Timothy 3:7; 2 Timothy 2:26), and are both times identified with Satan.

Although the Greek word *epitheumia* "passion" can be described as something good, its usage in the Pastoral Epistles "always describes strong sinful desire."[41] Towner suggests that these unleashed "passions" could be the kind that are open only to the person who has access to wealth, where normal rules and values are distorted.[42] These desires are coupled with "foolish," which is opposite of "wise" Greek (*sotheos*), and "harmful."

Some say that "ruin" (Greek *olethros*) means material destruction in this passage,[43] and that "destruction" (Greek *apoleia*) means spiritual destruction. Or it could mean that "the ultimate destiny of those who pursue riches is complete and total ruin.[44]

v. 10 *For the love of money is a root of all sorts of evil, and some by longing for it have wandered away from the faith and pierced themselves with many griefs.*

Several phrases in this verse merit our attention. Many theologians believe that Paul is citing current proverbial wisdom when he uses the phrase "the love of money." Kelly adds that a better reading of the text is: for evils of every kind are rooted in the love of money.[45] This seems close to saying, "for a root of all kinds of evil is the love of money."[46] The issue is that the desire or craving after money is at the core of a variety of evil things. Money, then, is not evil, but rather the excessive desire for it is evil. Because there is no definite article before "root" in Greek, it would be imprudent to say that love of money is the root-cause of all evil (sins).[47] John Stott offers a list of evils of which the love of (desire for) money is a major root or cause: Avarice leads to selfishness, cheating, fraud, perjury, and robbery, to envy, quarreling, and hatred, to violence and even murder. Greed lies behind marriages of convenience, perversions of justice, drug-pushing, pornography sales, blackmail and exploitation of the weak, the neglect of good causes, and the betrayal of friends.[48] Within the metaphor of a root, Paul urges us to do more than simply treat the problems caused by greed. We must tear out the root that produces the problem.[49] The phrase "have been led astray" (or wandered away) does not necessarily mean that they are apostate in the strict sense but that they are living out of accord with the gospel.[50] The idea of losing their way or "wandering from the faith" illustrates how the lust for more drives a wedge between the believer and God.[51] The "many griefs" can refer to broken relationships and loss of reputation.[52]

God knows our material needs and has promised to provide them. We are to cultivate contentment in Christ with the resources He provides (whether abundance or little), recognizing that earthly possessions are of no eternal value except as tools for accomplishing His will. When a healthy desire to improve our material condition gives way to the love of money and a passion to get rich, we have been seduced by false thinking that places us in extreme danger.

One way to distinguish between needs and wants is by maintaining a Christ-centered focus. As we align our wills with His ways, knowing that we are here to serve Him and not our own selfish desires, our perspective sharpens. We see eternity as our home and understand that our brief time on earth is an opportunity to affect eternity by what we do with the money God has entrusted to us.

In Proverbs 30:8-9, Agur's oracle provides us with a solution: "*Give me neither poverty nor riches; feed me with the food that is my portion, that I not be full and deny You and say, 'Who is the LORD?' Or that I not be in want and steal, and profane the name of my God*" (NAS). A steward's response to materialism is neither asceticism nor extravagance but rather to find the appropriate, individual balance between this world and other-world living. It is each one's responsibility to live always with the conviction that all things are God's. Every purchase, charge, or investment should be filtered through God's teaching on money.

Each person's focus, then, must be on God's individual provision from heaven, not looking at others to compare or judge but using every opportunity to manage God's unique provision as an act of worship and gratitude.

Think about it.

• *What constitutes joy?*

PART II

A Fresh View of the Godly Steward

CHAPTER SEVEN
Refresh: Peering into Eternity

Core Concepts

- What are the six key components of eternity given by the authors?

- How is eternity described?

- What does it mean to live as an alien and pilgrim?

> **Overview**
>
> *Eternity is mind-boggling to finite creatures—so much so that we sometimes avoid thinking about it and how it relates to our lives. However, eternity is at the core of our philosophy of money and possessions. To think about them apart from an eternal view always results in the futility of Solomon's chasing after the wind. Unfortunately, the deceitfulness of riches has the tendency to deter thinking with an eternal perspective, enticing us to live for the moment and its decaying treasures.*
>
> *Eternity is one of two lenses of understanding that enable the steward to discern God's earthly blessings. The second lens is ownership, which we address in the next chapter. If we forget that eternity is our home, we will live as if what we accumulate is all that matters.*

CREATED FOR ETERNITY

God created us in His image, and in doing so, placed eternity in our hearts (cf. Genesis 1:27, Ecclesiastes 5:11). Cultivating an eternal perspective helps us answer many of our practical giving, spending and saving questions.
A personal story (from Howard Dayton)

On Monday, October 25, 1999, the news reported an unfolding story. Air Force jets following a Lear jet from Orlando, Florida, were unable to communicate with its pilots. I learned later that two close friends, Robert Fraley and Van Ardan, were on that Lear as it carried them and golfer Payne Stewart to their deaths.

One of the most critical principles for us to understand is the reality of eternity. Robert and Van were men in their mid-forties who lived with an eternal perspective. Robert had framed these words in his workout area, "Take care of your body as though you will live forever; take care of your soul as if you will die tomorrow."

Because God loves us, He reveals in the Scriptures that there is a heaven and hell, that there is a coming judgment, and that He will grant eternal rewards unequally. The Lord wants the very best for us. Therefore, He wants to motivate us to invest our lives in such a way that we can enjoy an intimate relationship with Him now and receive the greatest possible rewards and responsibilities in heaven. Our failure to view our present lives through the lens of eternity is one of the biggest hindrances to seeing our lives and our assets in their true light. Yet Scripture states that the reality of our eternal future should determine the character of our present lives and the use of our money and possessions.

People who do not know the Lord look at life as an experience that begins at birth and ends at death. Looking to the future, they see no further than their own life span. With no eternal perspective, they think, *if this life is all there is, why deny myself any pleasure or possession?* Those who know Christ have an entirely different perspective. They know life is short: the preface—not the book; the preliminaries—not the main event. It is the testing period that will determine much of our experience in heaven.

Financial planners try to convince people to look ahead instead of simply focusing on today. "Don't think this year," they will tell you. "Think 30 years from now." The wise person does indeed think ahead, but far more than 30 years. Even 30 million years is insignificant in eternity. Someone once said, "He who provides for this life but takes no care for eternity is wise for a moment but a fool forever." Jesus said it this way, *"For what does it profit a man to gain the whole world, and forfeit his soul?"* (Mark 8:36, NAS).

Throughout the Bible, we are reminded that life on earth is brief. *"God is mindful that we are but dust"* (Psalm 103:14). Our earthly bodies are called *"tents"* (2 Peter 1:13), temporary dwelling places of our eternal souls. David recognized this and sought to gain God's perspective on the brevity of life. He asked of the Lord, *"Show me, O Lord, my life's end and the number of my days; let me know how fleeting my life is...Each person's life is but a breath. Man is a mere phantom as he goes to and fro: He bustles about, but only in vain; he heaps up wealth, not knowing who will get it"* (Psalm 39:4-6).

When a good friend (of Howard's) discovered she had only a short time to live, she told me of her radical change in perspective. "The most striking thing that's happened," she said, "is that I find myself almost totally uninterested in accumulating more things. Things used to matter to me, but now I find my thoughts are centered on Christ, my family, and other people."

Moses realized that true wisdom flows out of understanding that our lives are short. So he asked the Lord to help him number the days he had on earth. *"As for the days of our life, they contain seventy years, or if due to strength, eighty years...for soon it is gone and we fly away...So teach us to number our days, that we may present to You a heart of wisdom"* (Psalm 90:10, 12, NAS). I encourage you to number the days you estimate that you have left on earth. If I live as long as my father, I have about 8,500 days left. This has helped me focus on investing my life and resources in eternally important matters.

When I (Howard) served in the Navy, I was very interested in what was happening in the town in which I was stationed. However, as soon as I received orders discharging me in two months, I became what was called a "short-timer." My interest completely shifted from the town I was leaving to the town that would be my new home. In a similar way, when we comprehend that we are really "short-timers" on earth and will soon be going to our real home, our focus shifts to things that will be important in heaven. Author Matthew Henry said, "It ought to be the business of every day to prepare for our last day."

Eternity, on the other hand, *never ends*. It is forever. Imagine a cable running through the room where you are now. The cable runs to your right millions of light years all the way to the end of the universe; to your left, it runs to the other end of the universe. Now imagine that the cable to your left represents eternity past, and the cable to your right, eternity future. Place a small mark on the cable in front of you; the mark represents your brief life on earth.

Because most people do not have an eternal perspective, they live as if the mark were all there is. They make *mark* choices; living in *mark* houses, driving *mark* cars, wearing *mark* clothes, and raising *mark* children. A.W. Tozer referred to eternity as the "the long tomorrow." This is the backdrop against which all the questions of life and the handling of our resources must be answered.

ALIENS AND PILGRIMS

Scripture tells us several things about our identity and role on earth. First, *"Our citizenship is in heaven"* (Philippians 3:20), not earth. Second, *"We are ambassadors for Christ"* (2 Corinthians 5:20), representing Him on earth. Imagine yourself an ambassador from a country who goes to work in another country that is hostile to your own. Naturally, you will want to learn about this new place, see the sights, and become familiar with the people and culture. But suppose you eventually become so assimilated into this foreign country that you begin to regard it as your true home. Your allegiance wavers, and you gradually compromise your position as an ambassador, becoming increasingly ineffective in representing the best interests of your own country.

We must never become too much at home in this world or we will become ineffective in serving the cause of the kingdom we are here to represent. We are aliens, strangers, and pilgrims on earth. Peter wrote, *"Live your lives as strangers here in reverent fear"* (1 Peter 1:17). Later, he added, *"I urge you, as aliens and strangers in the world, to abstain from sinful desires"* (1 Peter 2:11). The King James translation uses the words *"strangers and pilgrims."* Pilgrims are unattached. They are travelers—not settlers—aware that the excessive accumulation of things can distract.

Material things are valuable to pilgrims but only as they facilitate their mission. Things can entrench us in the present world, acting as chains around our legs that keep us from moving in response to God. When our eyes focus on the visible, they cannot simultaneously focus on the invisible. *"So we fix our eyes not on what is seen, but on what is unseen. For what is seen is temporary, but what is unseen is eternal"* (2 Corinthians 4:18). Pilgrims of faith look to the next world. They see earthly possessions for what they are—useful for kingdom purposes, but far too flimsy to bear the weight of trust. Thomas à Kempis, author of *The Imitation of Christ,* said it this way, "Let temporal things serve your use, but the eternal be the object of your desire." There are two principles concerning our possessions that will help us gain a proper perspective of them.

WE LEAVE IT ALL BEHIND

After John D. Rockefeller died, his accountant was asked how much he left. The accountant responded, "He left it all." Job said it this way; *"Naked I came from my mother's womb, and naked I shall return there"* (Job 1:21, NAS). Paul wrote, *"We have brought nothing into the world, so we cannot take anything out of it either"* (1 Timothy 6:7, NAS). The psalmist observed, *"Do not be afraid when a man becomes rich, when the glory of his house is increased; for when he dies he will carry nothing away; his glory will not descend after him. Though while he lives he congratulates himself—and though men praise you when you do well for yourself—he shall go to the generation of his fathers"* (Psalm 49:16-20, NAS).

EVERYTHING WILL BE DESTROYED

Earthly goods will not last forever—they are destined for annihilation. *"The day of the Lord will come like a thief. The heavens will disappear with a roar; the elements will be destroyed by fire, and the earth and everything in it will be laid bare. Since everything will be destroyed in this way, what kind of people ought you to be? You ought to live holy and godly lives"* (2 Peter 3:10-11). Understanding the temporary nature of possessions should influence us as we consider spending decisions.

JUDGMENT

It is uncomfortable to think about judgment. But, because our Lord loves us so deeply, He wanted us to realize what would happen in the future. Therefore, God revealed to us that we all will be judged according to our deeds: *"He has fixed a day in which He will judge the world in righteousness"* (Acts 17:31, NAS). All of us should live each day with this awareness: *"They will have to give an account to Him who is ready to judge the living and the dead"* (1 Peter 4:5). God will judge us with total knowledge: *"Nothing in all creation is hidden from God's sight. Everything is uncovered and laid bare before the eyes of Him to whom we must give account"* (Hebrews 4:13). Because His knowledge is total, His judgment is comprehensive: *"Men will have to give account on the Day of Judgment, for every careless word they have spoken"* (Matthew 12:36). His judgment extends to what is hidden from people: *"God will bring every deed into judgment, including every hidden thing, whether it is good or evil"* (Ecclesiastes 12:14). He will even *"disclose the motives of each person's heart"* (1 Corinthians 4:5).

Judgment of God[1]

S. H. Travis, in his article "The Judgment of God" in the *New Dictionary of Theology,* explains four elements of God's judgment: First, all people will be judged (cf. Acts 10:42; Romans 14:10-12; Mark 8:38; 1 Corinthians 4:5; 1 Thessalonians 1:5-10). Dead or alive, Christian or non-Christian—all people will be judged. This judgment is tied into the final coming of Christ.

Second, judgment will be according to works (cf. Matthew 16:27; Romans 2:6; Revelation 22:12). This judgment does not conflict with justification by grace through faith; "it involves the obligation to work out our new status in practice. Thus, at the final judgment, a person's works will be the evidence of whether a living faith is present in him or not."[2]

Third, the final judgment will separate those who truly belong to Christ. Travis goes on to say, "it will not be arbitrarily imposed from on high. Rather, the verdict will underline and make known the self-judgment which men and women have chosen during the present life. There is a real sense in which, by the choices people make…they bring judgment on themselves"[3] (cf. John 3:19-20; Matthew 10:32-33; Romans 1:18-32).

Finally, salvation and condemnation are best understood in terms of relationship or non-relationship to God. "The criterion by which people's destinies will be determined is a double one—their failure to worship and serve God (cf. Romans 1:18-20) and their attitude to Christ—their relationship to Him, of which their deeds give evidence"[4] (cf. John 3:36).

After death, those who know Christ will spend eternity with the Lord in heaven, an incredibly wonderful place. What we seldom consider is that the entry point to heaven is a judgment. Scripture teaches that all believers in Christ will give an account of their lives to the Lord. *"We shall all stand before the judgment seat of God. ...So then each of us will give an account of himself to God"* (Romans 14:10, 12, NAS). The result of this will be the gain or loss of eternal rewards. In 1 Corinthians 3:13-15 we read, *"His work will be shown for what it is, because the [Judgment] Day will bring it to light. . . . If what he has built survives, he will receive his reward. If it is burned up, he will suffer loss."* Our works are what we have done with our time, influence, talents, and resources. God's Word does not treat this judgment as a meaningless formality before we get on to the real business of heaven but as a monumental event in which things of eternal significance are brought to light.

MOTIVATION AND REWARDS

Why should I follow Scripture's guidance on money and possessions when it is so much fun to do whatever I please with my resources? I'm a Christian. I know I'm going to heaven anyway. Why not have the best of both worlds; this one and the next? Though few of us would be honest enough to use such language, these questions reflect a common attitude.

The prospect of eternal rewards for our obedience is a neglected key to unlocking our motivation. Paul was motivated by the prospect of eternal rewards. He writes, *"I have fought the good fight, I have finished the course, I have kept the faith; in the future there is laid up for me the crown of righteousness, which the Lord, the righteous Judge, will award to me on that day"* (2 Timothy 4:7-8, NAS). The Lord appeals not only to our compassion but also to our eternal self-interest. *"Love your enemies, and do good, and lend, expecting nothing in return; and your reward will be great"* (Luke 6:35, NAS).

Our heavenly Father uses three things to motivate our obedience: the love of God, the fear of God, and the rewards of God. These are the same motivations that move my (Howard) children to obey me. My children love me, and sometimes this is sufficient for them to be obedient. But other times it isn't enough. In a healthy sense, they also fear me. They know I will discipline them for wrongdoing. They also know I will reward them with my words of approval and sometimes in tangible ways for doing right.

Unequal rewards in heaven

It is not as simple as saying, "I'll be in heaven and that's all that matters." On the contrary, Paul spoke about the loss of reward as a terrible loss. The receiving of rewards from Christ is a gain beyond our comprehension. Not all Christians will have the same rewards in heaven. John Wesley said, "I value all things only by the price they shall gain in eternity." God's kingdom was the reference point for him. He lived as he did, not because he treasured no things, but because he treasured the right things.

We often miss something in missionary martyr Jim Elliott's famous words, "He is no fool who gives what he cannot keep to gain what he cannot lose." We focus on Elliott's willingness to sacrifice, and so we should; however, we often overlook his motivation for gain. What separated him from many Christians was not that he did not want treasure but that he wanted *real* treasure. Remember God loves you deeply. Because He wants the best for you throughout eternity, God has revealed that today's sacrifices and service for Him will pay off forever.

IMPACTING ETERNITY TODAY

Our daily choices determine what will happen in the future. What we do in this life is of eternal importance. We only live on this earth once. *"It is appointed for men to die once and after this comes judgment"* (Hebrews 9:27, NAS). There is no such thing as reincarnation. Once our life on earth is over, we will never have another chance to move the hand of God through prayer, to share Christ with one who does not know the Savior, to give money to further God's kingdom, or to share with the needy.

Those who dabble in photography understand the effect of the "fixer." In developing a photograph, the negatives are immersed in several different solutions. The developing solution parallels this life. As long as the photograph is in the developing solution, it is subject to change. But when it is dropped in the fixer or "stop bath," it is permanently fixed, and the photograph is done. So it will be when we enter eternity: the life each of us lives on earth will be fixed as is, never to be revised.

Alfred Nobel was a Swedish chemist who made a fortune by inventing dynamite and explosives for weapons. When Nobel's brother died, a newspaper accidentally printed Alfred's obituary instead. He was described as a man who became rich by enabling people to kill each other with powerful weapons. Shaken from this assessment, Nobel resolved to use his fortune to reward accomplishments that benefit humanity. We now know those rewards as the Nobel Peace Prize. Let us put ourselves in Nobel's place. Let us read our own obituary, not as written by people, but as it would be written from heaven's point of view. Then let us use the rest of our lives to edit that obituary into what we really want it to be.

When I am face to face with Christ and look back on my life, I want to see that the things in which I invested my time, creativity, influence, and assets are big things to Him. I do not want to squander my life on things that will not matter throughout eternity. During Moses' time, Pharaoh was the most powerful person on earth. Pharaoh's daughter adopted Moses as an infant, giving him the opportunity to enjoy the wealth and prestige of a member of the royal family.

Hebrews 11:24-26 tells us what Moses later chose and why. *"By faith Moses, when he had grown up, refused to be called the son of Pharaoh's daughter, choosing rather to endure ill-treatment with the people of God, than to enjoy the passing pleasures of sin, considering the reproach of Christ greater riches than the treasures of Egypt; for he was looking to the reward"* (NAS). Because Moses was looking forward to the only real rewards that would last, he chose to become a Hebrew slave and was used by God in a remarkable way. What are the choices facing you now? How does an eternal perspective influence your decisions? Martin Luther said that on his calendar there were only two days: "today" and "*that* Day." May we invest all that we are and have today in light of *that* day."

Author Randy C. Alcorn graciously contributed much of this chapter from his outstanding book, *Money, Possessions and Eternity*. (Used by permission of Tyndale House Publishers, Inc. All rights reserved.)

Think about it

- *For what do you want to be remembered?*
- *In what way has your current spending behavior disregarded God's judgment of our deeds?*

CHAPTER EIGHT

Release: Let God Be God

Core concepts

- Describe how you will affirm the Lordship of your life through the principle of God's ownership.

- List three things God controls.

- Describe four characteristics of God as provider.

> *Overview*
>
> *Our perspective on money and possessions begins with a proper understanding of God's part in the equation. Understanding His part frees us from futile pursuits and enables us to focus on God's expectations as we steward His resources.*

OWNERSHIP

The Lord owns all our possessions. *"To the Lord your God belong . . . the earth and everything in it"* (Deuteronomy 10:14). *"The earth is the Lord's, and all it contains"* (Psalm 24:1, NAS). Scripture even reveals specific items God owns. Leviticus 25:23 identifies Him as the owner of all the land: *"The land, moreover, shall not be sold permanently, for the land is Mine"* (NAS). Haggai 2:8 says that He owns the precious metals: *"'The silver is Mine and the gold is Mine,' declares the Lord of hosts"* (NAS). In Psalm 50:10-12 we are told God owns the animals. *"Every beast of the forest is Mine, the cattle on a thousand hills. . . . Everything that moves in the field is Mine. If I were hungry I would not tell you, for the world is Mine, and all it contains"* (NAS) The Lord created all things, and He never transferred the ownership of His creation to people. In Colossians 1:17 we are told that *"In Him all things hold together."* At this very moment, the Lord holds everything together by His power. As we will see throughout this study, recognizing God's ownership is crucial in allowing Jesus Christ to become the Lord of our money and possessions.

Affirming God's Lordship through recognizing His ownership

Being genuine followers of Christ means transferring ownership of our possessions to the Lord. *"None of you can be My disciple who does not give up all his own possessions"* (Luke 14:33, NAS). We must give up claim to ownership of all we have. Sometimes the Lord will test us by asking if we are willing to give up the very possession that is most important to us. A vivid example of this in Scripture is when the Lord instructed Abraham, *"Take now your son, your only son, whom you love, Isaac . . . and offer him there as a burnt offering"* (Genesis 22:2, NAS). When Abraham obeyed, demonstrating his willingness to give up his most valuable possession, God responded, *"Do not lay a hand on the boy . . . now I know that you fear God, because you have not withheld from Me your son, your only son"* (Genesis 22:12).

When we acknowledge God's ownership, every spending decision becomes a spiritual decision. No longer do we ask, "Lord, what do You want me to do with *my* money?" It becomes, "Lord, what do You want me to do with *Your* money?" When we have this attitude and handle His money according to His wishes, spending and saving decisions become as spiritual as giving decisions.

The Lord's ownership also influences how we care for possessions. For example, because the Lord is the owner of where we live, we want to please Him by keeping His home or apartment cleaner and in better repair.

Consistently recognizing God's ownership can be difficult. It is easy to believe intellectually that God owns all you have but still live as if this were not true. Our culture suggests an opposing view. Everything around us—the media, even the law—says that what you possess, you own. Genuinely acknowledging God's ownership requires nothing less than a new way of thinking. Here are a number of practical suggestions to help you recognize God's ownership.

- For the next 30 days, meditate on 1 Chronicles 29:11-12 when you first awaken and just before going to sleep.
- Be careful in the use of personal pronouns in your daily conversation, substituting "Your(s)" or "the Lord's" for "my," "mine," and "ours."
- Ask the Lord to make you aware of His ownership and make you willing to give up ownership.
- Pray for this new way of thinking during the next 30 days.
- Establish the habit of acknowledging the Lord's ownership every time you purchase an item.

Recognizing the Lord's ownership is important in learning contentment. If you believe that you own a particular possession, the circumstances surrounding that possession will affect your attitude. If something good happens to it, you will be happy; if something bad, you will be discontent.

Shortly after my friend Jim came to grips with God's ownership, he purchased a car. He had driven the car only two days before someone rammed into the side of it. Jim's first reaction was "Lord, I don't know why You want a dent in Your car, but now You've got a big one!" Jim was learning contentment!

CONTROL

Besides being Creator and Owner, God is ultimately in control of every event that occurs upon the earth. *"We adore you as being in control of everything"* (1 Chronicles 29:11, TLB). *"Whatever the Lord pleases, He does, in heaven and in earth"* (Psalm 135:6, NAS). In the book of Daniel, King Nebuchadnezzar stated: *"I praised the*

Most High; I honored and glorified him who lives forever . . . All the peoples of the earth are regarded as nothing. He does as he pleases with the powers of heaven and the peoples of the earth. No one can hold back his hand or say to him: 'What have you done?'" (Daniel 4:34-35). The Lord is in control of even difficult events. *"I am the Lord, and there is no other, the One forming light and creating darkness, causing well-being and creating calamity; I am the Lord who does all these"* (Isaiah 45:6-7, NAS). It is important for us to realize that our heavenly Father uses even seemingly devastating circumstances for ultimate good in the lives of the godly. *"We know that God causes all things to work together for good to those who love God, to those who are called according to His purpose"* (Romans 8:28, NAS). The Lord allows difficult circumstances for three reasons.

1. He accomplishes His intention.

This is illustrated in the life of Joseph who was sold into slavery as a teenager by his jealous brothers. Joseph understood this later and responded to his brothers: *"Do not be distressed and do not be angry with yourselves for selling me here, because it was to save lives that God sent me ahead of you. . . . It was not you who sent me here, but God. . . . You intended to harm me, but God intended it for good to accomplish what is now being done, the saving of many lives"* (Genesis 45:5, 8; 50:20).

2. He develops our character.

Godly character, something that is precious in the sight of the Lord, often is developed during trying times. *"We also rejoice in our suffering, because we know that suffering produces perseverance; perseverance, character"* (Romans 5:3-4, NAS).

Stop for a moment and answer these questions:
- Considering that money is so linked to our character development, explain this statement: what we spend our money on reveals the object of our devotion.
- Why would God care so much about this area of our lives?
- What would godly financial motivation and management look like?

3. He disciplines His children.

"Those whom the Lord loves He disciplines. . . . He disciplines us for our good, so that we may share His holiness. All discipline for the moment seems not to be joyful, but sorrowful; yet to those who have been trained by it, afterwards it yields the peaceful fruit of righteousness" (Hebrews 12:6, 10-11, NAS). When we are disobedient, we can expect our loving Lord to discipline us, often through difficult circumstances that encourage

us to abandon our sin and "share His holiness." You can be at peace knowing that your loving heavenly Father is in control of every situation you will ever face, and He intends to use every one for a good purpose.

GOD IS PROVIDER

The Lord promises to provide our needs. *"Seek first his kingdom and his right- eousness, and all these things* [food and clothing] *will be given to you as well"* (Matthew 6:33). The same Lord who fed manna to the children of Israel during their 40 years of wandering in the wilderness and who fed 5,000 with only five loaves and two fish has promised to provide our needs. This is the same Lord who told Elijah, *"I have com- manded the ravens to provide for you . . . the ravens brought him bread and meat in the morning and bread and meat in the evening"* (1 Kings 17:4, 6, NAS).

God is both predictable and unpredictable.

He is totally predictable in His faithfulness to provide for our needs. What we cannot predict is *how* the Lord will provide. He uses various and often surprising means—an increase in income or a gift or a money-saving purchase. Regardless of how He chooses to provide for our needs, He is completely reliable. The Lord instructs us to be content when our basic needs are met. *"If we have food and clothing, we will be content with that"* (1 Timothy 6:8).

Charles Allen tells a story illustrating this principle. As World War II was drawing to a close, the Allied armies gathered up many hungry orphans and placed them in camps where they were well fed. Despite excellent care, they were afraid and slept poorly. Finally, a doctor came up with a solution. When the children were put to bed, he gave each of them a piece of bread to hold. Any hungry children could get more to eat, but when they were finished, they would still have this piece of bread just to hold, not to eat. The uneaten bread produced wonderful results. The children went to bed knowing that they would have food to eat the next day. That guarantee gave them restful and contented sleep. Similarly, the Lord has given us His guaran- tee—our "piece of bread." As we cling to His promises of provision, we can relax and be content. *"My God will supply all your needs according to His riches"* (Philippians 4:19, NAS).

He is Lord of the universe.

God, as He is revealed in Scripture, is very different from the way most people imagine Him to be. Our tendency is to shrink God down and fit Him into a man-like mold with human limitations. We do not understand the greatness of God, *"who stretched out the heavens and laid the foundations of the earth"* (Isaiah 51:13, NAS). We expand our perspective of God primarily through studying what the Bible tells us about Him.

Carefully review some of God's names and attributes: Creator, the Almighty, eternal, all-knowing, all-powerful, awesome, Lord of lords and King of kings. The Lord's power and ability are beyond our understanding. Astronomers estimate that there are more than 100 billion galaxies in the universe, each containing billions of stars. The distance from one end of a galaxy to the other is often measured in millions of light years. Though our sun is a relatively small star, it could contain more than one million earths, and it has temperatures of 20 million degrees at its center. Isaiah wrote, *"Lift up your eyes on high and see who has created these stars, the One who leads forth their host by number, He calls them all by name; because of the greatness of His might and the strength of His power, not one of them is missing"* (Isaiah 40:26, NAS).

He is Lord of the nations.

Examine how much greater the Lord is than mere nations and people. Isaiah 40:21-24 (NAS) tells us, *"Do you not know? Have you not heard? . . . It is He who sits above the circle of the earth, and its inhabitants are like grasshoppers . . . He it is who reduces rulers to nothing, who makes the judges of the earth meaningless. Scarcely have they been planted, scarcely have they been sown, scarcely has their stock taken root in the earth, but He merely blows on them, and they wither."* From Isaiah 40:15, 17 we read, *"The nations are like a drop from a bucket, and are regarded as a speck of dust on the scales. . . . All the nations are as nothing before Him, they are regarded by Him as less than nothing and meaningless"* (NAS). God doesn't fret over nations and their leaders as if He had no power to intervene. Acts 17:26 says, *"He [the Lord] . . . scattered the nations across the face of the earth. He decided beforehand which should rise and fall, and when. He determined their boundaries"* (TLB).

He is Lord of the individual.

God is intimately involved with each of us as individuals. *"You are familiar with all my ways. Before a word is on my tongue you know it completely, O Lord. . . . All the days ordained for me were written in your book before one of them came to be"* (Psalm 139:3-4, 16). The Lord is so involved in our lives that He reassures us, *"The very hairs of your head are all numbered"* (Matthew 10:30, NAS). Our heavenly Father is the One who knows us the best and loves us the most. God hung the stars in space, fashioned the earth's towering mountains and mighty oceans, and determined the destiny of nations. Jeremiah observed: *"Nothing is too difficult for You"* (Jeremiah 32:17, NAS). Yet God knows when a sparrow falls to the ground. Nothing in this study is more important than catching the vision of who God is and the part He plays in our finances.

SUMMARY OF GOD'S PART

The Lord did not design people to shoulder the responsibilities that only He can carry. Jesus said, *"Come to Me, all who are weary and heavy-laden, and I will give you rest. Take My yoke upon you. . . . For My yoke is easy and My burden is light"* (Matthew 11:28-30, NAS). God has assumed the burdens of ownership, control, and provision. For this reason, His yoke is easy, enabling us to enjoy the peace of God. For most of us, the problem is not recognizing God's part. Our culture contributes to this problem, assuming that God plays no part in financial matters. Another reason for this difficulty is that God has chosen to be invisible. Anything that is "out of sight" tends to be "out of mind." We get out of the habit of recognizing God's ownership, control, and provision. After learning God's part, some people think there is little responsibility remaining for us. However, the Lord has given us great responsibility, and we will consider that in the next chapter.

Think About it

- *In what ways do you try to take on God's role of ownership, control and provision?*

- *Why is it hard for you to let God do His part when it comes to money? What will you do to correct this practice?*

- *Think about someone in your life who really understands God's ownership of things. Write his or her name down and make an appointment to talk about how they cultivated God's ownership in their life.*

- *As a practical application of these concepts, complete the <u>Quit Claim Deed</u> on page 278.*

CHAPTER NINE

Fidelity: A Fresh Glance

Core Concepts

- Describe the two components of our part.

- In what way does faithfulness with a little matter equal faithfulness in a large matter?

- Describe how using money faithfully builds character.

- What are three benefits of faithfulness?

Overview

Having described God's responsibilities in our financial picture, we now examine ours. The word that best describes our role is "steward." A steward is a manager of someone else's possessions. The Lord has given us the authority to be stewards. "You made him ruler over the works of your [the Lord's] hands; you put everything under his feet" (Psalm 8:6). Our responsibility is summed up in this verse: "It is required in stewards that one be found trustworthy" (1 Corinthians 4:2, NAS). When God entrusts something to us, whether the gospel, money, possessions, relationships, health, education, abilities, etc., He requires us to manage it in a trustworthy or faithful manner according to His design and mission.

Before we can be faithful, we must know what we are required to do. Just as the purchaser of a complicated piece of machinery studies the manufacturer's manual to learn how to operate it, we need to examine the Creator's handbook—the Bible—to determine how He wants us to handle His possessions. As we begin to study our responsibilities, it's important to remember that God loves and cares for us deeply. He has given us these principles because He wants the best for us. Most people discover areas in which they have not been faithful. Don't become discouraged. Simply seek to apply faithfully what you learn.

We will look at two basic components that comprise our part of handling resources: faithfulness and contentment.

FAITHFULNESS

How we handle *His wealth* on earth impacts *our reward* in heaven and the riches of God's grace to us on earth; "we are but stewards of the manifold grace of God."[1]

Read the story of the unjust steward in chapter 16 of the Gospel of Luke. Context dictates our response to this example of faithfulness, and we must read the text in its normal meaning. The greatest difficulty in interpreting this story is the apparent conflict of an unjust person being commended by Christ.[2] But from Christ's every word and action throughout the Gospels, we know that He cannot be commending unethical behavior.

What we must observe and apply is Jesus' point about how to use money on earth. In verse nine, Jesus says: *"I say to you make friends for yourself by means of the mammon of unrighteousness; that when it fails they may receive you in the eternal dwellings"* (Luke 16:9, NAS). Jesus says first that we are to enable our comfortable reception to the happiness of another world by putting our possessions to good use for ourselves and others.[3] Matthew Henry enables us to further comprehend Jesus' recommendation by saying: "It is the wisdom of the men of this world so to manage their money as they may have the benefit of it in the hereafter, and not for the present only…now we should learn of them and make use of our money so that we may be the better off for it hereafter in another world (cf. Ecclesiastes 11:1)."[4]

Jesus' comment that *"the people of this world are more shrewd in dealing with their own kind than are the people of the light"* is not an invitation to walk away from the light of honesty and become dishonest people of darkness. Instead, he is pointing out how well the manager took care of himself. The implication is that we would take best care of ourselves by using our worldly wealth to influence others for eternity. With the understanding that Jesus commends the steward not for dealing falsely with his master but for acting wisely or shrewdly toward himself,[5] there is no contradiction or problem.

An additional point to be made is that Jesus is encouraging believers to use common sense with money, to be shrewd. *Shrewd* is a seldom-used adjective in our generation. In this case, it modifies "manager" or "steward," as "marked by keen awareness, sharp intelligence, and practicality." We are to use money with a keen mind, recognizing that worldly wealth is not to be trusted for happiness, but that it *can* be used for "the honor of God and the good of our brethren, that thus we may with them lay up in store a good bond, a good security, a good foundation for the time to come, for an eternity to come (cf. 1 Timothy 6:17-19)."[6]

Finally, Jesus indicated that the wise use of wealth would enable others to believe in the message of God and, in turn, lead them to accept God."[7]

Next, Luke 16:10-13 (NAS) says, *"He who is faithful in a very little thing is faithful also in much; and he who is unrighteous in a very little thing is unrighteous also in much. Therefore, if you have not been faithful in the use of unrighteous wealth* (worldly things/money), *who will entrust the true riches to you?"*

Faithfulness in the little things proves readiness for larger things. Jesus is connecting our fitness to handle things of deep and eternal value with how we now handle worldly wealth (little things by comparison).[8] Therefore, as overseers of God's goods, we develop faithfulness with what we are given as well as faithfulness in every area of our lives, including the possessions of others.

Being faithful with what we are given: We are to be faithful regardless of how much He has entrusted to us. The parable of the talents (a talent is a sum of money) illustrates this: *"It will be like a man going on a journey, who called his servants and entrusted his property to them. To one he gave five talents of money, to another two talents, and to another one talent"* (Matthew 25:14-15).[9] When the owner returned, he held each one responsible for faithfully managing his possessions. The owner praised the faithful servant who received the five talents: *"Well done, good and faithful [servant]. You were faithful with a few things, I will put you in charge of many things; enter into the joy of your master"* (Matthew 25:21, NAS). Interestingly, the servant who had been given two talents received the identical reward as the one who had been given the five talents (see Matthew 25:23). The Lord rewards faithfulness, regardless of the amount over which we are responsible. We are required to be faithful whether we are given much or little. As someone once said, "It's not what I would do if $1 million were my lot; it's what I am doing with the ten dollars I've got."

How do you know if a child is going to take good care of his first car? Observe how he cared for his bicycle. How do you know if a salesperson will do a competent job of serving a large client? Evaluate how she served a small client. If we have the character to be faithful with small things the Lord entrusts to us, He knows He can trust us with greater responsibilities. Small things are small things, but faithfulness with a small thing is a big thing.

Being faithful in every area: God wants us to be faithful in handling all of our money. Unfortunately, most Christians have been taught only how to handle 10 percent of their income God's way—the area of giving. Although giving is crucial, the other 90 percent is the lion's share, and most people have learned how to handle it from the world's perspective. As a result of not being taught to handle money biblically, many Christians have wrong attitudes toward possessions, often causing them to make incorrect financial decisions and suffer painful consequences.

Wasteful is not faithful. *"There was a rich man who had a manager (steward), and this manager was reported to him as squandering his possessions. And he called him and said to him, 'What is this I hear about you? Give an accounting of your management, for you can no longer be manager"* (Luke 16:1-2, NAS). Two principles from this passage apply to us. First, when we waste resources it becomes public knowledge and creates a poor testimony. *"This [steward] was reported to him as squandering his possessions."* Second, the Lord may remove us as stewards if we squander what He has given us. A contemporary example of this is a businessman who earned a fortune in just three years and then went on a spending spree. Two years later he informed his office staff that the company's finances were tight and everyone would need to economize.

Shortly thereafter, he left for an expensive vacation and had his office completely renovated at a cost of thousands of dollars. During his vacation the entire staff gathered in the newly decorated office to discuss his unbridled spending habits. The Lord soon removed this man from the privilege of being steward over much, and today he is on the verge of bankruptcy. The principle is applicable today: if we waste the possessions entrusted to us, we may not be given more.

Faithfulness with another's possessions: Faithfulness with another's possession will, in some measure, determine how much we are given. *"If you have not been faithful in the use of that which is another's, who will give you that which is your own?"* (Luke 16:12, NAS). We often overlook this principle. One of the most faithful men I (Howard) know rented a vehicle from a friend. While driving it, he was involved in an accident. After explaining the situation to the owner, he took the vehicle to the owner's mechanic and instructed him, "Completely restore it. Make it better than it was before the accident, and I will be responsible for the bill." What an example!

Are you faithful with others' possessions? Are you careless with your employer's office supplies? How about the time you report on your timecards? That time belongs to your employer if he is paying for it. When someone allows you to use something, are you careful to return it promptly and in good shape? Some people have not been entrusted with more because they have been unfaithful with the possessions of others. Please prayerfully review these principles of faithfulness.

CONTENTMENT

We have addressed this topic in previous chapters, but contentment is such a key issue in our relationship and understanding of money and ministry that it's worth mentioning again. If we attempt to serve two masters, we will never find peace. Paul reminds us that contentment comes through submission to Christ. Contentment is a process. Paul says, *"...for I have* learned *to be content in whatever circumstances I am. I know how to get along with humble means, and I also know how to live in prosperity; in any and every circumstance I have* learned *the secret of being filled and going hungry, both of having abundance and suffering need. I can do all things through Him who strengthens me"* (Philippians 4:11-13, NAS, emphasis mine). You may not get the job you really want after college. What happens then? Understand that the key to contentment does not reside in a different job or more education—even if those are prudent options. The key is always yielding to God's leading and expressing gratitude for His provision as you rely on Christ.

BENEFITS OF HANDLING MONEY FAITHFULLY

The faithful steward enjoys three benefits.

More intimate fellowship with Jesus Christ

Remember what the master said to the servant who had been faithful with his finances: *"Enter into the joy of your master"* (Matthew 25:21, NAS). We can enter into closer, more intimate fellowship with our Lord as we are faithful with the possessions He has given us. Someone once told me (Howard) that the Lord often allows a person to teach a subject because the teacher desperately needs it! That is true for me in the area of money. I have never met anyone who had more wrong attitudes about money or who handled money in a way more contrary to Scripture than I did. When I began to apply these principles, I experienced a dramatic improvement in my fellowship with the Lord. Each of these principles is intended to draw us closer to Christ.

The development of character

God uses money to refine our character. As David McConaugh explained in his book, *Money: the Acid Test* (written in 1918), "Money, most common of temporal things, involves uncommon and eternal consequences. Even though it may be done quite unconsciously, money molds people in the process of getting it, saving it, spending it, and giving it. Depending on how it's used, it proves to be a blessing or a curse. Either the person becomes master of the money, or the money becomes the master of the person. Our Lord uses money to test our lives and as an instrument to mold us into the likeness of Himself."[10]

All through Scripture there is a correlation between the development of character and the handling of money. Our checkbook and credit card statements provide an index to our character and values because they reveal what is most important to us: what we spend our money on.

Having our finances in order

As we apply God's principles to our finances, we will begin to get out of debt, spend more wisely, save for our future, and give more to the work of Christ. Having our finances in order enables us to avoid being a slave to them so we can focus more on serving the Lord through our vocation and the church.

Think About it

- *Is your relationship with Christ hindered by your financial behavior?*

- *Do you carefully consider the purchases you make with God's money?*

- *Are you being faithful with all the stuff He has given you?*

- *Are you dealing honestly with those for whom you work?*

PART III

Balance: The Way of the Godly Steward

Overview

Maintaining our balance can be difficult. Sometimes our enthusiasm for growth can lead us to unhealthy extremes. Just as the pursuit of money can become our god, so can an extreme avoidance of it that mistakes money—rather than the love of money—as being a root of evil. The goal of part three is to explore how we can live for Christ within our existing affluent culture while maintaining a godly perspective on faith and money.

So far, we have established why we need to study carefully the issue of stewardship. We have seen that God retains the major responsibilities of ownership, control, and provision. The remainder of the study focuses on our personal responses—our part of the equation—for which we will be held accountable as stewards of the resources God has entrusted to our care.

CHAPTER TEN

Honesty: God's Mandate

Core Concepts

- How was the community affected by the dishonest behavior of Achan? Of Ananias and Sapphira?

- Describe five reasons why Christians are to be honest.

- What three reasons are given in the text for the necessity of honesty in leaders?

Overview

Honesty: what could be simpler? At first it sounds too elementary to merit serious consideration in a financial study. Unfortunately, closer examination often reveals significant personal battles over the temptation to skew the truth in a way that benefits us.

We are called to be holy and to live a life worthy of our calling. We cannot be dishonest in the use of money and be simultaneously in close fellowship with God. Culture has desensitized many of us to the implications of dishonesty in our lives. Scripture gives us abundant insight into how God views dishonesty and the consequences it has on our spiritual development with Christ.

INTRODUCTION

I don't know how long, but it had been a while since I (Chad) had cleaned my shower. The slow drain finally forced my hand. With a new bottle of powerful tub cleaner in one yellow-gloved hand and a scrub brush in the other, I stepped in to do battle. Before long I began to see how bad it was. Emerging an hour later with a new appreciation for how white it could be, how the faucets could sparkle, I wondered why I was so surprised. It seems I had grown accustomed to the grime.

It just happened to be the night before I was to teach on honesty during an inter-session class. It occurred to me that the grime buildup in my tub is like dishonesty in our lives. Our hearts have a way of collecting grime without our realizing it. A little denial here, a half-truth there, and soon we are mired in a buildup of scum and muck that hinders our growth in Christ. We need routine heart exams to check for hints of dishonesty, especially with money.

LESSONS FROM THE LESS FORTUNATE: BIBLICAL EXAMPLES

One of my (Chad's) favorite Old Testament stories provides strong guidance and motivation for our pursuit of honesty. Take time now to read Joshua, chapter 7, making observations about Achan's dishonesty and its consequences. What principles do you observe about God's clear communication of His intentions?

1. The sin of Achan: Joshua 7

As you recall from your studies in the Old Testament historical books, Joshua and the children of Israel have recently conquered Jericho and are moving forward into the Promised Land. God tells Joshua to move on to Ai and conquer the city. In this context, we see the consequences of one man's disobedient, dishonest behavior.

Individual actions never occur in a vacuum. All of us live in community, and all of us have neighbors according to Jesus' definition. The consequences of our personal actions—bad or good—have powerful ripple effects beyond our expectations.

a. *Consequences of dishonesty:* We were created to live in community with other believers. We attempt to create biblical community in our churches and on our campuses, but we sometimes want its benefits without thinking through the real-life implications. One of those implications is the corporate discipline that may result from God's response to the sin of an individual.

Even though God deals with our sin individually through the substitutionary death of Christ, the community can be affected by not only the natural consequences of our sin but also God's discipline as He works to purify the body. As we see in Achan's example, his dishonest actions were not merely between him and God; they affected the whole community of Israel.

b. *The dishonesty process:* Achan's dishonest actions followed a process that is relevant to our study of money. We face the same process each day: (a) Achan saw (b) Achan coveted (c) Achan took for himself items strictly forbidden by God.

In this process of seeing, coveting, and taking, Achan became an accessory to the slaughter of 36 of his own people and brought God's wrath upon the community. Instead of leaving a righteous legacy for those he loved most, he was responsible for the stoning and burning of his entire family and their possessions.

Achan's story illustrates the inseparable link between our faith, finances and possessions. Sins of dishonesty are not surface irregularities that bear no direct correlation to our spiritual character; they reveal the core of our character and our unfitness for God's blessing (cf. Luke 16:11).

This example has nothing to do with the kind of sin we so often attribute to carnality—drinking, drugs, sex, or violence. This was about Achan willfully taking possessions for himself that were not his own. These possessions were to be placed in God's treasury. So Achan was actually robbing God, a sin God considered disgraceful:[1] a matter of dire consequence that required immediate restitution and resolution.

2. Ananias and Sapphira: Acts 5

Our second biblical example of dishonesty is the New Testament parallel to Achan's story. Just as Israel had been moving into the Promised Land, believers in "the better and greater covenant" (Hebrews 8:6 and 9:11-15) were being led by the Apostles to become the grace-filled body of Christ. Take time now to read Acts 5 carefully. Make observations about the dishonest behavior of Ananias and Sapphira and the consequences for their community of believers.

Ananias and Sapphira were following the example of Joseph, a Levite of Cypress known also as Barnabas, who sold property he owned on the Island of Cypress and gave all the proceeds to the Apostles.

When Ananias sold a piece of property, he conspired with his wife to keep a portion of the proceeds and present the rest to the apostles as though it were the entire amount. In this case, the sin was not keeping something forbidden; he was under no obligation to give anything. His sin was the deceit of false pretenses—making a show—and then lying to cover it up.

This passage teaches us several lessons.

a. *God's displeasure with sin (v. 4):* Deceit is not acceptable in the community of God's people. Ananias and Sapphira sold property but kept some of the proceeds back. In their desire for praise and recognition, they led the body to believe they had given all the proceeds to the needs of the community. Peter equated this sin as one from a heart that had been deceived by Satan.

b. *Example to others and us:* This act of dishonesty was a severe sin leading to death. God used it as an example to the greater body of believers (vs. 5, 11). During the transition from law to grace, God chose to make an example that would establish the necessity of absolute honesty within the church. Although it is clear that He does not visit those same consequences on every instance of dishonesty today, we must never be deceived into thinking that He hates sin and dishonesty any less.

3. What can we learn from these examples?

- God hates dishonest behavior. Congregations are only as effective as the honesty of the people.
- Our sin of dishonesty has consequences for all the community of believers.
- God's people are held to a higher standard as sons and daughters in whom the Spirit of the living God resides. We are to *"become blameless and pure,*

children of God without fault in a crooked and depraved generation, in which [we] shine like stars in the universe" (Philippians 2:15).

Honesty in society

All of us have to make daily decisions about whether to handle money honestly. Do we tell the cashier at the store when we receive too much change? Have we ever tried to sell something and been tempted not to tell the whole truth because we might lose the sale?

These decisions become even more difficult when everyone around us seems to be acting dishonestly. After pumping five dollars worth of gas in my truck, I (Howard) asked for a receipt, and the attendant made the receipt for ten dollars. When I pointed out the mistake, he replied, "Oh, just turn in the receipt to your company and you'll make a fast five bucks. After all, that's what many of the mail deliverers in this area do." When I heard that, my heart sank. The verse that came immediately to mind was Judges 17:6, *"Every man did what was right in his own eyes"* (NAS). People today formulate their own standards of honesty and then change them according to their circumstances.

Honesty in Scripture

Hundreds of verses in the Bible communicate the Lord's desire for us to be completely honest. For instance, Proverbs 20:23 reads, *"The Lord loathes all cheating and dishonesty"* (TLB). Proverbs 12:22, states, *"Lying lips are an abomination to the Lord"* (NAS). And in Proverbs 6:16-17 we read, *"The Lord hates...a lying tongue"* (NAS). As you study the verses in this chapter, notice how the Bible's standard of honesty contrasts with cultural norms.

The God of truth

Truthfulness is one of God's characteristics. He is repeatedly identified as the God of truth: *"I am ...the truth"* (John 14:6, NAS). The Lord commands us to reflect His honest and holy character: *"Be holy yourselves also in all your behavior; because it is written, 'You shall be holy, for I am holy'"* (1 Peter 1:15-16, NAS). In contrast to God's nature, John 8:44 describes the devil's character: *"He [the devil] was a murderer from the beginning, and does not stand in the truth because there is no truth in him. Whenever he speaks a lie, he speaks from his own nature, for he is a liar and the father of lies"* (NAS). The Lord wants us to become conformed to His honest character rather than to the dishonest nature of the devil.

Absolute honesty

God wants us to be totally honest for the following reasons.

1. To show that we really love God

Two of the Ten Commandments address honesty. *"You shall not steal. You shall not bear false witness against your neighbor"* (Exodus 20:15-16, NAS). Jesus told us, *"If you love Me, you will keep My commandments"* (John 14:15, NAS). Jesus Christ came to fulfill the law, not abolish it. Although we live under the new covenant of grace and there is no condemnation for those who are in Christ Jesus (Romans 8:1-2), the standard for righteous behavior has not been lowered. We will certainly struggle as we attempt to do God's will in our present state (Romans 7: 14-25), but Paul reminds us of the solution: *"But I say, walk in the Spirit and you will not carry out the desire of the flesh"* (Galatians 5:16, NAS).

We cannot practice dishonesty and simultaneously show love to God. When being dishonest, we are acting as if He doesn't even exist! We are acting as though God is not able to provide exactly what we need even though He has promised to do so (Matthew 6:33). We decide to take things into our own hands and meet our needs in our own dishonest way. We are also acting as if God is incapable of discovering our dishonesty and is powerless to discipline us. If we really believe God will discipline us, we will not consider acting dishonestly.

Honest behavior is an issue of faith. An honest decision may look foolish in light of what we can see, but the godly person knows Jesus Christ is alive even though invisible. Every honest decision strengthens our faith in God and helps us grow into a closer relationship with Christ. However, if we choose to be dishonest, we are really denying our Lord. It is impossible to love God with all our heart, soul, and mind if, at the same time, we are dishonest and acting as if He does not exist.

2. To show that we love our neighbor

The Lord requires honesty because dishonest behavior also violates the second great commandment, *"You shall love your neighbor as yourself"* (Mark 12:31, NAS). Romans 13:9-10 reads, *"If you love your neighbor as much as you love yourself, you will not want to harm or cheat him, or kill him or steal from him…love does no wrong to anyone"* (TLB). When we act dishonestly, we are stealing from another person. We may deceive ourselves into thinking it is a business, the government, or an insurance company that is suffering loss, but it is the business owners, fellow taxpayers, or policyholders from whom we are stealing. It is just as if we took the money from their wallets. Dishonesty always injures people. The victim is always a person.

3. To demonstrate credibility for evangelism

Our Lord requires honesty to enable us to demonstrate the reality of Jesus Christ to those who do not yet know Him. I will never forget the first time I (Howard) told a neighbor how he could come to know Christ as his personal Savior. He angrily responded, "Well, I know a man who always goes to church and talks a lot about Jesus, but watch out if you ever get in a business deal with him! He'd cheat his own grandmother! If that's what it means to be a Christian, I don't want any part of it!"

Our actions speak louder than our words. Just as we can influence people away from Jesus Christ, we can also influence people *for* Him by handling our money honestly (cf. Luke 16:9). Robert Newsom had been trying to sell a car for months. Finally, an interested buyer decided to purchase the car. However, at the last moment he said, "I'll buy this car, but only on one condition—you don't report this sale so I won't have to pay state sales tax." Although he was tempted, Robert responded, "I'm sorry, I can't do that because Jesus Christ is my Lord." Robert later said, "You should have seen the buyer's reaction. He almost went into shock!

Then an interesting thing happened. His attitude completely changed. Not only did he purchase the car, but also he eagerly joined my wife and me around our dinner table. Rarely have I seen anyone as open to the truth about knowing Jesus Christ in a personal way." Because Robert acted honestly even though it was going to cost him money (*"Prove yourselves to be blameless and innocent, children of God above reproach"*), he demonstrated to this person (*"a crooked and perverse generation"*) the reality of a personal faith in Jesus Christ (*"appear as lights in the world"*)—Philippians 2:15.

4. To confirm God's direction

Proverbs 4:24-26 reads, *"Put away from you a deceitful mouth and put devious lips far from you. Let your eyes look directly ahead, and let your gaze be fixed straight in front of you. Watch the path of your feet and all your ways will be established"* (NAS). Although Proverbs are general truths about life rather than absolute guarantees, this principle remains a tremendous comfort. As you are completely honest, *"all your ways will be established."*

Choosing to walk the narrow path of honesty eliminates the many possible avenues of dishonesty. Making decisions becomes simpler because the honest path is a clear path. "If only I had understood that truth before we bought our house," Raymond said. "But Donna and I wanted that house so much. We had too much debt to qualify for the mortgage, so the only way for us to buy the house was to hide some of our debts from the bank. It was the worst decision of my life. We were unable to meet the mortgage payment and pay our other debts too.

"The pressure built and was almost more than Donna could stand. Our dream house ended up causing a family nightmare. I not only lost the home but nearly lost my wife." Had Raymond and Donna been honest, the bank would not have approved the loan. They would not have been able to purchase that particular home. Had they prayed and waited, perhaps the Lord would have brought something more affordable, thus avoiding the pressure that almost ended their marriage. Honesty helps confirm God's direction.

5. Even small acts of dishonesty are harmful.

God requires us to be completely honest because even the smallest act of dishonesty is sin. And even the smallest sin interrupts our fellowship with the Lord and retards our maturity in Christ. The smallest "white lie" will harden our hearts, making our consciences increasingly insensitive to sin and deafening our ears to the still small voice of the Lord (cf. Ephesians 4:27, 30). This single cancer cell of small dishonesty multiplies and spreads to greater dishonesty. *"Whoever is dishonest with very little will also be dishonest with much"* (Luke 16:10).

An event in Abraham's life challenges us to be honest in small matters. In Genesis 14, the king of Sodom offered Abraham all the goods he (Abraham) had recovered when he successfully rescued the people of Sodom. But Abraham responded to the king, *"I have sworn to the Lord God Most High, possessor of heaven and earth, that I will not take a thread or a sandal thong or anything that is yours"* (Genesis 14:22-23, NAS). Just as Abraham was unwilling to take so much as a thread, we challenge you to make a similar commitment in this area of honesty.

Covenant not to steal a stamp or a photocopy or a paper clip or a long distance telephone call or a penny from your employer, the government, or anyone else. The people of God must be honest in even the smallest matters. To love God and our neighbors, to evangelize effectively, to confirm God's direction, and to develop a heart sensitive to God—is there any wonder that our Lord knows it is best for us to be completely honest?

Escaping the temptation of dishonesty

A friend was teaching these principles in a secular school when one student raised his hand and said, "I think we all would like to be the person you're talking about, but I know in my heart that if the right opportunity comes along, I'm going to be dishonest." I (Howard) think he is correct. Apart from living our lives yielded to the Holy Spirit, all of us will be dishonest. *"Live by the Spirit, and you will not gratify the desires of the sinful nature. For the sinful nature desires what is contrary to the Spirit, and the Spirit what is contrary to the sinful nature"* (Galatians 5:16-17). The character of our human nature is to act dishonestly. *"Out of men's hearts, come evil thoughts . . . theft . . . deceit"* (Mark 7:21-22).

The desire of the Spirit is for us to be totally honest. The absolutely honest life is supernatural. We need to submit ourselves entirely to Jesus Christ as Lord and allow Him to live His life through us. There is no other way. We heartily recommend a short book by Andrew Murray titled *Humility*. It is an excellent study for living your life yielded to Christ as Lord. The following practices will help you to develop the habit of honesty.

1. Practice the Golden Rule.

"Do not merely look out for your own personal interests, but also for the interests of others" (Philippians 2:4, NAS). This verse is better translated, "look intently" after the interests of others. The Lord used this passage to point out Warren's lack of concern for others when he was about to purchase some land. The seller knew nothing of its value. Warren had been secretly congratulating himself because he knew the purchase price he was offering was very low. Not once had he even considered what would be fair to the seller. He had concentrated solely on acquiring the property at the lowest possible price.

Warren reexamined the transaction in the light of "looking intently" after the seller's interests as well as his own. After an intense inner struggle, he concluded that he should pay more for the property to reflect its true value. Practicing the Golden Rule is sometimes costly, but its reward is a clear conscience before God and others.

2. Practice a healthy fear of the Lord.

When we talk of a healthy fear of the Lord, we do not mean that God is a big bully just waiting for the opportunity to punish us. Rather, He is a loving Father who, out of infinite love, disciplines His children for their benefit. *"He disciplines us for our good, so that we may share His holiness"* (Hebrews 12:10, NAS). One of the methods God uses to motivate us to honest living is this healthy fear. Proverbs 16:6 reads, *"By the fear of the Lord one keeps away from evil"* (NAS).

Hebrews 12:11 reminds us that discipline is painful: *"All discipline for the moment seems not to be joyful, but sorrowful"* (NAS). We are always better off to obey God's Word rather than make a decision that will prompt our loving Father to discipline us. Moreover, we believe our heavenly Father will not allow us to keep anything we have acquired dishonestly. Proverbs 13:11 reads, *"Wealth obtained by fraud dwindles"* (NAS). A friend (Howard's) purchased four azalea plants but the checkout clerk had only charged her for one. She knew it, but she left the store anyway without paying for the other three. She told me it was miraculous how quickly three of those plants died!

Think about this for a moment: If you are a parent and one of your children steals something, do you allow the child to keep it? Of course not, because it would damage the child's character to keep stolen property. Not only do you insist on its return, but also you usually want the child to experience enough discomfort to produce a lasting impression. For instance, you might have the child confess the theft to the store manager. When our heavenly Father lovingly disciplines us, He usually does it in such a way that we will not forget.

3. Practice avoiding dishonest people.

Scripture teaches that we are deeply influenced by those around us, either for good or for evil. David recognized this and said, *"My eyes shall be upon the faithful of the land, that they may dwell with me; he who walks in a blameless way is the one who will minister to me. He who practices deceit shall not dwell within my house; he who speaks falsehood shall not maintain his position before me"* (Psalm 101:6-7, NAS). Paul wrote, *"Do not be deceived: 'Bad company corrupts good morals'"* (1 Corinthians 15:33, NAS). Solomon was even stronger: *"He who is a partner with a thief hates his own life"* (Proverbs 29:24, NAS).

Obviously, we cannot isolate ourselves from every dishonest person. In fact, we are to be salt and light in the world. We should, however, be very cautious when choosing our close friends or considering a business relationship. If I observe a person who is dishonest in dealing with the government or in a small matter, I know this person will be dishonest in greater matters and probably in dealing with me. In our opinion, it is impossible for a person to be selectively honest. Either the person has made the commitment to be absolutely honest or that person's dishonesty will become more prevalent. It is much easier to remain absolutely honest if you are surrounded by others who are of like mind and conviction.

4. Practice giving.

We can reduce the temptation to act dishonestly by giving generously to those in need. *"He who steals must steal no longer, but rather he must labor performing with his own hands what is good, so that he will have something to share with him who has need"* (Ephesians 4:28, NAS). As we give, it draws us closer to Christ and reduces our incentive to steal. After all, if we are going to give something away, there is no reason to steal it!

What to do when we have been dishonest

Unfortunately, from time to time, we will act dishonestly. Once we recognize that we have been dishonest, we need to do the following.

1. Restore our fellowship with God.

Anytime we sin, we break our fellowship with our Lord, and we need to restore it. 1 John 1:9 tells us how: *"If we confess our sins, He is faithful and righteous to forgive us our sins and to cleanse us from all unrighteousness"* (NAS). We must agree with God that our dishonesty was sin, and then thankfully accept God's gracious forgiveness so we can again enjoy His fellowship. Remember, God loves us. He is kind and merciful. We take great comfort in these words: *"For we do not have a high priest (Christ) who cannot sympathize with our weaknesses, but One who has been tempted in all things as we are, yet without sin. Let us therefore draw near with confidence to the throne of grace, that we may receive mercy and may find grace to help in time of need"* (Hebrews 4:15-16, NAS). God is ready to forgive our dishonesty when we turn from it.

2. Restore our fellowship with the harmed person.

After our fellowship with Christ has been restored, we need to confess our dishonesty to the person we offended. *"Confess your sins to one another"* (James 5:16, NAS). Ouch! This hurts. Only a handful of people have confessed that they have wronged me (Howard). Interestingly, these people have become some of my closest friends—in part because of my respect for them. They so desired an honest relationship that they were willing to expose their sins.

This has been very hard for me. Several years ago I (Howard) went to someone I had wronged and confessed my sin—not that I hadn't had plenty of opportunities before then! In the past, however, my pride stood in the way. Afterward I sensed a great freedom in our relationship. I also discovered that the humbling pain of confession helps break the habit of dishonesty. A person's lack of financial prosperity may be a consequence of violating this principle. *"He who conceals his transgressions will not prosper, but he who confesses and forsakes them will find compassion"* (Proverbs 28:13, NAS).

3. Restore dishonestly acquired property.

If we have acquired anything dishonestly, we must return it to its rightful owner. *"Then it shall be, when he sins and becomes guilty, that he shall restore what he took by robbery . . . or anything about which he swore falsely; he shall make restitution for it in full and add to it one-fifth more. He shall give it to the one to whom it belongs"*

(Leviticus 6:4-5, NAS). Restitution is a tangible expression of repentance and an effort to correct a wrong. Zaccheus is a good New Testament example. He promised Jesus, *"If I have defrauded anyone of anything, I will give back four times as much"* (Luke 19:8, NAS). If it's not possible for restitution to be made, the property should be given to the Lord. Numbers 5:8 teaches, *"If the man has no relative to whom restitution may be made for the wrong, the restitution which is made for the wrong must go to the Lord for the priest"* (NAS).

Honesty required for leaders

The Lord is especially concerned with the honesty of leaders.

1. Influence of leaders

Leaders influence those who follow them. The owner of a trucking business began wearing cowboy boots to work. Within six months, all the men in his office were in boots. He suddenly changed to traditional business shoes and six months later all the men were wearing business shoes. In a similar way, a dishonest leader produces dishonest followers. *"If a ruler pays attention to falsehood, all his ministers become wicked"* (Proverbs 29:12, NAS). The leader of a business, church, or home must set the example of honesty in his or her personal life before those under his or her authority can be expected to do the same.

The president of a large international construction company was once asked why her company did not work in countries where bribes were a way of life. She responded, "We never build in those countries because we can't afford to. If my employees know we are acting dishonestly, they will eventually become thieves. Their dishonesty will ultimately cost us more than we could ever earn on a project."

During an effort to reduce expenses, a company discovered the employees making frequent personal long-distance telephone calls at the office and charging them to the company. The company president had unwittingly fueled this problem. He had reasoned that because he placed approximately the same number of long-distance calls for the company on his home phone as personal long-distance calls on the company phone, a detailed accounting was unnecessary. His employees, however, knew only of his calls at work. They concluded that if this practice was acceptable for the boss, it was acceptable for all. A leader should *"abstain from all appearance of evil"* (1 Thessalonians 5:22, KJV) because his or her actions influence others.

2. Selection of leaders

Dishonesty should disqualify a person from leadership. Listen to the counsel of Jethro, Moses' father-in-law. *"You shall select out of all the people able men who fear*

God, men of truth, those who hate dishonest gain; and you shall place these . . . as leaders of thousands, of hundreds, of fifties and of tens" (Exodus 18:21, NAS). Two of the four criteria for leadership selection dealt with honesty: *"men of truth, those who hate dishonest gain."* We believe the Lord wants us to continue to select leaders on the basis of these same character qualities.

3. Preservation of leaders

Not only are leaders selected, in part, by honest behavior, but they also retain these positions by honest behavior. *"A leader...who hates unjust gain will prolong his days"* (Proverbs 28:16, NAS). We have all witnessed the leaders of business or government who have been demoted because of personal corruption. How can a leader maintain the standard of absolute honesty? By becoming accountable! It is necessary to establish a system of checks and balances that do not usurp the leader's authority but provide a structure to ensure that the leader is accountable.

Bribes

A bribe is defined as anything given to influence a person to do something illegal or wrong. Taking bribes is clearly prohibited in Scripture: *"You shall not take a bribe, for a bribe blinds the clear-sighted and subverts the cause of the just"* (Exodus 23:8, NAS). A bribe is often disguised as a "gift" or "referral fee." Evaluate any such offer to confirm that it is not in reality a bribe.

SUMMARY

Honesty can be the area many Christians overlook in relation to finances. The sin of dishonesty will hinder our relationship with Christ. However, the law of grace reigns, as Paul says in Romans 6:1-2, *"What shall we say then? Are we to continue in sin so that grace may increase? May it never be (or more literally, God forbid!). How shall we who died to sin still live in it?"* (NAS)

We are all sinners saved by grace who need the Holy Spirit to show us where we need improvement so we can be honest with God, our families, the Christian community, and the world around us. Our goal is not to judge or condemn but to draw clearly the line of faithful obedience to Christ. It is a powerful testimony to be known by others as people who love enough to be honest in all things.

Think about it!

- *Perhaps dishonesty is one of the reasons some churches are ineffective. What are some sins that could hinder your church body?*

- *Can a congregation be blessed by God when its members act dishonestly?*

- *What does Achan's sin teach us about financial faithfulness within the body of Christ?*

- *Have you observed a congregation that has suffered or is suffering from someone's financial unfaithfulness? Explain.*

- *We have observed from this text that acting unfaithfully with finances can have corporate implications. How will you personally respond to the example of Achan in your relationship to money?*

- *From your own experience, describe three common beliefs the world holds regarding honesty and contrast them with God's desires for us.*

- *How has the world system influenced your thinking when you sin against God and others? Explain.*

CHAPTER ELEVEN

Thrive: The Blessing of Work

Core Concepts

- Describe two key misconceptions many people have about work.

- Describe specific God-given work abilities mentioned in the Old Testament.

- Identify four key elements about work from Solomon's perspective.

Overview

As we strive to serve Christ in our work, Scripture helps us put our lives and giftedness into perspective. I Peter 4:10-11 (NAS) reads, "As each one has received a special gift, employ it in serving one another as good stewards of the manifold grace of God. Whoever speaks is to do so as one who is speaking the utterances of God; whoever serves is to do so as one who is serving by strength which God supplies; so that in all things God may be glorified through Jesus Christ, to whom belongs the glory and dominion forever and ever. Amen."

Several key points come from this passage:
- *Each person has been gifted by God.*
- *We worship and bring Him glory through work.*
- *We are to serve in the strength of God.*

Furthermore, as we will see in subsequent passages, work is:
- *Ordained by God*
- *The legitimate means of making money*

MISCONCEPTIONS ABOUT WORK

Many people dread work and think of it as a necessary evil to be tolerated until retirement liberates them. Restaurants advertise "Happy hour" specials to greet weary workers with an "attitude adjustment," as if life has been on hold until work is over. This was never God's plan.

Work was established by God before the fall, which means it is inherently good. Genesis 2:15 (NAS) reads, *"Then the Lord God took the man and put him into the Garden of Eden to cultivate it and keep it."* To cultivate and keep implies that Adam was not placed in paradise to lounge around in a hammock drinking lemonade all day (as attractive as that might *seem*). God appointed Adam to be the steward or manager of God's creation. The honor of cultivating and keeping the garden was ordained by God before the consequences of sin.

When sin entered the world, it contaminated everything including the pleasure of work. Genesis 3:17 (NAS) reads, *"Cursed is the ground because of you; in toil you will eat of it all the days of your life."* God never cursed work; The earth was cursed because of the sin of Adam. Work, then, has taken a dramatic turn from being pure delight to being much harder than God intended. Although work has become more difficult, it has not been cursed, and it is still capable of fulfilling God's design for it.

Work was ordained by God to accomplish His purposes. One of those was to give man, made in His own image as the crown of His creation, the honor of creatively managing the splendor of God's own handiwork. This chapter also shows us God resting on the seventh day, setting the example that helps us stay refreshed and focused.

Biblical examples

Several biblical examples help us understand that God created work for our good and that He can bless what we do for Him on earth.

1. Genesis 1-2: God

God Himself worked in Trinity to create our world out of nothing. Genesis 1:2 mentions the Spirit: *"the Spirit of God was hovering over the waters."* When God is ready to create man, He states, *"Let us make man in our image"* Genesis 1:26). The New Testament makes Jesus' role in creation clear when the Gospel of John opens with a declaration that Jesus, the Word, *"was God"* and *"was with God in the beginning. Through him all things were made; without him nothing was made that has been made"* (John 1:1-2). Colossians 1:16-17 (NAS) says, *"For by Him (Christ) all things were created: things in heaven and on earth, visible and invisible, whether thrones or powers or rulers or authorities; all things were created by Him and for Him. He is before all things, and in Him all things hold together."* Our Triune God provides for us the foundational model for work.

2. Exodus 31:1-11 and 35:30—36:7: Bezalel and Oholiab

Perhaps you have never been introduced to Oholiab and Bezalel. Read these passages and make observations about how God called and equipped individuals to build the temple. Write down as many as you can before reading the list below, and then compare your list with this one.

a. Called by God: God calls specific people to accomplish specific things. God stirred the hearts of the people to build the temple. Remember that He has uniquely called and gifted you to serve Him in some way.

b. Craftsmen with many skills: Have you ever thought about God calling and gifting craftsmen? It is clear in this passage that God values people with building skills and He wants them to use those skills appropriately. God designed the heavens and earth. He crafted everything in our universe with excellence and precision. If you have the skills of craftsmanship, excel in those gifts as unto the Lord.

c. *Filled with the Spirit:* God filled these people with His Spirit to accomplish the task of building the temple. Remember, the Spirit was not available to the average person as He is to believers today. God's Spirit rested on only a select few in the Old Testament. In this situation, God's Spirit rested on those responsible to build and craft things for the Lord's house.

d. *Possessed wisdom and understanding from the Lord:* God gave these craftsmen wisdom and understanding to creatively apply their skills for accomplishing the task. God also gives us wisdom to serve Him in our particular ministries as we remain in Him. *"I am the vine; you are the branches. If a man remains in me and I in him, he will bear much fruit; apart from me you can do nothing"* (John 15:5).

e. *Designers of many things:* God gifts people with a variety of design capabilities. We learn in this passage that God enabled the workers to construct many different items for the temple. It is safe to assume that these people retained these abilities as a way to make a living and serve God.

f. *Diversified in their giftedness:* Equally important is the fact that there was a diversity of gifts among the workers. Each of us has a unique set of gifts that no one else possesses fully. It takes many people to accomplish God's work, both in building the temple and in building the body of Christ.

g. *Teachers/mentors pass on their skills to others:* These craftsmen passed on their skills to others. When God gives skills, a part of being faithful includes passing them on to others. Are you mentoring someone right now? Are you leaving a legacy of leadership or are you focused on yourself? Find someone to mentor, passing your skills and passion to the next generation.

h. *God gave skills to certain people:* We also observe that God selected certain people for building the temple. We are not given the opportunities or skills of others. Just as He gives every person a unique fingerprint, He gives every person a unique combination of gifts, aptitudes and personality traits. Focus on the strengths God has given you and don't worry about what others are doing with their skills and gifts.

3. Solomon's example: Ecclesiastes 2:4-11 (NAS)

Solomon worked hard. Ecclesiastes 2:4-6 and 11 reads, *"I enlarged my works: I built houses for myself, I planted vineyards for myself; I made gardens and parks for myself, and I planted in them all kinds of fruit trees; I made ponds of water for myself from which to irrigate a forest of growing trees...."*

We can learn at least four principles from Solomon's experience in relation to work.

a. *People:* Solomon required many skilled people to complete his projects: gardeners, landscape artists, masons, carpenters, architects, maintenance staff, etc. Where did those skills come from? God is the source of all of them. Each person is uniquely created and gifted to serve God *through what he or she does.*

b. *Purpose:* When we view work as merely a means to an end (supporting ourselves, for instance), we miss the point. Work as a divine endowment from our Creator enables us to exercise our gifts and find fulfillment in His purposes. We can make our work an act of worship that results in the gift of joy from God.

c. *Personal pleasure:* Did you notice how many times Solomon mentions that he did all those things for himself? No wonder he concluded that it was "vanity." When our motivation is selfish, simply doing things to please ourselves, we will always be disappointed in the end because the emphasis is on temporal accomplishments. Our work can have eternal purposes and implications. Please understand this: working *should* have personal benefits and allow us to experience dignity and significance in our efforts. However, if our focus is not to serve God through what we do, our shortsightedness will rob us of the eternal blessing our work could provide.

d. *Perspective:* Finally, we learn from Solomon that no matter how much stuff we have, build, buy, or design—no matter how much money we have—it will not bring ultimate fulfillment to our souls. Solomon is our greatest example of the futility of earthly stuff. He denied himself nothing and yet failed to finish well.

4. Paul's insight: 1 Timothy 5:8

Paul reminds us of the necessity of work in 1Timothy 5:8 (NAS). *"But if anyone does not provide for his own, and especially for those of his household, he has denied the faith and is worse than an unbeliever."*

Paul's letter to Timothy reminded believers in the community to provide for the widows. Some, having been convinced of Jesus' immediate return, were not even providing for the needs of their own families. Paul reminds them that work is essential for believers in Christ.

Sometimes our society unwittingly encourages laziness, not recognizing the trap it becomes. Paul reminds us in Colossians 3:23 (NAS) to *"do your work heartily."*

Putting it all together: work principles

Over a lifetime, the average person spends 100,000 hours working. Jobs often include some degree of dissatisfaction. Perhaps no statistic demonstrates this more than the frequency with which Americans change jobs. A survey found that the average man changes jobs every four and one-half years; the average woman, every three years. Boredom, lack of fulfillment, inadequate wages, and countless other pressures contribute to this discontentment. Doctors, housewives, salespersons, blue-collar workers, managers—all professions—have experienced similar frustrations. Understanding scriptural principles that relate to work will help you find satisfaction in your job. It will also place you in a position where the Lord can prosper you.

1. Biblical perspective of work

As we saw earlier, even before sin entered the human race, God instituted work. *"The Lord God took the man and put him into the garden of Eden to cultivate it and keep it"* (Genesis 2:15, NAS). The very first thing the Lord did with Adam was to put him to work. Despite what many believe, work was initiated for our benefit in the sinless environment of the Garden of Eden.

Work is so important that in Exodus 34:21 (NAS) God gives this command: *"You shall work six days."* In the New Testament, Paul is just as direct. *"If anyone is not willing to work, then he is not to eat"* (2 Thessalonians 3:10, NAS). Examine the verse carefully. It says, *"If anyone is not* willing *to work."* It did not say, *"If anyone cannot work."* This principle does not apply to those who are physically or mentally unable to work. It is for those who are able but *choose* not to work.

A close friend (Howard's) has a brother in his mid-thirties whose parents have always supported him. He has never had to face the responsibilities and hardships involved in a job. As a consequence, his character has not been properly developed. He is hopelessly immature in many areas of his life.

One of the primary purposes of work is to develop character. While the carpenter is building a house, the house is also building the carpenter. The carpenter's skill, diligence, manual dexterity, and judgment are refined. A job is not merely a task designed to earn money; it is also intended to produce godly character in the life of the worker.

2. Honest professions are honorable.

There is dignity in all types of honest work; Scripture does not elevate any profession above another. Biblical characters represent a wide variety of vocations. David was a shepherd and a king. Luke was a doctor. Lydia was a retailer who sold purple fabric. Daniel was a government worker. Paul was a tentmaker. The Lord Jesus was a carpenter. To God there is equal dignity in the labor of the automobile mechanic and the president of General Motors, in the labor of the pastor and a secretary serving the church.

3. God's part in work

Scripture reveals three responsibilities the Lord has in connection with work.

a. *God gives job skills.* Exodus 36:1 (NAS) illustrates this truth: *"Every skillful person in whom the Lord has put skill and understanding to know how to perform all the work…."* God has given each of us unique skills. People have a wide variety of abilities, manual skills, and intellectual capacities. It is not a matter of one person being better than another; it is simply a matter of having received different abilities.

b. *God gives success.* The life of Joseph is a perfect example of God helping a person to succeed. *"The Lord was with Joseph, so he became a successful man….His master saw that the Lord was with him and how the Lord caused all that he did to prosper"* (Genesis 39:2- 3, NAS). We have certain responsibilities, but it is ultimately God who gives success.

c. *God controls promotion.* Psalm 75:6-7 says, *"For promotion and power come from nowhere on earth, but only from God"* (NAS). As much as it may surprise you, our bosses are not the ones who control whether we will be promoted. Understanding this should have a tremendous impact on the way we perform as employees.

One of the major reasons people experience stress and frustration in their jobs is because they don't understand God's part in work. Stop now, and think about God's part for a few minutes. He gives you your skills and controls success and promotion. How should this perspective impact you and your job?

4. Our part in work

a. *We work for Christ.* Scripture reveals that we actually are serving the Lord in our work. *"Whatever you do, do your work heartily, as for the Lord rather than for men….It is the Lord Christ whom you serve"* (Colossians 3:23-24, NAS). Recognizing that we are really working for the Lord has profound implications. Consider your attitude toward work. If you could see Jesus Christ as your boss, would you try to be more faithful in your job? The most important question you need to answer every day as you begin your work is this: "For whom do I work?" You work for Christ.

b. *We are to work hard.* *"Whatever your hand finds to do, do it with all your might"* (Ecclesiastes 9:10). *"The precious possession of a man is diligence"* (Proverbs 12:27, NAS). In Scripture, hard work and diligence are encouraged; laziness is condemned: *"He also who is slack in his work is brother to him who destroys"* (Proverbs 18:9, NAS).

Paul's life was an example of hard work. *"With labor and hardship we kept working night and day so that we would not be a burden to any of you…in order to offer ourselves as a model for you, so that you would follow our example"* (2 Thessalonians 3:8-9, NAS).

Your work should be at such a level that people never equate laziness with God. Nothing less than hard work and the pursuit of excellence please the Lord. We are not required to be "super workers" who are perfect employees. Rather, the Lord expects us to do the best we can.

c. *Seek balance.* Hard work must balance with the other priorities of life. If your job demands so much of your time and energy that you neglect your relationship with Christ or your loved ones, you are working too much. You should determine whether the job is too demanding or your work habits need changing. If you tend to be a "workaholic," be careful that you don't forsake the other priorities of life.

Exodus 34:21 reads, *"You shall work six days, but on the seventh day you shall rest; even during plowing time and harvest you shall rest"* (NAS).

Rest can become an issue of faith. Is the Lord able to make our six days of work more productive than seven days? Yes! The Lord instituted weekly rest for our physical, mental, and spiritual health.

5. Employers' responsibilities

The godly employer performs a balancing act. The employer is to love, serve, and encourage employees. Yet the employer also is responsible to lead employees and to hold them accountable for the completion of their assigned tasks. Let's examine several principles that should govern an employer's conduct.

a. *Serve your employees.* The basis for biblical leadership is servanthood: *"Whoever wishes to become great among you shall be your servant"* (Matthew 20:26, NAS). Employers must balance efforts to make a profit with an unselfish concern for employees, treating them fairly and with genuine dignity. *"Masters [employers], grant your...[employees] justice and fairness, knowing that you too have a Master in heaven"* (Colossians 4:1, NAS).

Employers should attempt to be creative as they serve their employees. For example, they should consider investing time and money to educate and upgrade their employees' job skills. This will help employees grow in their capabilities, add value to the enterprise, and earn more.

b. *Be a good communicator.* It's especially important to listen to employee complaints. *"If I have despised the claim of my...[employees] when they filed a complaint against me, what then could I do when God arises? And when He calls me to account, what will I answer Him?"* (Job 31:13-15, NAS). A sensitive, listening ear is a tangible expression that you care about others. When a complaint is legitimate, the employer should take appropriate steps to solve the problem.

c. *Hold employees accountable.* Employers are responsible for ensuring that their employees know what is expected on the job. Employers should regularly evaluate employee performance and communicate their evaluations. If an employee does not perform satisfactorily and is unable or unwilling to improve, a personnel change may be required.

d. *Pay your employees a fair wage promptly.* The Bible warns employers to pay a fair wage. "[The Lord will judge] *those who oppress the wage earner in his wages*" (Malachi 3:5, NAS). It also commands prompt payment. *"You shall not oppress a hired [employee]....Give him his wages on his day before the sun sets...so that he will not cry against you to the Lord and it become sin"* (Deuteronomy 24:14-15, NAS).

e. *Pray for godly employees.* The Lord may choose to bless an employer for having a godly employee. Scripture gives two examples of this. First, *"Laban said to [Jacob], 'If I have found favor in your eyes, please stay with me...the Lord has blessed me because of you' "* (Genesis 30:27). Second, *"Joseph found favor in [Potiphar's] sight....It came about that from the time he made [Joseph] overseer in his house and over all that he owned, the Lord blessed the Egyptian's house on account of Joseph; thus the Lord's blessing was upon all that he owned, in the house and in the field"* (Genesis 39:4-5, NAS).

Because of this principle, I (Howard) wanted to employ Raymond, an especially godly construction worker. He was strong and did the work of two people. Far more important, however, was Raymond's influence over the project. There was less profanity and pilferage, and he was an excellent model to everyone. This principle is not a command, but we believe the wise employer will pray for the Lord to bring a "Raymond" to his or her company.

6. Employee's responsibilities

We can identify six major responsibilities of the godly employee by examining the story of Daniel in the lion's den. Daniel 6 begins with Darius, the king of Babylon, appointing 120 people to administer the government, and three people, one of whom was Daniel, to supervise those administrators. King Darius then promoted Daniel to govern the entire kingdom. Daniel's jealous employees looked for a way to get him removed. After failing, they asked King Darius to enact a law requiring everyone to worship only the king or to suffer death in the lion's den. Daniel refused to stop worshipping the Lord and was thrown to the lions, but God rescued him by sending an angel to shut the lions' mouths. Consider these six points of application of a godly employee as seen in Daniel.

a. *Honesty:* Daniel 6:4 (NAS) tells us that Daniel's fellow employees could find no dishonesty in him, and there was *"no… evidence of corruption"* in his work. Daniel was totally honest.

b. *Faithfulness:* *"He was faithful"* (Daniel 6:4, NAS). The godly employee establishes the goal of being faithful and excellent in work, and then works hard to reach that goal.

c. *Prayerfulness:* The godly employee is a person of prayer. *"When Daniel knew that the document was signed [restricting worship to the king alone]…he continued kneeling on his knees three times a day, praying and giving thanks before his God, as he had been doing previously"* (Daniel 6:10, NAS). Daniel governed the most powerful country of his day, a level of responsibility that few of us will ever face. Yet he knew the importance of making time for prayer. If you are not praying consistently, your work is suffering.

d. *Honors employer:* *"Daniel spoke to the king, 'O king, live forever!'"* (Daniel 6:21, NAS). What a remarkable response from Daniel. The king had been tricked into sentencing Daniel to the lion's den. Daniel's reaction was to honor his boss. Think how natural it would have been to say something like, "I'll show you! The God who sent His angel to shut the lions' mouths is now going to punish you!" Instead, he honored his boss. The godly employee always honors his or her superior. 1 Peter 2:18 reads, *"Servants [employees] be submissive to your masters [employers] with all respect, not only to those who are good and gentle, but also to those who are unreasonable."* One way to honor your employer is never to gossip behind your employer's back, even if he or she is not an ideal person.

e. *Honors fellow employees:* People may damage your reputation to secure a promotion over you or even to have you fired from your job. They tried to murder Daniel. Despite this, there is no evidence that Daniel did anything but honor his fellow employees. *"Do not slander a servant [employee] to his master [employer], or he will curse you"* (Proverbs 30:10).

The godly person avoids manipulation and office politics to secure a promotion. Your boss does not control your promotion; the Lord Himself does. We can be content in our jobs by being faithful, honoring superiors, and encouraging other employees. Having done this, we can rest, knowing that Christ will promote us if and when He chooses.

f. *Verbalizes faith:* King Darius may never have known about the Lord if Daniel had not communicated his faith at appropriate moments while at work. *"The king spoke and said to Daniel, 'Daniel, servant of the living God, has your God, whom you constantly serve, been able to deliver you from the lions?'"* (Daniel 6:20, NAS). King

Darius knew all about Daniel's faith because Daniel was verbally open about it. Daniel's influence, however, would not have been as powerful if he had not demonstrated honesty, faithfulness, and hard work. Listen to the words of Darius in response to Daniel's faith and God's deliverance: *"I issue a decree that in every part of my kingdom people must fear and reverence the God of Daniel. For he is the living God and he endures forever"* (Daniel 6:26).

Daniel influenced his employer, one of the most powerful people in the world, to believe in the only true God. You have that same opportunity in your own God-given sphere of work. A job well done builds a platform to tell others with whom you work about the reality of Christ. As we view our work from God's perspective, dissatisfaction will turn to contentment from a job well done, and drudgery will become excitement over the prospect of introducing others to the Savior.

Other work issues

1. Retirement

The dictionary defines retirement as "withdrawal from an occupation, to retreat from an active life." The goal of retirement is deeply ingrained in American culture. Many people retire and cease all labor to live a life filled with leisure. Numbers 8:24-26 is the only reference to retirement in Scripture. The instruction there applied only to the Levites who worked on the tabernacle. As long as one is physically and mentally capable, there is no scriptural basis for a person retiring and becoming unproductive. The concept of putting an older-but-able person "out to pasture" is unbiblical. Age is no obstacle in finishing the work the Lord has for you to accomplish. He will provide you with the necessary strength. For example, Moses was 80 years old when he began his 40-year adventure of leading the children of Israel. Scripture *does* imply that the type or the intensity of work may change as we grow older—a shifting of the gears to a less demanding pace to become more of an "elder seated at the gate." During this season of life we can use the experience and wisdom gained over a lifetime. If we have sufficient income to meet our needs apart from our job, we may choose to leave the job to invest more time in serving others in whatever way the Lord directs.

2. Ambition

Scripture does not condemn ambition. Paul was ambitious. *"We have as our ambition...to be pleasing to Him"* (2 Corinthians 5:9, NAS). However, our ambition should not be selfish. The Lord *"will render to each person according to his deeds...to those who are selfishly ambitious...wrath and indignation"* (Romans 2:6, 8). *"But if you have...selfish ambition in your heart, do not be arrogant and so lie against the truth. This wisdom is not that which comes down from above, but is earthly, natural, demonic. For where...selfish ambition exist[s], there is disorder and every evil thing"* (James 3:14-16, NAS). *"But you, are you seeking great things for yourself? Do not seek them"* (Jeremiah 45:5, NAS).

The Bible is not the enemy of ambition, only of the wrong type of ambition. The motivation for our ambition should be to please Christ. We should desire to become an increasingly faithful steward in using the possessions and skills God has given us. Our work should be done to please the Lord, doing it to the best of our ability.

3. Your calling

Each of us has a specific calling or purpose that the Lord intends for us. Ephesians 2:10 (NAS) reads, *"We are His workmanship, created in Christ Jesus for good works, which God prepared beforehand so that we would walk in them."* Study this passage carefully. *"We are His workmanship."* The Amplified Bible says, *"We are His handiwork."* Each of us has been given special physical, emotional, and mental abilities. You may have heard the expression, "After the Lord made you, He threw away the mold!" It's true! You are gifted uniquely. No one—past, present, or future—is exactly like you. The passage continues, *"created in Christ Jesus for good works, which God prepared beforehand so that we would walk in them."*

The Lord created each of us for a particular job, and He endowed us with the skills and desires to accomplish this work. This calling may be full-time Christian service as a vocation or it may be to serve Christ in a secular vocation. Often people struggle with whether God wants them to continue in their work once they commit their lives to Christ. Many feel they are not serving Christ in a significant way if they remain at their jobs. Nothing could be further from the truth. The key is for each person to determine God's call for his or her life.

Maria sat across from me (Chad) with tears in her eyes. She had just traveled from South America to visit the seminary where I worked in Dallas, Texas. A month earlier, her pastor had counseled her to quit her job as assistant to the president of the country and enroll in seminary so she could "pursue a vocation that had eternal significance."

"Now, what exactly is your position?" I asked, wanting to make sure I had an accurate picture of the situation.

"I am assistant to the President of my country," she said. During the course of the conversation, it became evident that she really enjoyed what she did and that she felt called to serve in her sphere of influence. But she was really confused by her pastor's perspective that she was having little eternal significance, and she wondered if God was telling her something through him.

Empathetic to Maria's situation and shocked by her pastor's counsel, I said, "Maria, it appears you have a wonderful opportunity to serve the Lord and influence the direction of your country." The rest of our discussion examined how God might be asking her to consider seminary training, but that He uses people in many areas of work.

Maria left my office with questions yet to ponder, but she felt a sense of release, understanding that she could serve the Lord and have a ministry right where she was. Do you struggle with the thought that if you are not a *full-time* missionary bouncing through some remote jungle or a pastor leading a group of God's people (as significant as these callings may be), then you are not *really* serving the Lord? Many of the students I encounter wrestle with this unfortunate stereotype of ministry.

In his book, *God Owns My Business*, Stanley Tam writes, "Although I believe in the application of good principles in business, I place far more confidence in the conviction that I have a call from God. I am convinced that His purpose for me is in the business world. My business is my pulpit."[1] To those who earn a living through secular pursuits, it is a great comfort to know that the "call" of holy vocation carries over into all walks of life. God strategically places His children everywhere!

4. Partnerships

Scripture discourages business partnerships with those who do not know Christ. In 2 Corinthians 6:14-17 (NAS) we read, *"Do not be bound together with unbelievers; for what partnership have righteousness and lawlessness, or what fellowship has light with darkness?...or what has a believer in common with an unbeliever?...Therefore, come out from their midst and be separate,' says the Lord."* Many have violated this principle and have suffered financially.

In our opinion, we should also be careful before entering into *any* partnership—even with another Christian. I would consider only a few people as partners. These are people I know well. I have observed their commitment to the Lord. I know their strengths and weaknesses and have seen them handle money faithfully. Never rush into a partnership! Before forming a partnership, put your understandings into writing. Develop this agreement with your future partner and be sure to include a way to end the partnership. If you are not able to agree in writing or too uncomfortable to attempt it, do not become partners.

5. Procrastination

A procrastinator is someone who, because of laziness or fear, has a habit of putting things off until later. Often this habit can develop into a serious character flaw. The Bible has many examples of godly people who were not procrastinators, and one of my favorite examples is Boaz. Naomi, the mother-in-law of Ruth, made this comment about Ruth's future husband, Boaz: *"Wait, my daughter, until you know how the matter turns out; for the man will not rest until he has settled it today"* (Ruth 3:18 NAS). Boaz had the reputation of a person who acted promptly.

Here are some practical suggestions to help overcome procrastination:
1. List the things you need to do each day.
2. Prayerfully review the list and prioritize it according to the tasks you need to accomplish first.
3. Finish the first task on your list before starting the second. Often that first task is the most difficult or the one you fear the most.
4. Ask the Lord to give you courage.

6. Wives working outside the home

For many reasons, women work in jobs of all kinds. Married women work to provide additional income for their families, to express their creativity, or because they enjoy their jobs. Single women work to provide for their needs. In our opinion, unless family finances prohibit it, it is wise during the children's early formative years for the mother to be home while the children are home. Titus 2:4-5 (NAS) reads, *"Encourage the young women to love their husbands, to love their children, to be sensible, pure, workers at home."* As the children mature, a mother will have increased freedom to pursue outside work. Proverbs 31:10-31 (NAS) reads, *"An excellent wife...does him* [her husband] *good and not evil all the days of her life. She looks for wool and flax and works with her hands....She brings her food from afar. She rises also while it is still night and gives food to her household....She considers a field and buys it; from her earnings she plants a vineyard....She stretches out her hands to the distaff, and her hands grasp the spindle. She extends her hand to the poor....She makes coverings for herself; her clothing is fine linen and purple. Her husband is known in the gates, when he sits among the elders of the land. She makes linen garments and sells them, and supplies belts to the tradesmen.... She looks well to the ways of her household, and does not eat the bread of idleness."*

Proverbs 31 paints a picture of the working wife living a balanced life with the thrust of her activity toward the home. Some women are gifted as homemakers, and there is no more important task than raising godly children. However, other women must work to earn income, or they have the skill and desire to work outside the home. Either way, it is a decision that the married couple should make together.

7. Two-income families

If both the husband and wife work outside the home, it is worth examining how much income, after taxes and expenses, the second wage contributes. (For this section, an online calculator can be found at *Crown.org/Tools/How Much does Mom Really Make*.) In the "Example 1" column of the worksheet, the following assumptions have been made; 40 hours a week at $9 per hour; giving ten percent of the gross income; federal income tax of 25 percent (a second income is added to the first and usually results in a higher tax bracket); state income tax of 5 percent; Social Security tax of 7.5 percent; ten trips per week of five miles at a cost of 25 cents a mile; lunch, snacks, and coffee breaks of $15 per week; eating out more often and using convenience foods add $35 a week to the budget; $20 for extra clothing and cleaning; $5 more is spent for grooming; extra child care of $45 a week.

In the "Example 2" column we assume earning $25 an hour, with all other assumptions remaining the same. These assumptions are for illustration only and may not represent your situation. Complete the exercise on the worksheet to determine your actual income after expenses. Couples often are surprised to learn that the income earned by a second working spouse is not as much as they had expected. Some wives have actually produced more net income (after reducing work-related expenses) when they decided to work in some creative way while staying at home. Of course, the financial benefits are not the only factors to evaluate. Consideration should also be given to the physical and emotional demands of working and how they affect a family.

Example 1

Your Monthly Gross Income:	1560
Tithe	156
Taxes	585
Net Spendable Income	819

Extra Job Expenses	
Child care	195
Clothing	87
Transportation and parking	54
Extra Food (lunches purchased at work)	65
Dining out (rather than cooking at home)	152
Miscellaneous (at work expenses)	22
Other expenses that can be avoided by working at home	50
Total expenses for working outside the home	625
Net Monthly Income (contribution from working outside the home)	194

Example 2

Your Monthly Gross Income:	4334
Tithe	433
Taxes	1625
Net Spendable Income	2276

Extra Job Expenses	
Child care	195
Clothing	87
Transportation and parking	54
Extra Food (lunches purchased at work)	65
Dining out (rather than cooking at home)	152
Miscellaneous (at work expenses)	22
Other expenses that can be avoided by working at home	50
Total expenses for working outside the home	625
Net Monthly Income (contribution from working outside the home)	1651

Worksheet

Your Monthly Gross Income:	
Tithe	
Taxes	
Net Spendable Income	

Extra Job Expenses	
Child care	
Clothing	
Transportation and parking	
Extra Food (lunches purchased at work)	
Dining out (rather than cooking at home)	
Miscellaneous (at work expenses)	
Other expenses that can be avoided by working at home	
Total expenses for working outside the home	
Net Monthly Income (contribution from working outside the home)	

Think about it!

- *Describe three ways you will implement a more biblical view of work into your situation (existing job, school, or potential new career).*

- *Are you serving God in a job that you are excited about and skilled at doing? If so, how will the principles you have just studied enhance your current position? If you do not have such a job, list at least three steps you need to take (your part) in locating a job that aligns with your gifts and calling.*

- *Does your pattern of work rob God and your family of the time and attention justified by their priority? What adjustments can you make to achieve balance in the next six months?*

CHAPTER TWELVE

Plugging in: The Importance of Counsel

Core Concepts

- Describe the hindrances to seeking counsel.
- What are the primary sources of counsel?
- Whose counsel should the believer avoid?
- What two things should you keep in mind when seeking counsel?
- What two things should you remember when someone seeks your counsel?

Overview

Plugging in to wise counsel, especially for money-related decisions, is essential for the godly steward. God intended for the church to be an interdependent body that ministers to one another in many ways, including intercession and giving wise counsel. In Paul's discourse on how the body is to function, he states, "Now to each one the manifestation of the Spirit is given for the common good. To one there is given through the Spirit the message of wisdom, to another the message of knowledge by means of the same Spirit..." (1 Corinthians 12:7-8). He goes on to teach that no part of the body can act independently, saying it has no need of the others. Yet we see it happen every day, whether through ignorance, pride or stubbornness. Accordingly, our study on counsel will be broken into two sections: hindrances to counsel and sources of counsel.

INTRODUCTION

The year was 1991. I (Chad) was eighteen and acted like it. Fresh out of high school with a well-paying job, my fast, bright orange 1976 Chevy Camaro was my dream car! I had bought it with hard-earned money before I even received my driver's license. I loved turning up the bass and cruising through town. In fact, I loved my car stereo almost as much as the car.

But some of my friends had louder stereos with more powerful bass. In my young mind, that was not acceptable! So without my parents' knowledge, I went to the best car stereo store in town. And wouldn't you know—they were running a special on new sub-woofers and amplifiers! I traded in my 10-inch bass speakers for 12-inch bass speakers, my 100-watt amplifier for a 300-watt version. I couldn't resist adding a new stereo deck and front speakers in the nifty "ninety days same as cash" deal for a grand total of two thousand dollars.

"No problem," I told the salesman. "I'll be good for the cash before ninety days."

"I'll have your car done tomorrow," he promised as he slid some papers in front of me. "Sign these so I can process your loan just in case."

To say I was excited is an understatement. *With what I have saved and my recent raise, I'll have this booming stereo paid off in no time,* I thought. That was before the Mustang muscle car I raced a month later got the best of my shiny orange Camaro. I had it made until that sickening thud when I power shifted from second to third. Blown transmission. I had to get that fixed first because I needed the car for work. Or at least I didn't want to walk. Sixty days turned into ninety days, followed by payments on two thousand dollars of stereo equipment. I spent years repaying that money, and I'm too ashamed to admit what the interest rate was. All that money for a stereo when the one I already had worked perfectly.

If I had not been so prideful, I would have sought counsel. I had a pretty good idea of what my parents would say; that's why I didn't ask. It was more important to me to impress my friends. I'm sure they were really impressed that I ended up with years of payments, lots of interest and lots of stress. I share this story with the hope that some of you will learn from my mistake and not do a similar thing. As Proverbs 12: 15 says, *"The way of a fool is right in his own eyes. But a wise man is he who listens to counsel"* (NAS). Let us be wise and listen to what God says about seeking the counsel of others.

HINDRANCES TO COUNSEL

Two attitudes keep us from seeking counsel. The first is pride. Our culture glamorizes independence with messages that imply, "Stand on your own two feet. You don't need anyone to help make your decisions for you!" Advertisers reinforce this independence to encourage impulse purchases that might be lost if buyers take time to seek counsel.

Second is the attitude of stubbornness. This attitude is characterized by the statement, "Don't confuse me with the facts. My mind is already made up!" We often resist seeking counsel because we do not want to learn the financial facts another person might discover. We don't want to be told we can't afford what we have already decided to buy.

God encourages us to use a great gift He has provided for our benefit—godly counselors. Proverbs 19:20 reads, *"Listen to advice and accept instruction, and in the end you will be wise."* And Proverbs 10:8 reads, *"The wise man is glad to be instructed, but a self-sufficient fool falls flat on his face"* (TLB). We seek counsel to secure insights, suggestions, and alternatives that will aid in making a proper decision. It is not the counselor's role to make the decision; we retain that responsibility.

INSUFFICIENCY OF FACTS ALONE

We need to assemble the facts that will influence our decisions, but we also need to seek God's direction. We must determine specifically what the Lord wants us to do, and this may be contrary to what the facts alone would dictate. This is illustrated in Numbers 13 and 14. Moses sent twelve spies into the Promised Land. They all returned with an identical assessment of the facts: It was a prosperous land, but terrifying giants lived there. Only two of the twelve spies, Joshua and Caleb, believed they should do what the Lord wanted them to do—go in and possess the Promised Land. Because the children of Israel relied only on the facts and did not act in faith on what the Lord wanted for them, they suffered 40 years of wandering in the wilderness until that generation died.

SOURCES OF COUNSEL

Before making important financial decisions, subject them to three sources of counsel.

1. Scripture: The counsel of the Lord

First, what does God's Word say about a particular issue? The Psalmist wrote, *"Your laws are both my light and my counselors"* (Psalm 119:24, TLB). *"Your commands make me wiser than my enemies....I have more insight than all my teachers, for I meditate on your statutes. I have more understanding than the elders for I have obeyed Your precepts"* (Psalm 119:98-100). When we think of people who are skilled in financial decision-making, we often think of experts or those who are older and more experienced. Yet Scripture tells us we can have more insight and wisdom by searching the Bible than those who are educated and experienced in the ways of the world's economy.

I would rather obey the truth of Scripture than risk the consequences of following my own inclinations or the opinions of people. The Bible makes this remarkable claim about itself: *"For the word of God is living and active and sharper than any two-edged sword, and...able to judge the thoughts and intentions of the heart"* (Hebrews 4:12, NAS). The truths in the Bible are timeless. It is a living book our Lord uses to communicate His direction to all generations. Most people are surprised to learn that the Bible contains over 2,350 verses dealing with money-related issues. Scripture is the very first filter through which we should put a financial decision. When it clearly answers the question, we do not have to go any further because the Bible contains the Lord's written, revealed will.

Let's look at an example. Bob and Barbara were faced with a difficult decision. Barbara's brother and his wife had just moved to Florida from Chicago. Because they experienced financial difficulties in Chicago, the bank would not loan them the money to purchase a home unless they had someone cosign the debt. They asked Bob and Barbara to cosign. Barbara thought they should, but Bob was reluctant. A friend referred them to the verses that warn against cosigning. When Barbara read the passages, she responded, "Who am I to argue with God? We shouldn't cosign." Bob was tremendously relieved. Two years later, Barbara's brother and his wife divorced and declared bankruptcy. Can you imagine the strain on Bob and Barbara's marriage if they had cosigned? Bob might have said, "Barbara, I can't believe your brother did this! You got me into this! I tried not to cosign, but you forced me!" Not only would Bob and Barbara have experienced marital strain, they probably would have gone under financially as well.

In addition to searching the Bible, we need to seek direction from the Lord through prayer and the ministry of His Spirit. This is extremely important because as we communicate with Him, our hearts are revealed and we are sensitized to His guidance. In Isaiah 9:6, Isaiah called the Lord *"Wonderful Counselor."* The Psalms also identify the Lord as our counselor. *"I [the Lord] will instruct you and teach you in the way which you should go; I will counsel you with My eye upon you"* (Psalm 32:8, NAS). *"You [the Lord] guide me with your counsel"* (Psalm 73:24). *"I will bless the Lord who has counseled me"* (Psalm 16:7, NAS).

Scripture provides numerous examples of the blessings of heeding God's counsel as well as the unfortunate consequences of not seeking it. After the children of Israel began their successful campaign to capture the Promised Land, the Gibeonites attempted to enter into a peace treaty with Israel. They deceived Israel's leaders into believing they were from a distant land. Joshua 9:14-15 (NAS) reads, *"The men of Israel took some of their* [Gibeonites] *provisions, and did not ask for the counsel of the Lord* [emphasis mine]. *Joshua made peace with them and made a covenant with them, to let them live."*

Because Israel failed to seek the Lord's counsel, the Promised Land remained populated with ungodly people, and Israel became ensnared by their false gods. The leaders simply accepted the "facts" they could see—facts that were designed to deceive. In many situations, only the Lord can reveal truth and proper direction to us. Only the Lord knows the future and the ultimate outcome of a decision.

A wonderful contrast is found in John 21:3-11. Peter and six of the other disciples had fished all night and caught nothing. Human wisdom dictated that it was time to pack it in, but Jesus appeared on the shore with supernatural wisdom. He told them to throw the net again and even told them where to throw it. The result was a net overflowing with 153 large fish. We are always more productive when we follow God's direction.

Throughout Scripture we are encouraged to wait on the Lord. Whenever you feel hurried or pressured or you are confused concerning a decision, go to a quiet place that will allow you to listen prayerfully for His still, small voice. The world around you screams "Hurry!" but our loving heavenly Father's advice is worth waiting for.

If the Bible provides clear direction, we know what to do. If it is not specific about an issue, and we can't discern the Lord's voice, we should subject our decision to the second source of counsel: godly people.

2. Godly people

"The godly man is a good counselor because he is just and fair and knows right from wrong" (Psalm 37:30-31, TLB). The Christian life is not one of independence from other Christians but of interdependence upon one other. God has not given any one person all the abilities he or she needs to be most productive.

a. *Spouse:* If you are married, the first person you need to consult is your spouse. Frankly, it has been a humbling experience for me (Howard) to seek the counsel of my wife, Bev, in financial matters, because she has no formal financial training. However, she has saved us a great deal of money by her wise counsel. Women tend to be gifted with a wonderfully sensitive and intuitive nature that is usually very accurate. Men tend to focus more objectively on the facts. The husband and wife need each other to achieve the proper balance for a correct decision.

I believe that the Lord honors the wife's "office" or "position" as helpmate to her husband. Many times the Lord communicates most clearly to a man through his wife. If you are a husband, let me be blunt. Regardless of her business background or her financial aptitude, you must cultivate and seek your wife's counsel. I (Howard) have committed never to proceed with a financial decision unless Bev agrees. There are additional benefits from seeking your spouse's counsel.

1. **It will preserve your relationship!**

    Since you and your spouse will both experience the consequences of decisions you make, you should strive to agree beforehand. Then, even if your choice proves to be disastrous, your relationship is not as vulnerable.

2. **It will honor your spouse and prepare him or her for the future.**

    Unfortunately, some in our culture suffer from a feeling of not being valuable. Seeking your spouse's counsel will help enormously in the development of a healthy and proper self-esteem. When a husband or wife seeks the other's advice, he or she actually is communicating, "I love you. I respect you. I value your insight." Consistently asking for advice also keeps your spouse informed of your true financial condition. This is important in the event you predecease your spouse or are unable to work. My (Howard's) father suffered a massive heart attack that incapacitated him for two years. Because he had kept my mother informed about his business, she was able to step in and operate it successfully until he recovered.

b. *Parents:* The second source of counsel is our parents. Proverbs 6:20-22 says, *"My son, observe the commandment of your father, and do not forsake the teaching of your mother; bind them continually on your heart; tie them around your neck. When you walk about, they will guide you; when you sleep, they will watch over you; and when you awake, they will talk to you"* (NAS).

Our parents have the benefit of years of experience, and they know us well. In our opinion, we should seek their counsel even if they do not yet know Christ or have not been wise money managers themselves. Over the years, it is not uncommon for a barrier to be erected between a child and parents. Asking their advice is a way to honor parents and build a bridge across any wall, since it is a compliment to anyone when you ask for advice; it is an expression of admiration. A word of caution: Although the husband and wife should seek the counsel of their parents, the advice of the parents should be subordinate to the advice of the spouse, especially if a family conflict materializes. *"A man will leave his father and mother and be united to his wife and they will become one flesh"* (Genesis 2:24).

c. *Experienced people:* We should also consult people experienced in the area in which we are attempting to make a decision. If you are considering a real estate investment, attempt to locate the most qualified real estate investor to counsel you. If you are going to purchase a car, ask a trustworthy automobile mechanic to examine the car and give you an opinion before purchasing it.

3. A multitude of counselors

We read in Proverbs 15:22, *"Without consultation, plans are frustrated, but with many counselors they succeed"* (NAS). Proverbs 11:14 says, *"Where there is no guidance the people fall, but in abundance of counselors there is victory"* (NAS). Each of us has limited knowledge and experience; we need the input of others who bring their own unique backgrounds to broaden our thinking with alternatives we would never have considered without their advice.

I meet regularly with a small group who share their lives and pray for each other. The members of this group know each other well. Over the years, each person has experienced a difficult circumstance or had to make a major decision. We have learned that when someone is subjected to a painful circumstance, it is difficult to make wise decisions. We have experienced the benefits and safety of having a group of people who can give loving, objective counsel even when it hurts. Because we know each other's weaknesses and strengths, it is easier to discern direction that is most appropriate for each one. And we are more receptive to constructive criticism when it comes from someone who cares for us.

Solomon describes the benefits of interdependence: *"Two are better than one because they have a good return for their labor. For if either of them falls, the one will lift up his companion. But woe to the one who falls when there is not another to lift him up. Furthermore, if two lie down together they keep warm, but how can one be warm alone? And if one can overpower him who is alone, two can resist him. A cord of three strands is not quickly torn apart"* (Ecclesiastes 4:9-12, NAS).

We often think of a multitude of counselors as being a resource pool to which we can go for independent, individual opinions. We might choose two or three different people whose counsel we respect on a given subject and conduct a private conversation with each of them to get a broader perspective. But it can be even more productive to gather counselors together. Frequently, the suggestions of one will trigger insights from another—sometimes in sharp disagreement. However, a common thread often develops, with the immediate interchange of ideas and perspectives leading to breakthroughs in direction and strategy.

This gathering together of a multitude of counselors requires some planning because of the various schedules of participants. Consideration for the value of their time dictates that you generally reserve this approach for major decisions. We encourage you to include your pastor among your counselors.

COUNSEL TO AVOID

1. The wicked

We need to avoid one particular source of counsel. *"How blessed is the man who does not walk in the counsel of the wicked"* (Psalm 1:1). The word "blessed" literally means to be "happy many times over." The definition of a "wicked" person is one who lives his or her life without regard for God. A wicked person may be one who does not yet personally know the Lord or one who knows Jesus Christ as Savior but is not following Him in obedience.

Facts and technical expertise may come from any source—Christian or otherwise—but you are responsible to make the final decision.

2. Fortune tellers, mediums, and spiritualists

The Bible prohibits seeking the advice of fortunetellers, mediums, or spiritualists: *"Do not turn to mediums or seek out spiritists, for you will be defiled by them. I am the Lord your God"* (Leviticus 19:31). Study this next passage carefully: *"Saul died because he was unfaithful to the Lord...and even consulted a medium for guidance, and did not inquire of the Lord. So the Lord put him to death"* (1 Chronicles 10:13-14). Saul died, in part, because he went to a medium. Not only should we avoid the counsel of these people but also anything they use in forecasting the future, such as horoscopes and all other practices of the occult.

3. Biased counsel

Be cautious of the counsel of the biased. When receiving financial advice, ask yourself this question: "What stake does this person have in the outcome of my decision? Does he or she stand to gain or lose from this decision?" If the advisor will profit, be cautious when evaluating this counsel and always seek a second unbiased opinion.

WHEN RECEIVING COUNSEL

When you are seeking advice, supply your counselor with all the important facts. Do not attempt to manipulate your advisor to give the answer you want by concealing information.

1. Major decisions

When faced with a major decision such as a job change or home purchase, go to a quiet place where you can spend uninterrupted time praying, reading Scripture, and seeking the Lord's direction. Many people have found it valuable to fast during this time.

2. Know your counselors

Be selective in choosing your counselors. Look for those who are gifted with wisdom and the courage to give you advice that may be contrary to your wishes. *"He who walks with the wise grows wise"* (Proverbs 13:20). Continually ask the Lord for wisdom. *"If any of you lacks wisdom, let him ask of God, who gives to all...and it will be given to him. But he must ask in faith without any doubting"* (James 1:5-6, NAS). As you seek counsel, do not be surprised if the answer comes out of your own mouth.

Interacting with others allows you to verbalize thoughts and feelings that may have been coalescing subconsciously.

WHEN OFFERING COUNSEL

Counseling others can be a frustrating experience unless you understand your proper role. Lovingly communicate truth to the best of your ability, and leave the results to God. Avoid preoccupation with whether people act on your recommendations. Some people are not yet prepared to follow advice. Others may recognize that your counsel might be inaccurate or incomplete. Be content to know that the Lord is in control of every counseling experience.

1. Observing confidentiality

The person seeking advice needs to know that nothing he or she says will be communicated to another person without permission. Only in an environment of trust will there be the candid dialogue that produces successful results.

2. When you do not know

Sometimes people come with problems or circumstances that are outside of our experience. The best way to serve is to respond with the simple statement, "I do not know," and refer them to someone who has expertise in their area of need. Avoid a guesswork answer that might feel comfortable at the moment but turn out to be inadequate.

SUMMARY

Seeking counsel is a necessary part of being faithful with God's resources. Recognizing that every money decision is a spiritual decision, we seek counsel from more than just financial planners when making significant decisions. We draw from a variety of carefully chosen counselors and, if married, include our spouse as a primary source of counsel. This has the dual benefit of leading to better decisions and enhancing open communication.

Think About it

- *Why do you avoid asking key people in your life about money issues? List at least three changes you will make to correct such behavior.*

- *Develop a list of key decisions you need to make in the next year regarding money, career, and lifestyle. For each decision, list three people whose counsel you will seek.*

- *How will you encourage people in your sphere of influence to seek counsel regarding money decisions? List two friends you will help in the next six months.*

CHAPTER THIRTEEN

Credit: Danger! Use with Caution

Core Concepts

- Contrast our culture's attitude about debt with how the Bible portrays debt.
- Describe four principles about debt that help the godly steward understand and avoid it.
- Define debt.
- Define borrowing.
- What are the ten steps to reaching "D-Day" debtless day?
- List the four types of debt described.

Overview

Credit is a powerful tool. The fact that our economy—the greatest in the world—is built on it should be proof enough. As with any powerful tool, extreme caution is required to avoid unintended consequences and serious injury. Cars, weapons, drugs, heavy machinery, classified information—all can be lifesavers or life takers. Credit can either enhance or destroy our lives depending on how we use it.

This chapter will emphasize the dangers of debt, not because credit is evil, but because the dangers are virtually ignored in today's culture. The engine that drives our economy depends on a growth in spending that cannot be sustained without significant credit. Powerful corporate interests create needs through advertising and then offer easy credit as the obvious (and very lucrative for them) path for fulfilling those needs. For that reason, we will attempt to bring balance by exposing common misuses of credit.

Matt, a student at the seminary where I (Chad) teach, sat across from my desk and ran his hands through his hair. He looked and sounded whipped. His fiancé had just pulled out of their wedding engagement—

Breaking the *Debt Cycle*

6 Church Becomes Debt Free Also

5 Needs Met; God Glorified; People Saved

4 Giving Goes Up

1 Church Recognizes the Problem

2 Church Teaches Stewardship

3 Family Debt is Reduced

with barely two months to go—because of his indebtedness. In desperation, he had come to me for counsel.

Imagine a part-time youth pastor with a huge heart for his students but no ministry budget. Can you see him rationalizing weekend fast-food splurges with the students as he attempts to build relationships that will enable him to minister to them? That is Matt. And when the expenses aren't reimbursed, they mount far beyond his ability to stay current.

As a young, successful professional, Matt holds a well-paying job at a local credit union. He is also a missionary kid, so he understands what it's like to live simply, and compared to many of his peers, he does live simply. He is witty and has a keen grasp on spiritual issues including head-knowledge of the Scriptures about money and debt.

Until he came to me for financial counseling, Matt had never taken time to worry about the credit card bills growing like grass during spring rains. He had been making minimum monthly payments on ten thousand dollars for the past ten years—but getting nowhere. His six credit card accounts and the money he owed to family for various "needs" now totaled over forty thousand dollars for this young man in his mid-thirties.

Matt finally recognized, through the Holy Spirit, that his life was being controlled by his indebtedness; he was a slave to it. His fiancé—the love of his life—had left him for this character issue, and his witness at work was hindered. He could no longer pile on debt for his youth group, nor could he imagine handling the expense of continuing seminary, even though he had not yet resorted to student loans to continue his studies. He was imprisoned by patterns of unhealthy behavior and years of undisciplined spending. Once he realized he could not effectively serve the Lord in this condition, he confessed his sinful behavior patterns of pride, lack of trust, and the desire to control his life through debt. We went to work on what would be a long journey back. Perhaps I've just described someone you know. Or perhaps you can relate in some way to Matt's situation.

THE WAY OF THE WORLD

Debt in America is growing. The Federal Reserve's latest numbers for consumer credit debt is 2.162 trillion.[1] When mortgages are included, the number increases to nearly 9 trillion.[2]

"Trillion" may be too large a number to be meaningful to you. Consider this chart showing the average non-mortgage debt load of Americans

Age	Debt
18-29	$8,636
30-39	$16,298
40-49	$18,659
50-59	$20,157
60-69	$15,964
70+	$6,500

in various age ranges. How do you compare with the average in your age range?
Source: Credit reporting agency Experian (www.NationalScoreIndex.com)

Personal consumer debt increases at the rate of $1,000 a second! We have so much personal debt in our country that the average person has been described as someone driving on a bond-financed highway, in a bank-financed car, fueled by charge card-financed gasoline, going to purchase furniture on an installment plan to put in a savings-and-loan-financed home!

We have become so accustomed to debt that we scarcely give it a second thought until we discover that we can't keep up with payments. By that time, there is no painless escape. The people of God must come to grips with what the Bible says about debt.

Take a moment to meditate on your spending and borrowing patterns. Ask yourself: "When was the last time I prayed about a significant purchase, asking God to provide before I went to the store and put it on the credit card?" Ask God to reveal the motivation for your spending and borrowing habits. How are you honoring God with those decisions?

PRINCIPLES FOR PRACTICE

Scripture does not say that debt is a sin, but it discourages the use of debt. Remember, God loves us and has given us financial principles for our benefit. Read the first portion of Romans 13:8 carefully from several different Bible translations: *"Owe no man any thing"* (KJV). *"Let no debt remain outstanding"* (NIV). *"Pay all your debts"* (TLB). *"Owe nothing to anyone"* (NAS). *"Keep out of debt and owe no man anything"* (AMPLIFIED).

This passage is not primarily about financial debt or a prohibition against it; it is a plea to fulfill the law in these last days by living the law of love. But it is also a very practical plea as the preceding verses mention taxes and revenue in their treatment of submission to authorities. The entire chapter urges us to live above reproach, and Paul's implication is that unpaid debts will quickly malign our reputation and witness. Notice that he does not say, "Never take on a debt." Rather, he says, *"Let no debt remain outstanding,"* which is more likely to mean "past due." We can infer from the tone of the entire chapter that living without any financial debt would be preferable, but it is inappropriate to turn that into a law prohibiting all debt for followers of Christ.

1. Debt is considered slavery.

Proverbs 22:7 reads: *"Just as the rich rule the poor, so the borrower is servant to the lender"* (TLB). When we are in debt, we are in a position of servitude to the lender. The deeper we are in debt, the more like servants we become. We do not have full freedom to decide where to spend our income because our money is already obligated to meet our debts. In 1 Corinthians 7:23 Paul writes, *"You were bought with a price; do not become slaves of men"* (NAS). Our Father made the ultimate sacrifice by giving His Son, the Lord Jesus Christ, to die for us. He now wants His children free to serve Him, not their lenders, in whatever way He chooses.

2. Debt is considered a curse.

In the Old Testament, being out of debt was one of the promised rewards for obedience. *"If you diligently obey the Lord your God, being careful to do all His commandments which I command you today, the Lord your God will set you high above all the nations of the earth. All these blessings will come upon you....You shall lend to many nations, but you shall not borrow"* (Deuteronomy 28:1, 2, 12). However, debt was one of the curses for disobedience. *"But it shall come about, if you do not obey the Lord your God, to observe to do all His commandments and His statutes with which I charge you today, that all these curses will come upon you and overtake you. ...The alien who is among you shall rise above you higher and higher, but you will go down lower and lower. He shall lend to you, but you will not lend to him; he shall be the head, and you will be the tail"* (Deuteronomy 28:15, 43-44, NAS).

3. Debt presumes upon tomorrow.

When we get into debt, we assume that we will earn enough in the future to pay the debt. We plan for our jobs to continue or our businesses or investments to be profitable. Scripture cautions us against presumption: *"Come now, you who say, 'Today or tomorrow we will go to such and such a city, and spend a year there and engage in business and make a profit.' Yet you do not know what your life will be like tomorrow. You are just a vapor that appears for a little while and then vanishes away. Instead, you ought to say, 'If the Lord wills, we will live and also do this or that'"* (James 4:13-15, NAS).

4. Debt may deny God an opportunity.

Ron Blue, an outstanding financial author, tells of a young man who wanted to go to seminary to become a missionary. The young man had no money and thought the only way he could afford seminary was to secure a student loan. However, this would have left him with $40,000 of debt by the time he graduated, which would have been impossible to pay back on a missionary's salary. After a great deal of prayer, he decided to enroll without the help of a student loan and to trust the Lord to meet his needs. He graduated without borrowing anything and grew in his appreciation for how God could creatively provide his needs. This was the most valuable lesson learned in seminary as he prepared for life on the mission field. Borrowing may deny God an opportunity to demonstrate His power.

Since debt is almost always viewed negatively in the Bible, we should be very careful about rationalizing our use of it so that we don't risk losing God's highest and best for us.

A WONDERFUL EXAMPLE: A LESSON FROM A WIDOW

2 Kings 4:1-7 gives us the story of God using Elisha to provide in a miraculous way for the widow of a former priest. It also suggests several principles for dealing with poverty and indebtedness.

Historical background: Elisha has just witnessed the sweeping away of his mentor and teacher, Elijah the prophet. God has confirmed that Elisha is now His mouthpiece.

Setting: A widow of one of Elisha's fellow prophets came to Elisha out of desperation. She and her sons were in debt to the extent that her sons were about to be taken as slaves in payment for the debt. This would remove her only hope for sustenance.

Spend some time reading this text before you go on. It does not provide any direct evidence as to the reason for the widow's destitution or whether it resulted from any failure on her husband's part to be financially faithful. For the sake of illustrating the first two general principles below, however, we will speculate that he made imprudent financial choices in spite of the fact that he "feared God." Once you have read the text, make observations from this example about how this widow was able to meet her financial obligations.

GENERAL PRINCIPLES

1. Service to God is no excuse for financial unfaithfulness.
2. Misuse of finances affects the entire family.
3. The consequences of financial mismanagement can be disastrous: slavery in this case.
4. God can take a little and provide much.

APPLICATIONS

1. Admit the problem: v.1. (Many people will not admit there is a problem.)
2. Seek help from a spiritual leader: v.2. (Are your spiritual leaders prepared to help?)
3. Recognize that the debt must be repaid: v.2. (Elisha did not allow her to shirk the family's responsibility to repay their debt. See also Psalm 37:21.)
4. Use existing resources: v.2. (Elisha reviewed her assets.)
5. Involve friends: v.3. (Elisha involved her neighbors/sphere of influence).
6. Don't underestimate God's ability: v.2. (A little oil in her hands became a lot in God's hands.)
7. Actively participate in the solution: v.3. (Go...)

8. Don't limit God to your way of thinking: v.3. (Elisha encouraged her: "Not just a few.")

9. Anticipate God's unique provision: v.4. (How He provides may be very creative.)

10. Involve the family: vs.4-5. (Financial hardship should not be hidden from children old enough to understand. Involving them in the solution can build both their character and self-esteem.)

11. Have a plan: v.3-4. (Elisha's instructions were specific.)

12. Follow through: v.5. (The widow did exactly as Elisha instructed.)

13. Be accountable to someone: v.7. (The widow reported to Elisha.)

14. Be responsible with blessings: v.7. (Pay the debt and live on the surplus. See also Proverbs 21:20.)

THE COST OF DEBT

The dictionary defines debt as "money that a person is obligated to pay to another." Debt includes outstanding credit card balances, bank loans, money borrowed from relatives, the home mortgage, and past-due medical bills. Regular monthly bills, such as utilities, are not considered debt if they are paid when due.

We need to understand the real cost of debt. Assume you have $5,560 in credit card debt at an 18 percent interest rate. This would cost $1,000 in interest annually. Study the chart below.

1. Amount of interest paid on $5,560 at 18%

Year 5	Year 10	Year 20	Year 30	Year 40
$5,000	$10,000	$20,000	$30,000	$40,000

2. Value of $1,000 invested annually, earning 12 percent

Year 5	Year 10	Year 20	Year 30	Year 40
$6,353	$17,549	$72,052	$241,333	$767,091

3. Amount lender earns from your interest payments at 18 percent interest

Year 5	Year 10	Year 20	Year 30	Year 40
$7,154	$23,521	$146,628	$790,948	$4,163,213

You can see what lenders have seen for a long time: the incredible impact of compounding interest. The lender will accumulate more than $4 million if you pay $1,000 a year for 40 years and the lender earns 18 percent on your payment! Obviously, lenders have expenses that prevent them from realizing a net 18% return on interest dollars paid in, but the business is still very lucrative. Can you see why you receive so many credit card solicitations? They are eager for you to become one of their big profit centers.

Now compare the $40,000 you paid in interest over 40 years with the $767,091 you could have accumulated by earning 12 percent on $1,000 invested each year. The monthly income on $767,091 earning 12 percent is $7,671—without ever touching the principal! Stop to consider this: When you assume debt of $5,560 and pay $1,000 a year in interest, that $1,000 per year, over 40 years, will cost you $767,091 in lost opportunity if you could have earned a 12 percent return on the same money. Debt has a much higher cost than many realize. The next time you are tempted to purchase something with debt, ask yourself if the long-term benefits of staying out of debt outweigh the short-term benefits of the purchase.

Home Mortgage

Original mortgage amount $100,000.00
Monthly mortgage payment at 10 percent interest = $877.57
Months paid x 360
Total payments $315,925.20

A 30-year home mortgage at a 10 percent interest rate will require you to pay more than *three times* the amount originally borrowed.

The Physical Cost of Debt

Debt also increases stress, which contributes to mental, physical, and emotional fatigue. It can stifle creativity and harm relationships. Many people raise their lifestyle through debt, only to discover that the burden of debt then controls their lifestyle. The car bumper sticker that reads, "I owe, I owe, it's off to work I go," is an unfortunate reality for too many people.

WHEN IS DEBT REASONABLE?

Scripture is silent on the subject of prudent debt. In our opinion, debt is acceptable for a home mortgage or for your business or vocation. When people use debt for these purposes, we believe they should adhere to the following three criteria.

- The item purchased is an asset with the potential to appreciate or produce an income.
- The value of an item equals or exceeds the amount owed against it.
- The debt should not be so high that repayment puts undue strain on the budget.

Here's how a home mortgage might qualify. Since houses have usually been an appreciating asset, a mortgage meets the first requirement. A reasonable down payment should ensure that the house can sell for at least enough to pay off the mortgage, meeting the second requirement. The third requirement dictates that the house be affordable, that the monthly payment will not strain the budget.

When people meet these criteria and assume some debt, we advise them to establish the goal of eliminating it as soon as possible. There is no assurance that the housing market will appreciate or that employment will continue uninterrupted. Freedom from debt relieves many hardships and opens many doors of opportunity.

THE PROCESS OF GETTING OUT OF DEBT

Consider these ten steps for getting out of debt. Although understanding them is easy, following them requires *hard work*. The goal is D-Day—Debtless Day—when you become absolutely free of debt.

1. Pray.

The same God who provided supernaturally for the widow In 2 Kings 4:1-7 is interested in your becoming free from debt. Seek the Lord's help and guidance in your journey toward Debtless Day. He may act immediately, as in the case of the widow, or slowly over time. In either case, prayer is essential. We see an exciting trend emerging: as people begin to eliminate debt, the Lord is blessing their faithfulness. Even if you can afford only a small monthly prepayment of your debt, please do it. The Lord can multiply your efforts.

2. Establish a written spending plan.

In our experience, few people in debt have been using a budget. They may have had one—neatly filed away in a drawer or loaded on their computer—but they have not been using it. A spending plan offers many benefits. Developing it enables you to analyze your spending patterns so that you can identify waste and unnecessary losses. The plan frees you from a lot of stress. Instead of laboring over each decision as it comes, you will have already made many of the decisions, making it much easier to follow through. It is an amazingly effective way to control impulse spending.

3. List everything you own.

Examine the list to determine whether you should sell anything and use the money to pay off debt. Golf clubs gathering dust in the garage or a car that's too expensive are examples.

4. List everything you owe.

Many people, particularly if they owe a lot of money, do not know exactly what they owe. They hope that ignoring the truth will somehow make it go away. You need to list your debts to determine your current financial situation.

5. Establish a debt repayment plan.

After you make your monthly payments, write down the amount paid and compute the balance due for each debt. This will give you a sense of accomplishment, which will encourage you to continue repaying all your debt.

If you are deeply in debt or have been past due on your payments to creditors, it is a good idea to send them a repayment schedule. A creditor will appreciate the fact that you have a concrete plan and have been concerned enough to share it. You must also decide which debts to pre-pay first. Base this decision on two factors: the size of the debts and the interest rate charged.

Focus on paying off the smallest high-interest debt first. You will be encouraged as it is eliminated, and this will free more cash to apply against other debts. After you pay off the first debt, add its payment to the payment for the next debt you wish to retire. After the second debt is paid off, add what you were paying on the first and second debts to the payment for the third and so forth.

6. Consider earning additional income.

Many people hold jobs that simply do not pay enough to meet their needs, even if they spend wisely. If you can earn additional income, decide in advance to pay off debts with the added earnings. We tend to spend more than we make, whether we earn much or little, so be careful about falling into the trap of spending the extra income.

7. Do not take on new debt: control the use of credit cards.

Many credit card solicitations offer low interest rates for a short introductory period. Not only does the rate increase—usually dramatically—at the end of the period, but card issuers can raise the rate at any time for a number of reasons. Some of those reasons would surprise you. For instance, if card issuers—in their sole judgment—believe that you have received too many other offers and that you could potentially take on too much credit, they can increase your rate. You would never know they have done it unless you carefully check your statement every month.

Credit cards are not sinful, but they are dangerous. More than one billion credit cards are currently in use, and only 40 percent of them are paid in full each month. People spend about one-third more when they use credit cards rather than cash because they don't feel as though they are spending real money—it's just plastic. As one shopper said to another, "I like credit cards lots more than money, because they go so much further!"

When we examine the finances of someone in debt, we use a simple rule of thumb to determine whether credit cards are too dangerous for them. If they do not pay the entire balance at the end of each month, we encourage them to perform some plastic surgery—any good scissors will do. (If you would like help stopping credit card offers, call 1-888-5-OPT-OUT.)

8. Be content with what you have.

The advertising industry uses powerful methods to get consumers to buy. Frequently the message is intended to create discontentment with what we have. An example is the American company that opened a new plant in Central America because the labor was relatively inexpensive. Everything went well until the villagers received their first paycheck; afterwards they did not return to work. Several days later, the manager went down to the village chief to determine the cause of this problem, and the chief responded, "Why should we work? We already have everything we need." The plant stood idle for two months until someone came up with the idea of sending a mail-order catalog to every villager. There has not been an employment problem since!

Note these three realities of our consumer-driven economy.

- The more television you watch, the more you spend.
- The more you look at catalogs and magazines, the more you spend.
- The more you shop, the more you spend.

Our (Howard's) family has been living proof of this. I could tell when my six-year old daughter had been watching television because she suddenly had to have a special glass from a fast-food restaurant. Limiting our television viewing also limits our wants.

9. Consider a radical change in lifestyle.

A growing number of people have lowered their standard of living significantly to get out of debt. Some have sold a home and moved to a smaller one or rented an apartment or moved in with family members. Many have sold automobiles with large monthly payments and have purchased inexpensive used cars for cash. In short, they have temporarily lowered their cost of living to become debt free more quickly.

10. Do not give up!

For some, this last step is the most difficult, but keeping the goal visible helps us keep its importance in mind. On October 29, 1941, Winston Churchill, Prime Minister of England, gave a commencement address. World War II was devastating all of Europe, and England's fate was in doubt. Churchill stood to address the crowd, saying, "Never give in. Never give in. Never, never, never—in nothing, great or small—give up except to convictions of honor." Then he sat down.

Never give up in your efforts to get out of debt. It may require hard work and sacrifice, but the freedom is worth the struggle.

ESCAPING THE AUTO-DEBT TRAP

Automobile loans are one of the leading causes of consumer indebtedness, with 70 percent of all car purchases being financed. To escape this trap, decide in advance to keep your car for at least three years longer than your existing car debt. Second, pay off your automobile loan. Third, continue paying the monthly car payment, but pay it into your own savings account. Then, when you are ready to replace your car, the saved cash plus what you get from selling your current car should be sufficient to buy a reliable used car without going into debt.

THE HOME MORTGAGE

If you own a home or plan to purchase one in the future, we want to encourage you to pay it off more rapidly than scheduled. When Bev (Howard's wife) and I first learned God's financial principles, we decided to work toward paying off everything, including our home mortgage. Frankly, this was an unrealistic goal for us at the time, but we began to explore how we might do it. Let's examine the payment schedule for a home mortgage. Please do not let the size of the mortgage or the interest rate hinder your thinking; this is for illustration purposes only. In the chart below, we are assuming a 30-year $100,000 mortgage at a 10 percent interest rate. The first year of the payment schedule looks like this.

Chart: Home Mortgage

Payment #	Payment Amt.	Interest	Principal	Balance
1 Jan	877.57	833.33	44.24	99,955.76
2 Feb	877.57	832.96	44.61	99,911.15
3 Mar	877.57	832.59	44.98	99,866.17
4 Apr	877.57	832.22	45.35	99,820.82
5 May	877.57	831.84	45.73	99,775.09
6 Jun	877.57	831.46	46.11	99,728.98
7 Jul	877.57	831.07	46.50	99,682.48
8 Aug	877.57	830.69	46.88	99,635.60
9 Sep	877.57	830.30	47.27	99,588.33
10 Oct	877.57	829.90	47.67	99,540.66
11 Nov	877.57	829.51	48.06	99,492.60
12 Dec	877.57	829.10	48.47	99,444.13
TOTALS	10,530.84	9,974.97	555.87	

As you can see, the payments during the early years are almost all interest. Of the $10,530 in payments made this first year, only $555 went toward principal reduction! In fact, it will be 23 1/2 years before the principal portion of the payment equals the interest portion. The goal of taking 30 years to pay off a home mortgage just doesn't seem too compelling.

Reducing that goal to 15 years makes it much more attractive. Several strategies will enable us to do that Here are two to consider.

The first is to increase the amount of our monthly payment by a regular amount. In our example, the required monthly payment is $877. Increasing the monthly payment by $197 for a payment of $1,074 will pay it off in 15 years. During those 15 years, we will have paid $35,467 in extra principal reduction, but we will have saved well over three times that much: $122,495 to be exact.

A second strategy is to prepay the next month's principal payment in addition to your regular monthly payment of $877. Doing this consistently for 15 years will pay off the entire mortgage. During the early years, the additional payment is low. In later years, the extra payment becomes much larger. The difficulty of the larger payment in later years may be offset somewhat by the effects of inflation and potential growth in earning power.

Before adopting either of these strategies, confirm that your mortgage can be prepaid without penalty; most mortgages can be. Finally, let your lender know what you are planning to do.

We often hear three arguments against early mortgage retirement. (1) Why pay off a low-interest home mortgage when you can get a better return elsewhere? (2) With inflation, the lender is being paid back with less valuable dollars during the life of the mortgage. (3) Since interest paid on a home mortgage is tax deductible, why lose the tax shelter?

Although these arguments have some merit, close examination shows that their benefits are often not as great as they appear. Earning a better return than the mortgage rate sounds good but usually entails considerable investment risk. It is a rare occurrence when the economic cycle allows a homeowner to earn more interest in a CD or treasury instrument than he pays on his mortgage. And the tax shelter? A homeowner in the 25% tax bracket gets the privilege of saving $250 in taxes for every $1,000 he pays in interest. It still costs him $750. If he didn't have to pay the interest, he could save the $1,000 payment, pay the $250 in taxes, and still be $750 ahead.

We recognize that the tax system in America is designed to reward indebtedness and penalize savings. We are taxed on interest earned, but interest paid on a home mortgage is a tax deduction. However, the Bible encourages saving and discourages debt. Our purpose is simply to challenge you to seek Christ with an open heart to learn what He wants you to do. For Bev and me (Howard), this turned into an exciting time as we began to pay off our mortgage. The Lord provided additional funds for us in an unexpected way, and today we do not owe anyone anything. This allowed me to take time off from my job to study and develop the Crown materials. God may have something similar for you. Our living costs are more modest now than they were before because we do not have house payments or any other debt.

INVESTMENT DEBT

Should you borrow money to make an investment? In our opinion, any investment for which you borrow (and any money invested as a down payment) should be the sole collateral for the debt. You should not put yourself in a position of guaranteeing repayment of an investment debt from other personal sources. At first this may appear to contradict the biblical instruction for godly people to repay their debts, but let's explore the issue further. For example, if we wanted to purchase a $70,000 rental house with $15,000 as the down payment, we would submit a loan application specifying the requirement of the house as sole security for the debt. We would explain to the lender that if, for any reason, we were unable to repay the loan, we would lose the $15,000 down payment, plus any other money we invested in the house, and the lender would own the house.

The lender must then make a business decision. Is the down payment sufficient? Is the house valuable enough? Is the housing market strong enough for the lender to feel secure about making the loan? In our opinion, the only circumstance under which we can be freed from the personal responsibility for a debt is when we have clearly communicated with the lender before obtaining the loan that we are not personally guaranteeing repayment of the loan. Some have responded that it is impossible to locate a lender willing to loan without a personal guarantee. Many of them, however, later admitted they had not made a sincere effort to obtain such a loan. We have repeatedly seen the Lord allow His children to secure this type of financing as they made it a matter of prayer.

Be sure to limit your potential loss to the money you invested (your equity) and the value of the investment itself. Any investment risks the possibility of difficult financial events over which you have no control. It is painful to lose your investment, but it is much more serious to risk all your assets on investment debt. Although this position may appear too conservative, we know many people who have become slaves of the lender and lost everything by guaranteeing debt on investments that went sour.

BUSINESS DEBT

We also encourage business owners to pray about eliminating business debt as well. A debt-free business provides wonderful stability and lowered stress.

CHURCH DEBT

Scripture does not specifically address whether a church may borrow money to build or expand its facility. In our opinion, such debt is permissible only if the church leadership clearly senses the leading of the Lord to do so. If a church borrows, we recommend that it raise as much money as possible for the down payment and establish a plan to pay off the debt as rapidly as possible. A growing number of churches have chosen to build without the use of any debt. Their members have been encouraged and have experienced growing faith as they have observed the Lord providing the necessary funds.

Some biblical examples should cause church leaders to think twice about following the world's example in taking on debt.

1 Chronicles 28 is a great example of God's people providing for the building of His temple. David led the operation and took the lead in giving. His enthusiasm to give from his own pocket moved the children of Israel so deeply that they responded with overwhelming generosity. The leadership finally had to tell the people "enough!"

An important value is the patience to seek God's guidance in funding. He may be willing to provide through other means but withhold that blessing because we jump ahead in our haste to complete a project.

The principle of leading by example as David did is still as valid today as it was in his time. Church leaders who demonstrate their commitment in a practical way are usually rewarded with generosity from their congregation.

DEBT REPAYMENT RESPONSIBILITIES

1. Prompt payment

Many people delay payments to creditors until payments are past due, even when they have the money. This is not biblical. Proverbs 3:27-28 reads, *"Do not withhold good from those to whom it is due, when it is in your power to do it. Do not say to your neighbor, 'Go, and come back, and tomorrow I will give it,' when you have it with you"* (NAS). Godly people should pay their debts and bills as promptly as they can. Some have a policy of trying to pay each bill the same day they receive it to demonstrate to others that knowing Jesus Christ has made them financially responsible.

2. Using your savings

We believe that it is wise not to use all your savings to pay off debt. Maintain a reasonable level of savings to provide for the unexpected. If you apply all your savings against debt and the unexpected occurs, you will probably be forced back into debt to fund the emergency.

3. Bankruptcy

A court can declare a person bankrupt and unable to pay his or her debts. Depending upon the type of bankruptcy, the court will either allow the debtor to develop a plan to repay his creditors or the court will distribute his property among the creditors as payment for the debts. A wave of bankruptcy is sweeping our country. Should a godly person declare bankruptcy? The answer is generally no. Psalm 37:21 tells us, *"The wicked borrows and does not pay back"* (NAS).

However, we believe that bankruptcy is permissible under two circumstances: 1) a creditor forces a person into bankruptcy or 2) counselors believe the debtor's emotional health is at stake because of inability to cope with the pressure of creditors. For example, a husband may desert his wife and children, leaving her with debts for which she is responsible. She may not have the resources to meet those obligations. The emotional trauma of an unwanted divorce, coupled with harassment from unsympathetic creditors, may be too much to bear. After a person goes through bankruptcy, he or she should seek counsel from an attorney to determine if it's legally permissible to attempt to repay the debt even though there is no obligation to do so. If it is allowable, every effort should be made to repay the debt. For a large debt, this may be a long-term goal that depends largely on the Lord's supernatural provision.

COSIGNING

Cosigning relates to debt. Anytime you cosign, you become legally responsible for the debt of another. It is just as if you went to the bank, borrowed the money, and gave it to your friend or relative who is asking you to cosign. A Federal Trade Commission study found that 50 percent of those who cosigned for bank loans ended up making the payment. Seventy-five percent of those who cosigned for finance company loans ended up making the payments! Unfortunately, few cosigners plan for this. The casualty rate is so high because the lender has already determined that the loan is a bad risk. That is why the lender won't make the loan without someone who is financially responsible to guarantee its repayment. Fortunately, Scripture speaks clearly about cosigning. Proverbs 17:18 reads, *"It is poor judgment to cosign another's note, to become responsible for his debts"* (TLB). The words "poor judgment" are better translated as "destitute of mind."

A parent often cosigns for his or her child's first car. The Watsons decided not to do this. They wanted to show their children the importance of not cosigning and to discourage them from using debt. Instead, they trained them to plan and save for the cash purchase of their first car.

If you have already cosigned for a loan, the Scripture gives you counsel. Proverbs 6:1-5 reads, *"Son, if you endorse a note for someone you hardly know, guaranteeing his debt, you are in serious trouble. You may have trapped yourself by your agreement. Quick! Get out of it if you possibly can! Swallow your pride; don't let embarrassment stand in the way. Go and beg to have your name erased. Don't put it off…. If you can get out of this trap you have saved yourself like a deer that escapes from a hunter or a bird from the net"* (TLB). Please use sound judgment and never cosign.

Think About it!

- *If you are currently burdened by debt, list at least four things you will do to eliminate it as soon as possible.*

- *How will you avoid needless debt in the future? List three strategies.*

- *If you are in school, what can you do to reduce your need for educational loans?*

- *If you are thinking about pursuing graduate school, how can you do it with the least amount of debt possible?*

CHAPTER FOURTEEN

Store It Up: Giving's Big Picture

Core concepts

- What are two essential elements of giving?

- What is the purpose of giving? In what way does giving fuel the Great Commission?

- Describe how giving is worship.

- What are six steps in the process of giving?

- Describe the attitude of the giver.

- What are four advantages of giving?

- Discuss how we determine the amount to give.

- To what organizations and places should we give?

Overview

Sometimes we overlook the fact that God rewards every sacrifice, every gift, every act of service. Nothing escapes His attention, and His compensation plan exceeds our wildest dreams. Our desire to give to Him out of pure gratitude should grow as we understand His forgiveness and redemption in spite of our depravity.

Although we desire to have the purest possible motivation—and our attitude in giving is extremely important to God—Jesus makes a strong appeal for us to be self-serving in the best possible way. Matthew 6:20 reads, "But store up for yourselves treasures in heaven, where neither moth nor rust destroys, and where thieves do not break in and steal; for where your treasure is, there your heart will be also" (NAS). As we set our eyes and efforts on that which is eternal, we make the only investment that is guaranteed to never disappoint. That is our focus as we study the eternal perspective and rewards of the godly steward.

INTRODUCTION

Several years ago a young couple in one of my (Chad) wife's Crown small groups was severely in debt but committed to climbing out. Imagine a situation so bleak that Deb, the wife, was working three jobs, one of them as a late-night checker in a local supermarket. Near closing time one evening, a female customer whom Deb had finished checking out asked if Deb could help put the groceries in her car. Somewhat hesitant, Deb complied. In the parking lot, the lady turned and asked Deb where *her* car was. Confused, Deb said, "It's on the side of the store, why?"

"Well," the lady replied, "God told me that I was supposed to buy these groceries and give them to you!"

Stunned, Deb silently thanked the Lord for His provision, having wondered how they would buy food the next week. This generous customer knew from experience what Jesus meant when He said, *"it's more blessed to give than to receive"* (Acts 20:35b).

Giving is not the most popular subject among believers. Matthew 6:20 and Acts 20:35b—verses we have just cited—if taken to heart, would make giving a very popular subject, but the fear of not having enough or being used by a manipulative leader makes many churchgoers oversensitive at the mere mention of it. That is an unfortunate victory for the enemy because giving is a deeply spiritual matter that affects every believer's heart.

If every regular churchgoer actually gave ten percent to the church, churches would never have to ask for money. They would still be well advised to teach on the subject for the welfare of their members—as a means of expressing gratitude to God, enriching their own lives, blessing others, and conforming to God's image. God, by His loving nature, is a giver (cf. John 3:16). He calls us, who have been created in His image, to conform to His image. He is delighted when we experience His joy in our pursuit of God-like giving.

We give both vertically and horizontally, and both planes are bidirectional. All giving finds its origin in God's giving directed toward us. We respond vertically to Him as we recognize His ownership and give back to Him.

When we give horizontally (to family, church, and our biblical "neighbor"), we reflect God's giving in an imperfect but very meaningful way. And just as God both gives and receives back from us on the vertical plane, we both give to and receive from one another on the horizontal. The miraculous part of this is that when we give horizontally, the benefits are not confined to that horizontal plane. God Himself actually benefits as though we were giving to Him. Jesus' story of the sheep and goats in Matthew 25:34-45 gives us a powerful picture of God identifying with the poor. And once again, He enters the equation by rewarding us.

PURPOSE OF GIVING

Why do we give? Why should we give? God gives us our answers to these questions in His interaction with us. As our ideal example of giving, God created the universe and gave us a splendor-filled home to oversee. His act of creating us in His image is a merciful gift of love. He invites us to be in relationship with Him and remedies our refusal by sending His very own Son to redeem us from slavery to sin. Because our best efforts come up short, God gives yet again by exchanging our little faith for an infinite righteousness we could never earn. *"But now a righteousness from God, apart from law, has been made known [given], to which the Law and the Prophets testify"* (Romans 3:21). In Romans 5:6, 8 we read, *"...at just the right time, when we were still powerless, Christ died for the ungodly....But God demonstrates his own love for us in this: While we were still sinners, Christ died for us."* That is ceaseless giving that deserves our ceaseless gratitude!

GIVING MEETS NEEDS THROUGH PEOPLE.

In most cases, God meets needs through the generosity of His people—the body of Christ. Together, we are ministers of His manifold grace. We see clear examples of this truth in 2 Corinthians 9:10-15.

    a. *Giving is a proof of true discipleship.*

    b. *Giving supplies the needs of God's servants and His church.*

    c. *Giving enables us to be "Christ in the flesh" to others and participate in His work on earth.*

GIVING IS WORSHIP.

Giving, as a component of the spiritual life—the life of a steward—must be seen primarily as an act of worship to God. As we give God our lives daily, we give Him our constant *worship;* in fact, everything we do that is true and honorable is worship to Him. It always includes some element of sacrifice: our will, our way, even our wants. When we give, we say, "not my will but yours, Father." When we give, we say, "Your way is better than mine." When we give, we value the needs of others above our selfish wants.

GIVING IS A MATTER OF THE HEART.

Although we are to surrender everything to God—our time, talent and treasure—this course focuses on money, so we will devote most of our giving discussion to financial resources. Understanding that everything originates from God and ultimately belongs to Him, the issue of giving is less about percentages and more about our hearts. When our question centers on how much we *must* give, we miss the point. Paul helps us find the point when he applauds the Macedonians in 2 Corinthians 8:5 for giving *"themselves first to the Lord and then to us in keeping with God's will."* That is the heart formula that will never fail to please God as it meets the needs He wants to meet. And rather than feeling manipulated or coerced, our hearts will experience the same *"overwhelming joy"* they did (v. 2).

"For where your treasure is, there your heart will be also" (Matthew 6:21). This poignant statement by Jesus gives us a method for finding our heart and assessing its loyalty. What do we treasure? What do we fear losing? What will we fight to keep? What do we dream about getting? In answer to these questions, many people would create a list of *things*. Some would choose fame, some would choose the love of a person, some would choose health; most would choose something they hope to receive. A special few would choose what they hope to give.

God's desire is that we would treasure Him, that we would desire an intimate relationship with Him above all else. He knows that when that happens, we will automatically excel in giving.

ATTITUDE

God evaluates our actions on the basis of our attitude. God's attitude toward giving is best summed up in John 3:16: *"For God so loved the world that He gave His one and only son."* Note the sequence. Because God loved, He gave. Because God is love, He is also a giver. He set the example of giving motivated by love. An attitude of love in giving is crucial: *"If I give all I possess to the poor . . . but have not love, I gain nothing"* (1 Corinthians 13:3). It is difficult to imagine anything more commendable than giving everything to the poor. However, giving with the wrong attitude, without love, is of no benefit to the giver. From God's perspective, the attitude is more important than the amount.

Jesus emphasized this in Matthew 23:23: *"Woe to you, teachers of the law and Pharisees, you hypocrites! You give a tenth of your spices— mint, dill and cumin. But you have neglected the more important matters of the law—justice, mercy and faithfulness. You should have practiced the latter without neglecting the former."* The Pharisees had been careful to give the tithe (10 percent) down to the last mint leaf in their gardens. Christ rebuked them, however, because He looks past the amount of the gift to the heart of the giver. The reason we can give out of a heart filled with love is that our gifts are actually given to the Lord Himself. We see an example of this in Numbers 18:24, where God declared that He would give to the Levites as their inheritance *"the tithes that the Israelites present as an offering to the Lord"* [emphasis mine].

If giving is merely to a church, a ministry, or a needy person, it is only charity. But if it is given to the Lord, it becomes an act of worship. Because God is our Creator, our Savior, and our faithful Provider, we can express our gratefulness and love by giving our gifts to Him. For example, when the offering plate is passed at church, we should remind ourselves that we are giving our gift to the Lord Himself.

In addition to giving out of a heart filled with love, we are to give cheerfully. *"Each man should give what he has decided in his heart to give, not reluctantly or under compulsion, for God loves a cheerful giver"* (2 Corinthians 9:7). The original Greek word for cheerful is *hilarios*, which is translated into the English word "hilarious." We are to be hilarious givers. Unfortunately, there is usually little hilarity in the pews during the offering. Instead, the atmosphere is more like a dentist's waiting room where patients know a painful procedure is about to occur.

How do we develop this hilarity in our giving? Consider the early churches of Macedonia. *"We want you to know about the grace that God has given the Macedonian churches. Out of the most severe trial, their overflowing joy and their extreme poverty welled up in rich generosity"* (2 Corinthians 8:1-2).

How did the Macedonians, who were in terrible circumstances, *"severe trial and extreme poverty,"* still manage to give with *"overflowing joy"*? The answer is in verse 5: *"They first gave themselves to the Lord and to us by the will of God."* The key to cheerful giving is to submit ourselves to Christ and ask Him to direct how much He wants us to give. Only then are we in a position to experience any of the advantages of giving with the proper attitude. Stop and examine yourself. What is your attitude toward giving?

ADVANTAGES OF GIVING

Gifts obviously benefit the recipients. The church continues its ministry, the hungry are fed, the naked are clothed, and missionaries are sent. But gifts given with the proper attitude benefit the giver even more than the receiver. *"Remembering the words the Lord Jesus himself said: 'It is more blessed to give than to receive'"* (Acts 20:35). As we examine Scripture, we find that the giver benefits in four significant areas.

1. Increase in intimacy

Above all else, giving directs our attention and heart to Christ. Matthew 6:21 tells us, *"For where your treasure is, there your heart will be also."* This is why it is so necessary to give each gift to the person of Jesus Christ. When you give your gift to Him, your heart will automatically be drawn to the Lord. Also remember that giving is one of the responsibilities of the steward, and the more faithful we are in fulfilling these responsibilities, the more we can *"share your Master's happiness"* (Matthew 25:21). Nothing in life can compare to entering into His joy and knowing Christ more intimately.

2. Increase in character

Our heavenly Father wants us as His children to be conformed to the image of His Son. The character of Christ is that of an unselfish giver. Unfortunately, humans are selfish by nature. One of the ways we become conformed to Christ is by regular giving. Someone once said, "Giving is not God's way of raising money; it is God's way of raising people into the likeness of His Son."

3. Increase in heaven

Matthew 6:20 reads, *"Store up for yourselves treasures in heaven, where moth and rust do not destroy, and where thieves do not break in and steal."* He wants us to know that we can invest for eternity. Paul wrote, *"Not that I am looking for a gift, but I am looking for what may be credited to your account"* (Philippians 4:17). There is an account for each of us in heaven, which we will be able to enjoy for eternity. And while it is true that "we can't take it with us," Scripture teaches that we can make deposits to our heavenly account before we die.

4. Increase on earth

Many people have a hard time believing that giving results in material blessings flowing back to the giver. But study the following passages. Proverbs 11:24-25 says, *"One man gives freely, yet gains even more; another withholds unduly, but comes to poverty. A generous man will prosper; he who refreshes others will himself be refreshed."*

Examine 2 Corinthians 9:6-11. *"He who sows sparingly will also reap sparingly, and he who sows bountifully will also reap bountifully. . . . God is able to make all grace abound to you, so that always having all sufficiency in everything, you may have an abundance for every good deed; as it is written, 'He scattered abroad, He gave to the poor, His righteousness endures forever.' Now He who supplies seed to the sower and bread for food, will supply and multiply your seed for sowing and increase the harvest of your righteousness; you will be enriched in everything for all liberality"* (NAS). These verses clearly teach that giving results in a material increase: *"will also reap bountifully . . . always having all sufficiency in everything . . . may have an abundance . . . will supply and multiply your seed . . . you will be enriched in everything."* But note carefully *why* the Lord is returning an increase materially: *"Always having all sufficiency in everything, you may have an abundance for every good deed . . . will supply and multiply your seed for sowing . . . you will be enriched in everything for all liberality."*

As shown in the diagram below the Lord produces an increase so that we may give more and have our needs met at the same time.

Give

Material Increase

Needs Met

One reason the Lord gives a material increase in response to our giving is that He wants us to recognize that He is encouraging it. God has chosen to be invisible, but He wants us to experience His reality. When we give, we should do so with a sense of anticipating the Lord to provide a material increase, even though we do not know when or how He may choose to provide it. From our experience, He can be very creative! Remember, the giver can experience the advantages of giving only when he or she gives cheerfully out of a heart filled with love, not when the motive of giving is just to get.

GIVING AND THE GREAT COMMISSION

Jesus says in Matthew 28:19-20, to *"go therefore and make disciples of all nations, baptizing them in the name of the Father and of the Son and of the Holy Spirit, and teaching them to obey everything I commanded you. And surely I am with you always, to the very end of the age."* This passage, commonly called the Great Commission, has important implications for our giving.

Jesus provides in these two verses our basic and most important marching orders: to reach out to others in His name. In order to fulfill this commission, we must have both willing hearts and the resources to go; people and money are both necessary.

In the book of Exodus, God made the Israelites willing to go and the Egyptians willing to generously supply them. In the book of Ezra, God worked in the heart of several Persian Kings to enable the Jews to go to Jerusalem to build the temple, again supplying through their neighbors and later, through the royal treasury. This is a familiar pattern, often used by God: motivating people both to do the work and to supply the resources.

As followers of Jesus Christ, our mission is to align our goals with God's in order to fulfill His purposes. This means both going and supplying as He leads us to participate with Him in His work of redemption.

PROCESS OF GIVING (1 CORINTHIANS 16:1-2)

During Paul's third missionary journey, one of his objectives was to take up a collection for the church in Jerusalem. Paul provides counsel on the process of giving by reminding the Corinthians to follow the precedent given to the churches in Galatia. This suggests that Paul's process for giving is applicable to more than just one congregation. As we shall observe, giving should be a systematic, thoughtful, and personal process. 1 Corinthians 12:1-2 says, *"Now concerning the collection for the saints, as I directed the churches of Galatia, so do you also. On the first day of every week let each one of you put aside and save, as he may prosper, that no collections be made when I come"* (NAS). In verse two, we observe the process for faithful giving.

1. **Priority** (first day) v. 2 *"On the first day…"* Paul is affirming the need to make giving a priority in our lives. We give first.

2. **Regular** (weekly) v. 2 *"of every week…"* Giving should be a regular occurrence in our lives. If we give once a year or sporadically, the needs of others will not be met on a regular basis.

3. **Individual** (each one) v. 2 *"let each one of you…"* Giving is an individual or family matter in which all should participate.

4. **Specific** (sum) v. 2 *"put aside and save (sum…)"* We put aside from the rest of our money a specific sum for the needs of others. This requires a decision in which the heart should be involved: *"let each one do just as he has purposed in his heart; not grudgingly or under compulsion…"* (2 Corinthians 9:7).

5. **Proportional** v. 2 *"in keeping with income."* The NAS says *"as he may prosper."* This suggests a generosity that goes beyond a mere ten percent.

6. **Timely distribution** v. 2 *"When I come"* Paul's desire for the Corinthians to plan their giving allowed them to do it effectively and without haste. Among other things, he knew that giving is contagious, that as people planned and responded in advance, their generosity would snowball, creating an additional blessing both for them as well as the recipients in Jerusalem. When God's people give with consistency, church leaders can focus more on direct ministry than on fund-raising.

This thoughtful methodology for giving should be our pattern today.

AMOUNT TO GIVE

Let's survey what the Scripture says about how much to give. Before the Old Testament Law was given, there were two instances of giving with a known amount. In Genesis 14:20, Abraham gave ten percent—a tithe—after the rescue of his nephew Lot. And in Genesis 28:22, Jacob promised to give the Lord a tenth of all his possessions if God brought him safely through his journey. Mosaic law required a tithe. The Lord severely rebuked the children of Israel in Malachi 3:8-9 for not tithing properly: *"Will a man rob God? Yet you are robbing Me! But you say, 'How have we robbed You?' In tithes and offerings. You are cursed with a curse, for you are robbing Me, the whole nation of you!"* In addition to the tithe, various offerings were prescribed. The Lord also made special provisions for the needs of the poor. Every seven years, all debts were forgiven; every 50 years, land was returned to the original land-owning families. There were also special rules for harvesting that allowed the poor to glean behind the harvesters.

God made another significant provision for the poor in Deuteronomy 15:7-8: *"If there is a poor man with you, one of your brothers, in any of your towns in your land which the Lord your God is giving you, you shall not harden your heart, nor close your hand from your poor brother; but you shall freely open your hand to him, and shall generously lend him sufficient for his need in whatever he lacks."* Even under the law, the extent of giving was not solely determined by a fixed percentage but was to adjust to the needs of the surrounding people.

The New Testament teaches that we are to give generously in proportion to the material blessing we receive (cf. 1 Corinthians 16:1-2; 2 Corinthians 9:6-15) with a joy that is rooted in our deep love for God because He has given and forgiven us more that we could ever repay (John 3:16; Matthew 18:21-35). It also commends sacrificial giving (2 Corinthians 8:1-4). While the New Testament never says that ten percent is *the* amount to give, it is systematic and easy to compute. A danger of settling on ten percent as a standard is that it can be treated as simply another bill to be paid; without the correct attitude I do not put myself in a position to receive the blessings God has for me in giving. Another potential danger is the assumption that once I have given ten percent I have fulfilled all my obligations to give. For many Christians, ten percent should be the beginning of giving, not the limit.

As you wrestle with this question of amounts, first give yourself to the Lord (2 Corinthians 8:5). Submit yourself to Him. Earnestly seek His will for you concerning giving. Ask Him to help you obey Christ's leading. We are convinced that giving ten percent is merely the foundation of joyful, God-directed proportional giving as the Lord increases our portion (2 Corinthians 9:6-15).

C.S. Lewis aptly places the question of how much to give in proper perspective: "I do not believe one can settle how much we ought to give. I am afraid the only safe rule is to give more than we can spare. In other words, if our expenditure on comforts, luxuries, amusements, etc., is up to the standard common among those with the same income as our own, we are probably giving away too little. If our charities do not at all pinch or hamper us, I should say they are too small. There ought to be things we should like to do and cannot do because our charitable expenditure excludes them."

PLACES FOR GIVING

Scripture instructs us to give to three areas. The specifics of to whom and in what proportion depend on what God communicates to the heart of each believer.

Two Areas: Giving to the local church and Christian ministries

The Bible teaches funding the ministry. The Old Testament priesthood was to receive specific support: *"I give to the Levites all the tithes in Israel...in return for the work they do"* (Numbers 18:21). And the New Testament teaching on ministerial support is just as strong. Unfortunately, some have wrongly taught poverty for Christian workers. That position is not scriptural. *"Pastors who do their work well should be paid well and should be highly appreciated, especially those who work hard at both preaching and teaching"* (1 Timothy 5:17, TLB).

How many Christian workers have been driven to distraction from their ministry by inadequate support? God never communicated that His servants are to exist at the level of bare subsistence. As someone has said, "The poor and starving pastor should exist only among poor and starving people."

People ask us if we give only through our church. In our case, the answer is no. However, giving to the local church should be a priority. We give a minimum of ten percent of our regular income through our church, because this is a tangible expression of our commitment to it. But we also give to others who minister to us. *"The one who is taught the word is to share all good things with the one who teaches"* (Galatians 6:6).

A Third Area: Giving to the poor

In some way we cannot fully understand, Jesus, the Creator of all things, personally identifies Himself with the poor. Compassion for the needy around us should always prompt action as we emulate Christ's example. Sometimes this concern should come before our comfort, too. During Christ's earthly ministry, He gave consistently to the poor. It is especially revealing that, during the Last Supper after Jesus told Judas to do what he was going to do quickly, the following comment occurs: *"No one at the meal understood why Jesus said this to him. Since Judas had charge of the money, some thought Jesus was telling him to buy what was needed for the Feast, or to give something to the poor"* (John 13:28-29). Giving to the needy was such a consistent part of Jesus' life that the disciples assumed he might have been sending Judas to give to the poor.

After Paul met with the disciples to announce his ministry to the Gentiles, this statement is made: *"All they [the disciples] asked was that we should continue to* remember the poor—the very thing I was eager to do" (Galatians 2:10). Imagine all the issues the disciples could have discussed with Paul, but the only one they mentioned was to remember the poor. That should tell us something!

Three areas of our Christian life are affected by giving or lack of giving to the less fortunate.

1. Prayer

A lack of giving to the poor could be a source of unanswered prayer. *"Is not this the kind of fasting I have chosen . . . to share your food with the hungry and to provide the poor wanderer with shelter? . . . Then you will call, and the Lord will answer"* (Isaiah 58:6-9). *"If a man shuts his ears to the cry of the poor, he too will cry out and not be answered"* (Proverbs 21:13). The principle in these passages is that we invite God to treat us in the same way as we treat the needy around us. When we do not respond to their pleas, God may not answer ours.

2. Provision

God's provision to us is partially conditioned by our giving to the needy. *"He who gives to the poor will never want, but he who shuts his eyes will have many curses"* (Proverbs 28:27). This Proverb teaches the wisdom of giving to those in need to avoid God's disfavor. A mirror reflection of this is Paul's encouragement to the Corinthians: *"Whoever sows sparingly will also reap sparingly, and whoever sows generously will also reap generously"* (2 Corinthians 9:6).

3. Knowing Jesus Christ intimately

Those who do not share with the poor do not know the Lord as intimately as they could. *"'He defended the cause of the poor and needy, and so all went well. Is that not what it means to know me?" declares the Lord"* (Jeremiah 22:16). Giving to the poor has been discouraged, in part, because of government programs. It is good for a government to be compassionate and try to improve the living conditions of those in poverty, but they tend to do it impersonally. The church should always be at the forefront of ministering to the physical as well as the spiritual needs of people. Always remember that the church is you.

If you are not engaging in some meaningful way with needy people, please consider asking the Lord to bring such a person into your life. Ask Him to give you the desire to minister to Him in that way so that you can learn what it really means to give and to reflect His image. This will be a significant step in maturing your relationship with Christ. Mother Theresa is probably the best example in our time of serving the poor in a loving, compassionate way. May we be able to echo Job's statement: *"I rescued the poor who cried for help, and the fatherless who had none to assist him. . . . I made the widow's heart sing. . . . I was eyes to the blind and feet to the lame. I was a father to the needy; I took up the case of the stranger"* (Job 29:12-16).

Secular charities

Numerous secular charities (schools, fraternal orders, organizations that fight diseases) compete vigorously for our gift dollars. Scripture does not address whether we should give to these charities. However, our family has decided not to regularly support these organizations with our gifts. Our reason is that while many people support secular charities, only those who know the Lord support the ministries of Christ. However, we occasionally give to secular charities when the solicitor is a friend we want to encourage or influence for Christ or we sense the Lord's prompting to give.

OTHER TYPES OF GIVING

While giving our money is a primary focus for us in this study of faith and money, we should also give in other ways.

Giving our time

Time can be an extremely valuable gift. It is an unusual resource in the sense that everyone has the same amount of it each day, each month, each year—a constant that no amount of money can alter. One person has more time than money; he would gladly trade some of his time for more money. Another has more money than time; the demands on his schedule have such economic impact that he would gladly trade a lot of money for more time. Which is more meaningful to God? Probably the one that is more meaningful to you. Never forget what means the most to Him: your heart.

In the discussion of time and money as appropriate gifts to God, recognize that He desires and deserves both from us. Giving your time to nurture your relationship with God, to serve your family, your church, and your neighbor—all of these represent a spiritual act of worship.

Giving our talent

Equally important in our conversation regarding giving is the issue of giving our talents to further God's mission on earth. God has uniquely gifted each of us in some way. When we serve Him with our talents, we emulate Christ. Christ had a specific mission on earth and was endowed with the capacity to fulfill it. He could have chosen to use that capacity for some lesser purpose, which was the goal of Satan's temptation, but He chose to yield His capacity to the will of the Father. We face the same temptation to serve our human desires rather than focusing on God's mission for us.

One of Satan's deceptions is to get us to focus on "doing great things for God" in the sense that they will be greatly noticed and applauded. We look back at giants of the faith in the Bible and throughout history, and we would love to join their ranks. That is not an evil ambition unless it takes God's place in our hearts, becoming an unworthy goal because of distorted priorities and motivation. Simon, in Acts 8:9-23 provides a classic example of this tendency that often afflicts exceptionally talented people.

We need to guard our hearts against impurities and run from unhealthy spiritual competition. *"If anyone thinks he is something when he is nothing, he deceives himself. Each one should test his own actions. Then he can take pride in himself, without comparing himself to somebody else, for each one should carry his own load"* (Galatians 6:3-5). God has given each of us our "own load" and equipped us with the gifts we need to carry it. Paul explains this in great detail in 1 Corinthians 12 as he describes how the body of Christ works. Following a considerable list of specific gifts, he says in verse 11, *"All these are the work of one and the same Spirit, and he gives them to each one, just as he determines."* God gives us our role and His Spirit equips us for it. This is "our load," whether great or small in our eyes. Faithfulness to God in carrying this load is far more important than a grandiose vision inspired by our flesh.

A different but related temptation is to accomplish God's purpose by using our gifts apart from His empowerment. Any public ministry, including the pastorate, is vulnerable to judging its effectiveness solely by the response of people. Obviously, a higher standard is in order because many people respond to false teachers. One such standard is time alone with God to receive His empowerment. Jesus Himself modeled this. Since our time alone with God is not easily measured and evaluated in the public square, it is easy to underestimate its importance. Eternity, however, measures and evaluates it perfectly.

Some talents by their very nature are oriented toward public performance. The applause of an appreciative audience can be very motivating. That doesn't invalidate an honest expression of appreciation and encouragement; it merely places a responsibility on the performer to receive it in the right spirit and to guard his or her heart against the inherent temptations. Any desire to give our talent to God requires that we give it honestly and with the purest possible motives. *"For the word of God is* living and active. Sharper than any double-edged sword, it penetrates even to dividing soul and spirit, joints and marrow; it judges the thoughts and attitudes of the heart. Nothing in all creation is hidden from God's sight. Everything is uncovered and laid bare before the eyes of him to whom we must give account" (Hebrews 4:12-13).

> ### Think About it!
>
> • If God were to look at your current giving, would he consider you loyal to His purposes on earth or focused on your own pleasure?
>
> • If you lack an effective strategy for giving to God's work around the world, what are the top three things you need to do to get started?
>
> • Do you allow the fear of legalistic giving to hinder regular giving to God?

CHAPTER FIFTEEN

Growing in Faith and Giving

Core concepts

- Describe Fowler's six stages of faith.

Overview

Connecting the issue of money to our faith development is a major theme throughout this course. In the last chapter, we saw how giving demonstrates our true belief about faith and money. But how do we know if we are on the right track with our giving?

Finding ways to assess progress is challenging. Dr. Wes Willmer has devised a helpful approach by modifying James Fowler's stages of faith. We have provided a chart that offers the value of comparison-at-a-glance. It is not based on hard science and is not intended to represent a rigid grid, but it should help you identify your present position and set appropriate growth goals. I (Chad) have found this section to be one of the most practical tools in the classroom and believe you will find it helpful, too.

STAGES OF GIVING[1]

James Fowler, in *Stages of Faith: The Psychology of Human Development,* uses the well-established theoretical models of Piaget, Selman, and Kohlberg and maps out six stages of faith. Besides using these existing developmental models, he conducted interviews with people from a variety of religious backgrounds. M. Scott Peck calls this work "the classic book on the subject of faith development."[2] As Fowler explains in the introduction, "Theories can be exciting and powerful, giving us names for our experiences and ways to understand and express what we have lived."[3] This theory put forth by Fowler helps explain our growth in faith through six stages. The stages help us answer important questions:

- For what goals or organizations are you pouring out your life?
- To whom or what are you committed in life? In death?
- What activities receive your best time?
- With whom do you share your most sacred hopes?

In other words, they help us answer the all-important question: Who is master of your life?

Using Fowler's six stages of faith, Table 1 outlines six stages, or benchmarks, of spiritual formation to measure our maturity in giving and the use of possessions. The purpose of this measurement is not to become legalistic or to produce guilt but to spur growth in our journey. It can help us identify the next steps in our life of faith, give us a vision for our destination, and assist us in creating a plan to get there. Thomas Schmidt, in talking about Christian discipleship, refers to it as a journey: "We begin at different points and we move at different rates . . . but the biblical message is clear enough about this destination."[4]

These stages are intended to be a general guide. Keep in mind that the Christian life is a relationship that balances *being* and *doing*. The stages are not unidirectional; we can move from one to another at different times in our lives. One easy analogy would be to relate the stages to our age, i.e., Stage 1 - toddler, Stage 3 - adolescent, etc., up to mature adulthood at Stage 6. Although this is a convenient way to conceptualize these developmental stages, it would be inaccurate to imply that they actually occur in some age-related way. Some people may die of old age without ever growing out of stage 1. Some young people, on the other hand, may demonstrate surprising spiritual maturity. Many people spend their entire lives at stage two or three. Some people become Christians during midlife or later and progress very quickly, even seeming to skip stages as they mature in their faith and use of possessions. Since our use of possessions is an accurate barometer of our faith, this chart helps us see the connection between faith and stewardship.[5]

Here are the stages of faith along with their characteristics and the corresponding stages of stewardship (cf. *Table 1: Correlation of Faith Maturity with Stewardship*, p. 178).

Stage 1—Imitator

Imagine a young girl with a one-dollar allowance. Before Sunday school class, her dad tells her to put a dime in the offering plate. Although she does not realize the reason for giving, she obeys out of necessity. She has also seen her parents put something in the church offering plate. Another example could be an adult who puts a dollar or two into the offering plate at church because it is the thing to do.

These beginning points in faith and use of possessions can be best described as imitating or mimicking. Little about the faith is understood, and giving is generally done at someone else's suggestion. The primary awareness is the physical act of doing.

This first-stage giving behavior is learned from other believers. This can be a problem when money is the silent subject of the church—seldom taught clearly or understood. Teaching at this first stage ideally takes place with small, digestible pieces of information, consistent with the analogy of feeding a small child.

Some people never grow out of stage 1.

Stage 2—Modeler

Principles are seen as "black and white" in a world of reciprocal fairness, e.g., "eye for an eye." If the person is aware of the concept of a tithe of ten percent or more, he will generally try to make a radical change to make this a life pattern—at least for a while. Seldom, however, does this pattern last. Stage 2 behavior is similar to that of an eight- to eleven-year-old child with inconsistent behavior.

Stage 2 givers may frequently put something in the offering plate solely because they feel it is the right thing to do. Like children, they are subject to strong swings in their giving. One day they strongly support God's kingdom work, and the next day their own personal needs have priority. Feelings of guilt than swing them back to strong devotion. The pendulum goes back and forth during this "literal faith" stage, because of the lack of internal value structures to stabilize lifestyle and behavior. Regular, substantial giving is not a priority.

In this modeler stage, a perfectionist attitude sometimes develops. The person in this modeler stage might say, "Look, I am doing this the correct way. What's wrong with the rest of you? Why don't you give at a more generous level?" This "If I can do it, why can't you?" attitude swings with the pendulum of performance. Some people never grow beyond stage 2.

Stage 3—Conformer

Some depth begins to develop. Seeing the effects and benefits of giving makes an impact. There is a better understanding of moral and biblical reasons for giving. The focus, however, tends to remain on a horizontal plane, fulfilling practical needs of others and satisfying a sense of personal obligation.

Conformers give when it is convenient, are motivated by tax benefits, and will readily give small amounts for recognition. Debt may not be a problem for them. Their giving is probably in the two percent range—leftovers rather than firstfruits.

Conformers are typically self-centered givers with a strong compartmentalization of faith and finances. There is little connection between their belief in a personal God and how they handle their possessions. Many Christians are in this category and remain there throughout their lives, never becoming liberated by understanding the vital link between their eternal souls and earthly possessions.

Stage 4—Individual

Stage 4 begins a transformation in the understanding of giving. A connection is made between spiritual growth and the proper use of possessions. Giving becomes more joyful as the needs of others are given a higher priority.

Stage 4 givers are like young adults stepping out with more confidence in their faith and giving. Giving is less defined by others and becomes more of a personal concern as part of faith. Lifestyle changes may become evident as they recognize God's call to give to Him first and trust Him to provide. No matter what method they employ, their effort to give to God first deepens their faith and gives them an increased desire to serve His eternal kingdom.

During the individual stage, the vertical issues of soul development become internalized, and giving becomes a lifestyle of faith.

Stage 5—Generous (Proverbs 22:9)

As Gary Thomas has written, "Fulfillment comes in being vessels of the generous heart of God by giving of our wealth and substance."[6] God made us to give ourselves away to get our lives back. In Stage 5, there is less dependence on earthly possessions for security and more dependence upon God. Continued vertical soul growth results in generous givers becoming role models and desiring to teach others about the significance of giving. Giving becomes much more integrated into their spiritual lives as they realize that their giving fulfills a deep human need.

Stage 6—Mature Steward

As mature stewards, we develop a firm conviction that God owns everything, just as it is written in Psalm 24:1, *"The earth is the Lord's, and all it contains, the world and those who dwell in it"* (NAS). Mature stewards give without needing to know where their money will come from, and they give more generously so that others can experience spiritual and material benefits.

Vertical understanding or "spiritual giving" matures as well. They see how powerful God is when they depend on Him rather than on worldly things. This understanding and use of possessions transforms their character as they grow in spirit. Just as God *"gave His one and only Son"* (John 3:16), they imitate God's deep giving. They can say along with Paul, *"…I have learned to be content in whatever circumstances I am. I know how to get along with humble means, and I also know how to live in prosperity; in any and every circumstance I have learned the secret of being filled and going hungry, both of having abundance and suffering need. I can do all things through Him who strengthens me"* (Philippians 4:11-13, NAS).

Table 1: Correlation of Faith Maturity with Stewardship

STAGES	FAITH CHARACTERISTICS (FROM FOWLER)	STEWARDSHIP PATTERNS
STAGE 1: IMITATOR	Like a child, marked by imagination and influenced by stories and examples of others.	Is able to mimic the examples of others in giving when shown or instructed.
STAGE 2: MODELER	Takes beliefs and moral rules literally.	Perception of God is largely formed by friends.
STAGE 3: CONFORMER	Faith becomes a basis for love, acceptance, and identity; faith shapes most aspects of life and is shaped mainly by relationships. Faith does not yet form a cohesive "philosophy of life."	Gives because it is the thing to do. Likes recognition, tax benefits, and other personal gain from giving.
STAGE 4: INDIVIDUAL	Begins to "own" personal faith. Faith is less defined by others. Growing ability to examine and question personal beliefs.	Starts to give in proportion to what God has given. Danger of becoming prideful regarding giving. Wonders why others do not give more.
STAGE 5: GENEROUS GIVER	Grasps the main ideas of individualized faith and individual practices. Becomes interested in developing the faith of others.	Recognizes that all possessions come from God. Begins to give on own initiative rather than from obligation or routine. Derives joy from giving.
STAGE 6: MATURE STEWARD	Little regard for self. Focuses on God and then on others. Free from man-made rules.	Recognizes the role of a faithful steward of God's possessions. More concerned with treasures in heaven than on earth. Content with daily provision.

SUMMARY

These six stages help to assess our use of earthly possessions and our growth as stewards. All stages have value, but we should continue to mature in our faith and stewardship. How do you know if you are growing spiritually? Determine where you fit in the stages of giving. Consider the pattern and speed of your past growth. Since Jesus said in Matthew 6:21 that *"where your treasure is there your heart will be also,"* your giving reveals the devotion and loyalty of your heart.

Content for this chapter was adapted from *God & Your Stuff* by Wesley Willmer copyright 2002. Used by permission of NavPress - www.navpress.com. All rights reserved.

> **Think About it!**
>
> • *Compared to the stages of faith given above, where would you place yourself? What steps will you take to move toward being a mature steward?*

CHAPTER SIXTEEN

Using Your Head While You Live by Faith

Core concepts

- List three goals for investing.
- Describe the difference between provision and presumption.
- What is the best and first step to investing?
- What are three goals of investing?
- What are the three characteristics of a risky investment?
- What are the two types of savings?
- List each of the five steps for saving.

Overview

This chapter examines the biblical foundation for investing and offers principles for investing wisely. It also considers the role of insurance and offers some practical counsel. Our frequent theme of avoiding extremes is a common sense approach to both of these important components of financial stewardship.

BIBLICAL FOUNDATIONS FOR INVESTING

In earlier chapters we have demonstrated that money is not evil but that the wrong attitude toward it is sinful. 1 Timothy 6:10 clearly identifies loving money as a wrong attitude that results in unwanted consequences: *"The love of money is a root of all sorts of evil"* (NAS).

Scripture encourages us to save. *"The wise man saves for the future, but the foolish man spends whatever he gets"* (Proverbs 21:20, TLB). The ant is commended for saving for a future need. *"Four things on earth are small, yet they are extremely wise: ants are creatures of little strength, yet they store up their food in the summer"* (Proverbs 30:24-25).

We call saving the "Joseph principle" because Joseph saved during seven years of plenty to survive during seven years of famine. The logical connection between wealth and saving implies that many godly people in the Bible were also savers. Job, Abraham, and David serve as examples of extremely wealthy men who did not allow their wealth to interfere with their relationship with the Lord. In both the Old and New Testaments we find examples of people who used their wealth—wealth that was most likely accumulated through saving—for Kingdom purposes.

How, then, do we explain Matthew 6:19-21, which seems to speak against saving and investing? *"Do not store up for yourselves treasures on earth, where moth and rust destroy, and where thieves break in and steal; but store up for yourselves treasures in heaven . . . for where your treasure is, there your heart will be also"* (NAS). Jesus clarifies this issue in the parable of a rich man who laid up treasures for himself. *"The land of a rich man was very productive. And he began reasoning to himself, saying, 'What shall I do, since I have no place to store my crops?' Then he said, 'This is what I will do: I will tear down my barns and build larger ones, and there I will store all my grain and my goods. And I will say to my soul, "Soul, you have many goods laid up for many years to come; take your ease, eat, drink and be merry." But God said to him, 'You fool! This very night your soul is required of you; and now who will own what you have prepared?' So is the man who lays up treasures for himself and is not rich toward God* (Luke 12:16-21).

A key word in this parable is "all." Jesus called the rich man a fool because he saved (by his own admission) *all* of his goods. He stored them up for his own use. He did not balance his saving with generous giving. We should save and invest only when we also are giving to the Lord. Why? *"Where your treasure is, there your heart will be also"* (Matthew 6:21). If we concentrate solely on saving and investing, our focus and affection will gravitate to those possessions. If we balance our saving and investing by giving generously to the Lord first, our treasure and heart can remain with Him.

Investment goals

Before you develop your individual investment strategy, you must establish investment goals. We believe three goals are acceptable for investing.

1. To provide for you and your family: In 1 Timothy 5:8 we read, *"If anyone does not provide for his own, and especially for those of his household, he has denied the faith and is worse than an unbeliever"* (NAS). This principle extends to providing for your needs in old age and leaving an inheritance to any children you may have.

2. To become free financially to serve the Lord: One objective of saving is to reduce our dependence on a salary to meet our needs. This affords us the freedom to invest more volunteer time in ministry if this is God's plan for us. The more income our savings and investments produce, the less we are dependent on income from our jobs. Some have saved enough to be free one day a week; others are in a position to be full-time volunteers without the need to earn salaries.

3. To operate your business: Another purpose for saving and investing is to accumulate enough capital to open and operate a business without going into debt. The amount of money will vary substantially depending on the requirements of the business.

How much is enough?

We never want to allow saving to become hoarding, which was the rich man's problem in Luke 12. Hoarding is perverted saving that is motivated by greed or fear.

Consider this analogy. When runners break the tape at the finish line, they rarely continue running. However, some people who have already achieved the three acceptable investment goals continue accumulating. We believe that each of us should establish a maximum amount we will accumulate for personal use, and once we have "finished this race," we should give away the portion of our current income that we had earmarked for saving. This "finish line" on accumulation protects us against the dangers of hoarding.

Investment goals to avoid

One investment goal—the desire to become rich—is extremely dangerous. 1 Timothy 6:9 states, *"Those who want to get rich fall into temptation and a snare and many foolish and harmful desires which plunge men into ruin and destruction"* (NAS). Paul does not qualify his warning by saying *many* or *most* of "those who want to get rich"; his statement is all-inclusive and is logically interpreted as *everyone* who wants to get rich will *"fall into temptation and a snare and many foolish and harmful desires which plunge men into ruin and destruction."* For this reason, we classify the desire to become rich as an illegitimate investment goal.

For most of my life, I (Howard) wanted to become rich—not just a little rich—enormously rich! Dealing with this biblical warning has been painful. Sometimes, even now, I vacillate between wanting to get rich and wanting to be a faithful steward. When I want to get rich, I am self-centered. My motivations for wanting to get rich may vary—pride, greed, or a fearful desire to prepare for survival in an uncertain economic future. When I want to be a faithful steward, I am Christ-centered in my thoughts and attitudes, and a pure heart motivates my actions; I am serving Christ and growing closer to Him.

The next verse, 1 Timothy 6:10, amplifies the warning by presenting an even more graphic picture: *"For the love of money is a root of all sorts of evil, and some by longing for it have wandered away from the faith and pierced themselves with many griefs."* I (Howard) have witnessed this firsthand. I admired and respected the man who led me to Christ. However, he became consumed by a desire to get rich. He divorced his wife and abandoned his four young sons. He denied Christ repeatedly and left the faith. It is easy to say that no thinking person would invite those consequences, but the deceptions of Satan wreak havoc with our thinking.

It is difficult to separate the desire to get rich from the practice of making money our master. If money is the primary motivator of our plans, it *is* our master. Although we may argue that it is just one of many interests we serve, Jesus sees through our rationalizations and closes that option. *"No one can serve two masters. Either he will hate the one and love the other, or he will be devoted to the one and despise the other. You cannot serve both God and Money"* (Matthew 6:24). Notice that this text does not prohibit having money; it prohibits serving money. This important distinction enables us to use money without allowing it to become our master. But when we want to get rich, we are devoted to money. We may not feel as though we hate or despise God, but we are putting something else ahead of His will in our lives. This is always idolatry.

We are of the opinion that our heavenly Father usually will not allow His children to prosper when they are motivated to get rich. Wanting to get rich—loving money—closely parallels greed. And *"greed . . . amounts to idolatry"* (Colossians 3:5, NAS). The Father watches closely over His children to ensure that we will not be drawn away from loving Him with all of our heart.

Please understand that we are not saying it is wrong to become rich. We rejoice seeing God prosper a person who has been ambitious in faithful stewardship. Nothing is wrong with becoming wealthy when it is a by-product of being a faithful steward.

Overcoming the temptation to get rich

How can you overcome the temptation to get rich? By remembering to split and submit. Paul continues his warning to Timothy with this counsel in verse 11: *"flee from these things* [the desire to get rich], *you man of God, and pursue righteousness, godliness, faith, love, perseverance and gentleness"* (NAS). When you become aware of your desire to become rich, you must run from that temptation and replace it with the pursuit of godliness. Analyze what triggers your desire. I (Howard) discovered an unrecognized habit of dreaming about becoming rich whenever I would take a long automobile trip alone. I started to break the habit by replacing it with a new one. Listening to Christian music helped me concentrate on the Lord while I drove. I chose to flee the temptation of wandering, unguided thoughts.

The second part of the formula is to submit. We remind ourselves of our true master and consciously renew our submission to Jesus as Lord. We can do this with perfect confidence in His ability to understand and help us because He overcame a massive temptation to become rich.

After Christ fasted 40 days in the wilderness, the devil tempted Him three times. The final temptation is recorded in Luke 4:5-7: *"He* [the devil] *led Him* [Jesus] *up and showed Him all the kingdoms of the world in a moment of time. And the devil said to Him, 'I will give You all this domain and its glory…if You worship me'"* (NAS). Jesus was exposed to all the kingdoms of the world in an instant of time, but He was able to resist that temptation because He was submitted entirely to the Father and empowered by the same Holy Spirit who lives in us.

SAVING

Once we have established our investment goals, the first step is to begin saving. Unfortunately, most people are not consistent savers. The average person in our country is three weeks away from bankruptcy with little or no money saved, significant debt, and total dependence on next week's paycheck to keep the budget afloat.

Saving is the opposite of being in debt. Saving is making provision for tomorrow, while debt is presumption upon tomorrow. Saving is denying expenditures today so we will have something to spend in the future. One of the major reasons most people are poor savers is that they do not practice self-denial. When we want something, we want it now! That is true for all of us. The difference is that some have learned to control that impulse and others have not.

How to save and how much to save

The most effective way to save is to do it every time you receive income. The first check you write should be your gift to the Lord, and the second check should go to your savings. An automatic payroll deduction can help ensure that a portion of your income is saved regularly. Some save income from tax refunds or bonuses. If you immediately save a portion of your income each time you are paid, you will save more.

The Bible does not teach a percentage to save. The only example it gives is Joseph's plan to prepare for the lean times ahead. That plan called for a saving rate of just over 14 percent. It is only an example, however, not a mandate or a prescription. Based on widely accepted counsel, we recommend establishing a goal of saving 10 percent of your income. This may not be possible initially, but begin the habit of saving—even if it's only a dollar a month.

Two types of savings

1. Long-term savings: Long-term savings are intended to fund long-term needs and goals. Pensions and retirement accounts fall into this category. Except for extreme emergencies, these savings should not be used for any other purpose. They could be called "never-to-spend savings."

2. Short-term savings: Short-term savings are for buying or replacing items such as appliances or cars and making major home repairs. These funds should be in an account that is liquid and easily accessible—interest-bearing accounts, some mutual funds, and so forth. A second category of short-term savings should be set aside for emergencies: an illness, loss of job, or other interruption of income. Financial experts recommend you save the equivalent of three to six months of income for this fund.

INVESTING PRINCIPLES

People place some of their savings in investments in the hope of receiving income or growth in value. The purpose of this CROWN FINANCIAL MINISTRIES course is not to recommend any specific investments. **No one is authorized to use affiliation with CROWN to promote the sale of any investments or financial services.** Our objective is to draw attention to the scriptural framework for saving and investing. Visit Crown's Web site, www.crown.org, for more detailed information on investing.

1. Steady plodding

"Steady plodding brings prosperity, hasty speculation brings poverty" (Proverbs 21:5, TLB). The original Hebrew words for *"steady plodding"* picture a person filling a large barrel one handful at a time. Little by little the barrel is filled to overflowing. The fundamental principle for becoming a successful investor is to spend less than you earn. Then save and invest the difference over a long period of time.

Examine various investments. Almost all of them are well suited for "steady plodding." A home mortgage is paid off after years of steady payments. Savings grow because of compounding interest, and a business can increase steadily in value through the years as its potential is developed.

2. Understanding compound interest

A wealthy man was asked if he had seen the Seven Wonders of the World. He responded, "No, but I do know the eighth wonder of the world—compound interest." Understanding how compounding works is very important. There are three variables in compounding: the amount you save, the percentage rate you earn, and the length of time you save.

a. *The amount:* The amount you save is determined by your income and how much you spend for living expenses, giving, and debt. It is our hope that you will increase the amount available for saving as you apply the biblical principles in this course.

b. *Rate of return:* The second variable is the rate you earn on an investment. The following table demonstrates how an investment of $1,000 a year grows at various rates:

Percent	5 years	10 years	20 years	30 years	40 years
6%	5,975	13,972	38,993	83,802	164,048
8%	6,336	15,645	49,423	122,346	279,781
10%	6,716	17,531	63,003	180,943	486,851
12%	7,115	19,655	80,699	270,293	859,142

As you can see, the increase in the rate has a remarkable effect on the amount accumulated, and the longer the term, the more dramatic the effect. A two percent increase almost doubles the amount over 40 years. However, be careful not to make investments that are too risky in order to achieve a high return. The risk/reward ratio is a general law of investing: any higher rate of return assumes a higher rate of risk.

c. *Time:* Time is the third factor. Answer this question: Who do you think would accumulate more by age 65, a person who started to save $1,000 a year at age 21, saved for eight years, and then completely stopped, or a person who saved $1,000 a year for 37 years who started at age 29? Assume they both earned 10 percent. One person actually invested $8,000; the other, $37,000. Who ends up with more at age 65? Study the chart on the following page.

Incredibly, the person who saved only $8,000 accumulated more because that person started saving earlier. The moral of this illustration: start saving now.

This graph may help you better visualize the benefits of starting now. If a person faithfully saves $2.74 each day—$1,000 a year—and earns 10 percent, at the end of 40 years the savings will grow to $486,852 and will be earning $4,057 each month. Steady plodding pays. However, if the person waits one year before starting, then saves for 39 years, $45,260 less will accumulate. Start saving today.

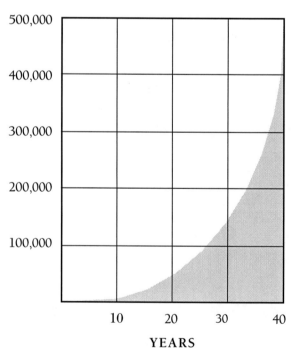

YEARS

$1,000 invested each year, earning 10%

INDIVIDUAL A			INDIVIDUAL B		
Age	Contribution	Year-End Value	Age	Contribution	Year-End Value
21	$1,000	$1,100	21	0	0
22	1,000	2,310	22	0	0
23	1,000	3,641	23	0	0
24	1,000	5,105	24	0	0
25	1,000	6,716	25	0	0
26	1,000	8,487	26	0	0
27	1,000	10,436	27	0	0
28	1,000	12,579	28	0	0
29	0	13,837	29	$1,000	$1,100
30	0	15,221	30	1,000	2,310
31	0	16,743	31	1,000	3,641
32	0	18,417	32	1,000	5,105
33	0	20,259	33	1,000	6,716
34	0	22,284	34	1,000	8,487
35	0	24,513	35	1,000	10,436
36	0	26,964	36	1,000	12,579
37	0	29,661	37	1,000	14,937
38	0	32,627	38	1,000	17,531
39	0	35,889	39	1,000	20,384
40	0	39,478	40	1,000	23,523
41	0	43,426	41	1,000	26,975
42	0	47,769	42	1,000	30,772
43	0	52,546	43	1,000	34,950
44	0	57,800	44	1,000	39,545
45	0	63,580	45	1,000	44,599
46	0	69,938	46	1,000	50,159
47	0	76,932	47	1,000	56,275
48	0	84,625	48	1,000	63,003
49	0	93,088	49	1,000	70,403
50	0	103,397	50	1,000	78,543
51	0	112,636	51	1,000	87,497
52	0	123,898	52	1,000	97,347
53	0	136,290	53	1,000	108,182
54	0	149,919	54	1,000	120,100
55	0	164,911	55	1,000	133,210
56	0	181,402	56	1,000	147,631
57	0	199,542	57	1,000	163,494
58	0	219,496	58	1,000	180,943
59	0	241,446	59	1,000	200,138
60	0	265,590	60	1,000	221,252
61	0	292,149	61	1,000	244,477
62	0	321,364	62	1,000	270,024
63	0	353,501	63	1,000	298,127
64	0	388,851	64	1,000	329,039
65	0	**$427,736**	65	$1,000	**$363,043**

Total Investment $8,000 **Total Investment** $37,000

3. Avoiding risky investments

"There is another serious problem I have seen everywhere—savings are put into risky investments that turn sour, and soon there is nothing left to pass on to one's son. The man who speculates is soon back to where he began—with nothing" (Ecclesiastes 5:13-15, TLB).

Scripture warns us to avoid risky investments, yet each year thousands of people lose money in highly speculative and sometimes fraudulent investments. How many times have you heard of people losing their life's savings on some get-rich-quick scheme? Sadly, it seems that Christians are particularly vulnerable to such schemes because they trust others who appear to live by the same values they do. We have known of investment scandals in churches where "wolves in sheep's clothing fleeced the flock." Below are three characteristics that will help you identify a risky investment.

1. The promise of an unusually high profit or interest rate that is "practically guaranteed."

2. The requirement to decide quickly, leaving no opportunity to investigate either the investment or the promoter who is selling it. The promoter often presents himself as doing you a "favor" by allowing you to invest.

3. Little or no mention of the risk of loss, and the requirement of little or no effort on your part. Sometimes a portion of the profits are said to be "dedicated to the Lord's work." Before participating in any investment, please be patient and do your homework.

4. Diversity

"Divide your portion to seven, or even to eight, for you do not know what misfortune may occur on the earth" (Ecclesiastes 11:2, NAS).

No investment on this earth is guaranteed. Money can be lost on any investment. The government can make private possession of gold illegal. The value of real estate can decrease. Money can be inflated until it is valueless. The stock market can perform well or crash. My (Howard's) father's friend, Mr. Russell, was very successful in the stock market. When I was young he used to advise me, "When you grow up, invest in the stock market. It's the one sure way to become financially independent." When I was 25, I met Mr. Russell again. The stock market was in the midst of a significant decline. He said, "I've done a great deal of research on the stock market and the *Titanic*. Do you know the only difference between the two? The *Titanic* had a musical band!" The perfect investment does not exist. We need to diversify. Consider the following steps as you diversify. We recommend that you not skip any of the steps. Begin with step one, and then take each step at a time.

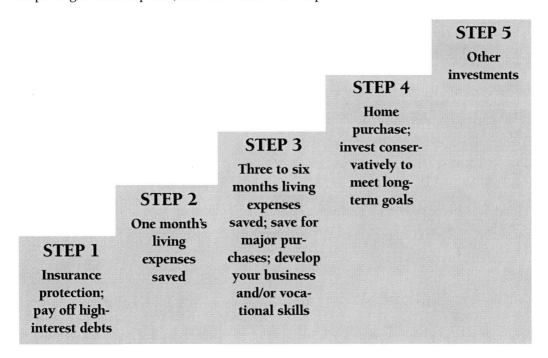

STEP 1

Insurance protection; pay off high-interest debts

STEP 2

One month's living expenses saved

STEP 3

Three to six months living expenses saved; save for major purchases; develop your business and/or vocational skills

STEP 4

Home purchase; invest conservatively to meet long-term goals

STEP 5

Other investments

5. Counting the cost

Every investment includes costs: financial costs, time commitments, efforts required and sometimes even emotional stress. For example, a rental house will require time and effort to rent and maintain. If the tenant is irresponsible, you may have to try to collect rent from someone who does not want to pay; talk about emotions! Before you decide on any investment, carefully consider all the costs.

OTHER ISSUES

1. Gambling and lotteries

Lotteries and gambling of all types are sweeping our country. A recent study discovered that people spend 15 times more money on gambling than they donate to churches! The average church member gives $20 a year to international missions, and the average person gambles $1,174 annually. Sadly, millions of compulsive gamblers regularly lose their incomes. Their stories are heartbreaking. The Bible does not specifically prohibit gambling. However, many gamble in an attempt to get rich quick. This is a violation of Scripture. In our opinion, a godly person should *never* participate in gambling or lotteries—even for entertainment. We should not expose ourselves to the risk of becoming compulsive gamblers; neither should we support an industry that enslaves so many.

2. Inheritance

Parents should attempt to leave an inheritance to their children. *"A good man leaves an inheritance to his children's children"* (Proverbs 13:22, NAS). It is wise to with-hold inheritances until the recipients have been trained to be wise stewards. *"An inheritance gained hurriedly at the beginning will not be blessed in the end"* (Proverbs 20:21, NAS). In our opinion, you should provide in your will for gradual distribution over several years or until heirs are mature enough to handle the responsibility of money. Select those you trust to supervise young heirs until they are capable stewards. *"As long as the heir is a child, he does not differ at all from a slave although he is owner of everything, but he is under guardians and managers until the date set by the father"* (Galatians 4:1-2, NAS).

3. Wills

It is important to prepare financially for your death. As Isaiah told Hezekiah, *"Thus says the Lord, 'Set your house in order, for you shall die'"* (2 Kings 20:1, NAS). Someday, if the Lord does not return first, you will die. One of the greatest gifts you can leave your loved ones for that emotional time is an organized estate and a proper-ly prepared will or revocable living trust. If you do not have a current will or trust, please make an appointment soon with an attorney to prepare one.

THE CHALLENGES OF WEALTH

God loves us deeply. Consider what Jesus said in John 15:9, *"Just as the Father has loved me, I have also loved you"* (NAS). Imagine the depth of love God the Father has for God the Son. In the same way, He loves you! Just as a loving earthly father desires a close relationship with his children, so our heavenly Father hungers for such a relationship with each of us. Understanding human nature perfectly, God knows the particular challenge wealth presents as a potential barrier to an intimate relationship with Him.

If you have a measure of wealth, the Lord is not disappointed or surprised; rather, He intentionally entrusted it to you for a purpose. In 1 Timothy 6:17-19, the Lord issues a set of instructions designed to help those with resources to remain undistracted from loving Him.

1. Do not be conceited.

"Instruct those who are rich in this present world not to be conceited" (1 Timothy 6:17, NAS). Wealth tends to produce pride. For several years we (Howard) drove two vehicles. The first was an old pickup truck that cost $100. It looked as if it cost $100! When I drove that truck to the bank drive-in window to write a check for cash, I was humble. I knew the cashier would take a look at that beat-up truck and check my account carefully to confirm that I had sufficient funds in it. I was so patient! When I received the money, I was so grateful. I drove away with a song in my heart and praises on my lips. Our other vehicle was a well-preserved, second-hand car that was expensive when it was new. When I drove that car to the bank, I appeared to be a different person. I was a person of means who deserved a certain amount of respect. I was not quite as patient when the cashier examined my account, and when I received the money, I was not as grateful. Wealth often leads to conceit.

James 1:9-10 addresses this issue: *"The brother of humble circumstances is to glory in his high position; and the rich man is to glory in his humiliation, because like flowering grass he will pass away"* (NAS).

The poor should be encouraged as children of the King of kings, while the rich are to remain humble, because life is short. If you have been entrusted with some wealth, remain humble before the Lord and other people.

2. Put no confidence in your assets.

"Instruct those who are rich in this present world not . . . to fix their hope on the uncertainty of riches, but on God, who richly supplies us with all things to enjoy" (1 Timothy 6:17, NAS). This is a struggle for many. It is easy to trust in money, because money can buy things. We tend to trust in the seen rather than in the invisible living God. We need to remind ourselves that possessions can be lost and that the Lord alone can be fully trusted.

3. Give generously.

"Instruct them to do good, to be rich in good works, to be generous and ready to share, storing up for themselves the treasure of a good foundation for the future, so that they may take hold of that which is life indeed" (1 Timothy 6:18-19, NAS). Paul commands the wealthy to be generous and then encourages them with two benefits of giving: (1) eternal treasures that they will enjoy in the future, and (2) the blessing of *"taking hold of that which is life indeed."* By exercising generosity, they can live the fulfilling life God intends for them.

INSURANCE

Overview

Some say insurance is in direct opposition to faith and that we should have faith in God to provide no matter what. I (Chad) know very sincere believers who have this conviction. This section is not an attempt to dishonor their convictions but rather to offer biblical information in support of an informed discussion.

The essence of insurance is a pooling of risk so that the financial burden of a covered loss (illness, death, accident, theft, etc.) is shared among many people who have exposure to such a loss. As each covered person pays a small amount in advance, funds become available to reimburse insured losses.

Having defined insurance, we now step back and think through some previous lessons about faith and money. The practical question of insurance takes us back to earlier discussions on trust, faith, and eternity. Our perspective on these foundational issues will influence how we view and use insurance. Is it the object of our trust? Of course it is to some degree—otherwise we would never buy it. But are we placing our ultimate trust in it? If our ultimate faith and trust is in the human institution of an insurance company and its ability to protect us, our trust is shortsighted and misplaced. Insurance can never protect us against loss—only against its financial consequences.

If, however, we recognize God's protection coupled with His expectation for us to be prudent managers of all resources, our perspective changes. Managing resources includes managing risks that carry financial consequences. Using appropriate tools to manage those financial risks is an essential part of a good steward's responsibility.

Biblical principles

We make no claim that the Bible teaches us to buy insurance, but today's cultural equivalent of what the faithful servants in Matthew 15:14-18 did would include the use of insurance to manage risk and avoid exposing assets to the threat of loss without remedy.

1 Timothy 5:8 gives this stern warning: *"If anyone does not provide for his relatives, and especially for his immediate family, he has denied the faith and is worse than an unbeliever."* Obeying this injunction through the appropriate use of insurance to provide for family could be, in our modern age, a wise application of the principle.

Consider 2 Corinthians 8:14-15, where Paul describes how the body of Christ is to help one another. The Corinthians' abundance was to supply the Macedonian churches' needs. In return, when the Corinthians might suffer need, the Macedonians' excess would help the Corinthians. This excellent example of community—of God's people helping one another rather than hoarding wealth—results in what Paul calls equality. This is also one function of insurance: spreading the burden of financial losses to avoid the devastation of some people while others escape any burden whatsoever.

Regardless of the extent to which insurance might mitigate the effects of loss, the church should always be the leader in reaching out to aid the suffering. Are we currently cultivating a heart that eagerly uses what God has so graciously given us to help others? *"Each of you should look not only to your own interests, but also to the interests of others"* (Philippians 2:4).

Future expectation

Insurance cannot protect us from loss other than its financial consequences. The future is and always will be an unknown to us. We constantly balance the knowledge that God will take care of us (cf. Luke 12:22-34) with wisely planning for the future (Proverbs 6:6-8). We cannot expect a human institution to protect us from all problems.

COMMON TYPES OF INSURANCE[1]

1. Homeowner's insurance

A homeowner's insurance policy covers the majority of risks to your home and contents. It also covers some personal liability in the event of someone being injured on your property. It is important to know the difference between *actual cash value* insurance and *guaranteed* [true] *replacement value.*

Actual cash value refers to the depreciated value of items covered in an insured loss. A policy that pays on this basis might allow $100 for a sofa that is several years old even though it might cost five or ten times that much to replace it with a new one. *Guaranteed replacement value* means that your structure and contents are covered at 100 percent of the cost to replace them with new items of like kind. This policy provision is obviously more expensive, but is generally considered well worth the small increase in premium.

2. Dwelling insurance

Dwelling insurance is not as comprehensive as homeowner's insurance but is often just as expensive. Because of age, condition, or location, some homes are not insurable under homeowner's policies.

3. Renter's insurance

Renter's insurance covers the replacement value of your furniture and personal property. It also provides liability coverage if someone is hurt as a result of your negligence or the negligence of your children. An example of this is someone falling over a toy or slipping on ice outside the home. In addition to insurance for your home, there are other insurance plans for condominiums, mobile homes, and apartment complexes. See your agent for more details about the type of policy that best fits your needs.

Keep in mind that any type of insurance should be considered on a need-versus-cost basis. You don't *need* renter's insurance if you can afford to replace all your personal property or cover a liability suit resulting from negligence. You might, however, still think it prudent to pay a comparatively small premium to protect your investment.

4. Automobile insurance

Liability insurance covers the other person's costs in the event of an accident. As of this writing, only five states do not require liability insurance on all vehicles. Even if your state does not require it, you should carry it. Potential liability is great, and the cost of liability insurance is relatively small. One "at fault" accident can put you in debt for the rest of your life. Remember Proverbs 22:3: *"A prudent man sees danger and takes refuge, but the simple keep going and suffer for it."*

Additional coverages protect your interests in your car and its contents. Evaluate those on a need-versus-cost basis. An old car—no matter how reliable—would not likely have enough replacement value to justify comprehensive coverage.

5. Life insurance

The purpose of life insurance is to continue providing for your dependents if you die. Unfortunately, some Christians seem to think their responsibility to care for their families (1 Timothy 5:8) ends at the moment of their death. Their families suffer not only the great emotional loss of a spouse and/or parent, but the loss of a breadwinner as well. This often results in poor decisions made in hasty desperation—decisions that would have been unnecessary with the affordable purchase of the right kind of insurance in the right amount. At the opposite extreme are Christians with far more insurance than they need.

FINAL NOTE

This information covers basic biblical principles that apply to insurance. Although your specific question may not have been addressed, you can still take these principles and apply them to your particular situation. Seek a qualified, trustworthy agent for answers to your specific questions and needs. Your state insurance commissioner's office can also provide assistance.

Think About it!

- *How will you balance trusting God for your financial future with your responsibility to faithfully manage the resources God has given you?*

- *Are you over-insured? Uninsured? Underinsured?*

- *Are you trusting more in your investments to provide for your future than you are trusting in God? How do you discern the difference?*

SELECTED BIBLIOGRAPHY

Adie, D.K., Wealth, Christian view of. Evangelical Dictionary of Theology, Ed., Walter Elwell Baker Book House: Grand Rapids, 2001.

Alcorn, Randy, Money, Possessions and Eternity, Tyndale House Publishers: Wheaton, IL, 2003, revised edition.

Alcorn, Randy, The Treasure Principle, Tyndale House Publishers: Wheaton, IL, 2002.

Badcock, Gary, The Way of Life: A Theology of Christian Vocation, William B. Eerdmans Publishing Company: Grand Rapids, 1998.

Barnett, Jake, Wealth & Wisdom: A Biblical Perspective on Possessions, NAVPRESS: Colorado Springs, CO, 1987.

Bassler, Jouette, God & Mammon: Asking for Money in the New Testament, Abingdon Press: Nashville, 1991.

Beisner, E. Calvin, Prosperity And Poverty: The Compassionate Use of Resources in a World of Scarcity, Crossway Books: IL, 1988.

Blomberg, Craig L., Wealth. Theological Dictionary of the Bible, Ed., Walter Elwell, Baker Book House: Grand Rapids, 1996.

Blomberg, Craig L., Degrees of Rewards in the Kingdom of Heaven?, Journal of Evangelical Theological Society, 35/2 June 1992, pp. 159-172.

Blomberg, Craig L., Neither Poverty nor Riches: A Biblical Theology of Material Possessions, InterVarsity Press: Downers Grove, IL 1999, ed. D.A. Carson.

Blue, Ron, Generous Giving: Finding Contentment Through Giving, Zondervan: Grand Rapids, 1997.

Blue, Ron, Raising Money-Smart Kids: How to Teach Your Children the Secrets of Earning, Saving, Investing, and Spending Wisely, Thomas Nelson Publishers: Nashville, TN, 1992.

Blue, Ron, Storm Shelter: Protecting Your Personal Finances, Thomas Nelson Publishers: Nashville, TN, 1994.

Budd, Michael, L., & Brimlow, Robert W., Christianity Incorporated: How Big Business is Buying the Church, Brazos Press: Grand Rapids, 2002.

Burkett, Larry, Business By The Book: The Complete Guide of Biblical Principles for the Workplace, Thomas Nelson Publishers: Nashville, 1998.

Burkett, Larry, How to Manage Your Money, Moody Press: Chicago, IL, 1991, 1975.

Burkett, Larry, The WORD on Finances, Moody Press: Chicago, IL, 1994.

Carson, D.A., & Woodbridge, John, D., ed. God & Culture: Essays in Honor of Carl F. H. Henry, William B. Eerdmans Publishing Company: Grand Rapids, 1993.

Clapp, Rodney, ed., The Consuming Passion: Christianity & the Consumer Culture, Inter Varsity: Downers Grove, IL, 1998.

Crosson, Russ, A Life Well Spent: The Eternal Rewards of Investing Yourself & Your Money in Your Family, Ron Blue & Company: Atlanta, 1994.

Dayton, Howard, Your Money Counts: The Biblical Guide To Earning, Spending, Saving, Investing, Giving, and Getting Out of Debt, Crown Financial Ministries: Gainesville, GA, 1996.

Ellis, E.E. Pastoral Letters, Dictionary of Paul and his Letters, Ed. G.F. Hawthorne, R.P. Martin, and D.G. Reid, InterVarsity Press: Downers Grove, 1993.

Eskridge, Larry, & Noll, Mark A., ed., More Money More Ministry: Money and Evangelicals in Recent North American History, William B. Eerdmans Publishing Co., Grand Rapids, MI, 2000.

Evans, W., Wealth, Wealthy. The International Standard Bible Encyclopedia, Ed. James Orr. WM. B. Eerdmans Publishing: Grand Rapids, 1939.

Fehrenbacher, Scott, Put Your Money Where Your Morals Are: A Guide To Values-Based Investing, Broadman & Holman: Nashville, 2001.

Field, D.H., Ethics, New Dictionary of Theology, InterVarsity Press: Downers Grove,1988.

Foster, Richard J., The Challenge of the Disciplined Life: Christian Reflections on Money, Sex and Power, Harper Collins: San Francisco, 1985.

Getz, Gene, Biblical Theology of Material Possessions, Moody Press: Chicago, IL, 1990.

Getz, Gene, Real Prosperity: Biblical Principles of Material Possessions, Moody Press: Chicago, IL, 1990.

Gonzales, Justo L., Faith & Wealth: History of Early Christian Ideas on the Origin, Significance, and Use of Money, Harper & Row: New York, 1990.

Goudzwaard, Bob, Idols of Our Time, InterVarsity Press: Downers Grove, IL, 1981.

Grant, C.F., The Economic Background of the Gospels, Russell & Russell: New York, 1926.

Guinness, OS, Doing Well and Doing Good: Money, Giving and Caring in a Free Society, Trinity Forum Study Series, NavPress: Colorado Springs, 2001.

Halteman, Jim, Market Capitalism & Christianity, Baker Book House: Grand Rapids, 1988.

Halteman, Jim, The Clashing Worlds of Economics and Faith, Herald Press: Scottdale, PA, 1995.

House, H. Wayne, Christian Ministries and the Law: What Church and Para-church Leaders Should Know, Baker Books: 1992.

Kapoor, Jack R., Dlabay, Les, R., & Hughes, Robert, J., Personal Finance, Richard D. Irwin Publishing: Boston, MA, 1991 second edition (or current).

Kelly, J.N.D., The Pastoral Epistles, Blacks New Testament Commentary, Ed. Henry Chadwick, Hendrickson Publishers: London, 1998.

Knight, G.E., The Pastoral Epistles, The New International Greek Testament Commentary, Eds., I Howard Marshall and W. Ward Gasque, William B. Eerdmans Publishing Co.: Grand Rapids, 1992.

MacArthur, John, Whose Money Is It Anyway? Word Publishing: Nashville, 2000.

Marshall, I. H, A critical and exegetical commentary on the Pastoral Epistles, International Critical Commentary, T & T Clark: Edinburg, 1999.

Mathewson, Dave, L., The Parable of the Unjust Steward (Luke 16:1-3): A Reexamination of the Traditional Views in Light of Recent Challenges, Journal of Evangelical Theological Society, 38:1 (March 1995), pp. 29-39.

McNamara, Patrick, H., More than Money: Portraits of Transformative Stewardship, The Alban Institute Press: Bethesda, MD, 1999.

Miller, Arthur F & William Hendricks, Why You Can't Be Anything You Want to Be, Zondervan Publishing House: Grand Rapids, 1999.

Montgomery, Bill, Christians and Their Money, Montgomery Associates: Exton, PA, c1996.

Morton, Scott, Funding Your Ministry: Whether You're Gifted or Not!, Dawson Media & NavPress: Colorado Springs, CO, 1999.

Mounce, W. D. Pastoral Epistles, Word Biblical Commentary, Eds, Bruce M. Metzger, David A. Hubbard & Glenn W. Barker, Thomas Nelson Publishers, Nashville, 2000.

Murchie, David, The New Testament View of Wealth Accumulation, Journal of Evangelical Theological Society, 21:4 (December 1978), pp. 335-344.

O'Brien, P.T. Letters, forms of, Dictionary of Paul and his Letters, Ed. G.F. Hawthorne, R.P. Martin, and D.G. Reid, InterVarsity Press: Downers Grove, 1993.

Olford, Stephen, F., The Grace of Giving: Thoughts on Financial Stewardship, Zondervan Publishing House: Grand Rapids, MI, 1972.

Pollock, David, Business Management in the Local Church, Moody Press: Chicago, IL, 1996.

Pryor, Austin, Sound Mind Investing: A Step-by-Step Guide to Financial Stability and Growth, Austin Pryor: 2000.

Robinson, Hadden, Decision-Making by The Book, Victor Books: Wheaton, IL, 1991.

Rodin, R., Scott, Stewards in the Kingdom: A Theology of Life in All Its Fullness, InverVarsity Press: Downers Grove: IL, 2000.

Russell, Bob, Money: A Users Manual, Multnomah Books: Oregon, 1997.

Schlereth, Thomas, J., ed., Material Culture Studies in America, The American Association for State and Local History, Nashville, 1982.

Schlossberg, Herbert, Idols for Destruction: Christian Faith and Its Confrontation with American Society, Thomas Nelson: New York, 1983.

Schneider, John, Godly Materialism: Rethinking Money & Possessions, Intervarsity Press: Downers Grove, IL, 1994.

Schneider, John, The Good of Affluence: Seeking God in a Culture of Wealth, William B. Eerdmans: Grand Rapids, MI, 2002.

Schultz, A. C., Wealth. Baker's Dictionary of Theology, Ed. E. F. Harrison, Baker Book House: Grand Rapids, 1960.

Sedgwick, Peter H., Market Economy and Christian Ethics, Cambridge University Press: Cambridge, UK; New York: 1999.

Sherman, Doug & Hendricks, William, Your Work Matters to God, NavPress: Colorado Springs, 1987.

Speer, William, God's Rule for Christian Giving: A Practical Essay on the Science of Christian Economy, Presbyterian Board of Publication: Philadelphia, 1875.

Stott, J.R. W., The Message of 1 Timothy & Titus, Bible Speaks Today, InterVarsity Press: Downers Grove, 1996.

Swindoll, Charles, R. The Mystery of God's Will, Word Publishing: Nashville, TN, 1999.

Thomas, Robert, Evangelical Hermeneutics: The Old Versus the New, Kregel: Grand Rapids, 2002.

Tolson, Chester, L., Proven Principles for Finding Funds: A Guide for Church and Non-profit Leaders, Baker Books: Grand Rapids, 2003.

Towner, P. H., 1-2 Timothy & Titus, The IVP New Testament Commentary Series, Ed. Grant R. Osborne, InterVarsity Press: Downers Grove, IL,1994.

Tozer, A.W., The Pursuit of God, Christian Publications: Harrisburg, PA, 1958.

Unger, M., F., Measurement of, Money, The New Unger's Bible Dictionary, Ed., R.K., Harrision, Moody Press: Chicago, 1998.

Watson, P.J., Jones, N.D., & Morris, R.J., (2004). Religious orientation and attitudes toward money: relationships with narcissism and the influence of gender, Mental Health, Religion & Culture. Vol.7, 4.

Wesley, John, The Bicentennial Edition of the Works of John Wesley, vol. 2 ed. Frank Baker, Abingdon: Nashville, TN, 1985.

Willmer, Wesley K. Ed., Money for Ministries, Victor Books, Scripture Press: Wheaton, IL, 1989.

Willmer, Wesley K., God and Your Stuff: The Vital Link between Your Possessions and Your Soul, NavPress: Colorado Springs, CO, 2002.

Wuthnow, Robert, God and Mammon in America, Free Press: New York, NY, 1994.

Wuthnow, Robert, The Crisis in the Churches: Spiritual Malaise, Fiscal Woe, Oxford University Press: New York, 1997.

ENDNOTES

Chapter 1

1. Fear, as one of the main reasons pastors do not teach on money, is well documented in a study done by Saint Meinrad School of Theology called "The Reluctant Steward" in 1992, and the follow up study "The Reluctant Steward Revisited" in 2002. This study is primarily of mainline Protestant and Catholic Church pastors and lay people and validates the fact that one of the main reasons pastors do not teach on the issue of money is fear. Although only 11 percent of the churches surveyed were evangelical, the same conclusions are expressed across theological convictions. For further information on "The Reluctant Steward" contact Saint Meinad School of Theology for a copy of the study. The study is a fascinating window in the issues related to the topic of teaching and communication of money among pastors, seminary institutions, and denominations.

2. See above study.

3. See Wuthnow, Robert, (1994). *God and Mammon in America,* The Free Press: New York, for a sociological glimpse of how people view and use money. The research gathered by Robert Wuthnow is powerful and is helpful in solidifying the indication that religious teaching has not taken root in our thinking and actions related to the faith and money issue. See especially pp. 5,6 and 9

4. Adie, D.K., (2001). Wealth, Christian view of. *Evangelical Dictionary of Theology*, Ed., Walter Elwell Baker Book House: Grand Rapids. See especially pp. 1262-1263.

5. George Barna, (1997) *The Second Coming of the Church*, Nashville: Word Publishing. See chap. 1.

6. Jesus reminded us in Matthew 6.21 that where our treasure is so our hearts will be also. This means that to which we are most devoted (what we hold most dear) will evidence itself in how we handle money and spend our time. Often, practically, our behavior shows that we want to serve money *and* God.

7. See Wuthnow, Robert, (1994). *God and Mammon in America,* The Free Press: New York. See especially chap. 3 and 5.

8. The terms "culture of affluence" comes from John Schneider in his significant work, *The Good of Affluence: Seeking God in a Culture of Wealth*, Wm B Eerdmans Publishing Co: Grand Rapids, 2002. Dr. Schneider talks about living in our culture of capitalism and further develops his perspective on how we are to live in this culture of wealth. His perspective and teaching on the enjoying the goodness of God's material blessings has influenced my thinking.

9. According to the lending agency, Nellie Mae.

10. The entire "Manna from Heaven" study can be viewed and downloaded from the seminary Web site: www.auburnseminary.org/studies/pubs.html. Although this study is primarily of mainline institutions the results are essentially the same as evangelical institutions and very enlightening. The Manna from heaven study is currently being updated and should proved more recent data on the state of the seminary student in relation to financial faithfulness. It is with sadness that I personally believe these numbers will only worsen as a result of continued lack of recognition of the importance of personal financial teaching among training institutions. Being on the cutting-edge of reaching the next generation of stewards with God's principles of finance, I can personally attest to the lack of training seminary students receive in

faith and money issues. Save only a slim handful, many schools do not even connect the dots of faith and money beyond giving and church administration. And if such a course is offered it is usually an elective few students see the need to take. I suppose only when things get too bad that the decision makers at institutions will seek God in this area, ask for guidance and recognize that the issue of money and faith is of more personal, theological and practical importance than one more course in Greek or Hebrew, for example. The present study and others like The Reluctant Steward by Saint Meinrad School of Theology indicate that pastors are struggling with the faith and money issues not Greek or Hebrew issues, and yet they are simply not trained biblically to respond with conviction, clarity and compassion. In my view, we can do better to equip the future leaders of God's church handle resources God has entrusted to them: from people, possessions and projects. If you are looking for models for such training contact Talbot School of Theology, or Phoenix Seminary who currently actively partner with Crown Financial Ministries to meet students' needs in the area of faith and money training.

11. Alcorn, Randy; "Money, Possessions & Eternity," Tyndale House Publishers: Wheaton, IL, 2003, p. 5.

Chapter 2

1. Cf. the powerful chapter, Money & Misery by David Meyers in The Consuming Passion: Christianity and the consumer culture, InterVarsity Press: Downers Grove 1998.

2. George Fooshee, *You can be Financially Free*, Old Tappan, NJ: Revell, 1976.

3. Statement made by Howard Hendricks.

4. US News & World Report

5. See Speer footnote in introduction.

6. Matthew 25:21, NIV.

7. Matthew 6:24, NIV.

8. According to the College Board in 2002 and the National Association of Student Financial Aid Officers (NASFO) in 2002. See also the Wall Street Journal article: In Too Deep? What to do about debts, December 25, 2002. The revolving debt numbers referenced in the article come from the Federal Reserve.

9. See Personal Income and Outlays, U.S. Department of Commerce, Bureau of Economic Analysis, Personal Income And Outlays: September 2005. Personal income increased $173.5 billion, or 1.7 percent, and disposable personal income (DPI) increased $171.2 billion, or 1.9 percent, in September, according to the Bureau of Economic Analysis. Personal consumption expenditures (PCE) increased $44.1 billion, or 0.5 percent. In August, personal income decreased $94.9 billion, or 0.9 percent, DPI decreased $95.4 billion, or 1.1 percent, and PCE decreased $48.4 billion, or 0.5 percent, based on revised estimates. The September and August estimates of personal income reflect the effects of Hurricanes Rita and Katrina, which hit the Gulf Coast of the United States. Rental income of persons and proprietors' income together were reduced by about $5 billion (at an annual rate) in September and about $240 billion (at an annual rate) in August to reflect the uninsured losses of residential and business property. "Other current transfer receipts from business (net)" were boosted by about $7 billion (at an annual rate) in September and about $120 billion (at an annual rate) in August to reflect insurance benefits paid to persons. Excluding these effects, personal income increased $50.8 billion, or 0.5 percent in September, after increasing $26.0 billion, or 0.3 percent in August. Personal saving — DPI less personal outlays — was a negative $32.0 billion in September, compared with a negative $158.0 billion in August. Personal saving as a percentage of disposable personal income was a negative 0.4 percent in September, compared with a negative 1.8 percent in August. Negative personal saving reflects personal outlays that exceed disposable personal income. Saving from current income may be near zero or negative when outlays are financed by borrowing (including borrowing financed through credit cards or home equity loans), by selling investments or other assets, or by using savings from previous periods. http://www.bea.gov/bea/newsrel/pinewsrelease.htm

10. Cf. 2002 study by Myvesta a credit counseling organization that found student between the ages of 16-24 scored lower than 50% on basic finance questions.

11. According to a study conducted by Christian Stewardship Association in 2002.

Chapter 3

1. For a full detailed account of the history of understanding of money, see Justo Gonzalez, *Faith & Wealth: A History of early Christian Ideas on the Origin, Significance, and Use of Money*, Harper & Row Publishers: San Francisco, 1990. The information on these charts was gleaned from this significant work.

2. Rodin, Scott, R., *Stewards in the Kingdom: A Theology of Life in All Its Fullness*, InterVarsity Press: Downers Grove, 2000, p. 16-19.

3. Ibid, p. 120.

4. Howard Hendricks, *Living By the Book,* Moody Press: Chicago, p. 95.

Chapter 4

1. Works consulted for this chapter are from the following theological dictionary articles: Adie, D.K., (2001). Wealth, Christian view of. *Evangelical Dictionary of Theology*, Ed., Walter Elwell Baker Book House: Grand Rapids; Blomberg, C., L., (1996). Wealth. *Theological Dictionary of the Bible*, Ed., Walter Elwell, Baker Book House: Grand Rapids; Evans, W. (1939). Wealth, Wealthy. *The International Standard Bible Encyclopedia*, Ed. James Orr. WM. B. Eerdmans Publishing: Grand Rapids; Schultz, A. C., (1960) Wealth. *Baker's Dictionary of Theology*, Ed. E. F. Harrison, Baker Book House: Grand Rapids; Unger, M., F., (1998) Measurement of, Money, Ed., R.K., Harrision, *The New Unger's Bible Dictionary*, Moody Press: Chicago.

2. Adie, D. K. Wealth, Christian View of, in *Evangelical Dictionary of Theology*, Ed. Walter A. Elwell, Baker Book house: Grand Rapids, 2001, page 1261.

3. Adie, D. K. Wealth, Christian View of, in *Evangelical Dictionary of Theology*, Ed. Walter A. Elwell, Baker Book house: Grand Rapids, 2001, page 1262.

4. Blomberg, C.L., Wealth, in *Theological Dictionary of the Bible*, Ed. Walter A. Elwell, Baker Book House: Grand Rapids, 1996. page 814.

5. Blomberg, C.L., Wealth, in *Theological Dictionary of the Bible*, Ed. Walter A. Elwell, Baker Book House: Grand Rapids, 1996. page 814.

6. Adie, D. K. Wealth, Christian View of, in *Evangelical Dictionary of Theology*, Ed. Walter A. Elwell, Baker Book house: Grand Rapids, 2001, page 1261.

7. Adie, D. K. Wealth, Christian View of, in *Evangelical Dictionary of Theology*, Ed. Walter A. Elwell, Baker Book house: Grand Rapids, 2001, page 1261.

Chapter 5

1. This section and the following five distinctive components of the nature of Christian spirituality are based on the article, *Spirituality* by J.M. Houston, Evangelical Dictionary of Theology, Ed. Walter A. Elwell, Baker Book House, Grand Rapids, 2001, 1138-1143.

2. This chart has been modified and adapted from a sermon by John Erwin, interim pastor of Cypress Church in Cypress, California.

3. Jeffrey L. Sheler, "Nearer My God to Thee," *U.S. News and World Report*, May 3, 2004, p. 59.

4. The Barna research group has provided convincing data regarding this reality in studies taken on the behavior of the church. See www.barna.org.

5. cf. Jenkins, Natalie H., *You Paid How Much for That?: how to win at money without losing at love*, San Francisco: Jossey-Bass, c2002. See especially page 14. A 1991 study, by Howard Markman published from the University of Denver. One of the questions: What is the number one thing that you and your partner argue about most?" "Money is the most common conflict area for couples whether they remain happily married or get a divorce. Couples who stay together have money issues. Couples who don't stay

together have (and will likely continue to have) money issues. The difference between those who stay together and those who don't isn't *whether* they have money issues. The key difference lies in *how* couples manage their money issues. So money, per se, doesn't cause divorce, but it is the most difficult topic of all for the average couple."

6. Romans 5:6-8.

7. I'm indebted to Randy Alcorn's teaching on the subject of materialism as seen in his book entitled, *Money Possessions & Eternity*. Many of the concepts highlighted in this section are concepts I've thought about, adapted or revised, and reaffirmed for our study.

8. The idea of "Christ-awareness" comes from Oswald Chambers. He provides a powerful devotion related to the idea that our goal in life is not to become self-aware, but rather to become "Christ-aware." As we become more Christ-aware our selfishness decreases. This is in contrast to much teaching today. Christian self-help books abound. Christ never calls us to become self-aware. He calls us rather to Himself, to deny self and follow Him.

9. According to David Myer, page 60 in his chapter entitled *Money & Misery*. For a more thorough read on the discontinuity between money and happiness, see the same chapter in, *The Consuming Passion: Christianity and the Consumer Culture*, ed. by Robert Clapp, pages 50-75.

Chapter 6

1. Stott, J.R. W., (1996). The Message of 1 Timothy & Titus, *Bible Speaks Today*, InterVarsity Press: Downers Grove. p. 145. See also Towner, P. H., (1994). 1-2 Timothy & Titus, *The IVP New Testament Commentary Series*, Ed. Grant R. Osborne, InterVarsity Press: Downers Grove, IL. p.134.

2. Arnold, C.E., *Dictionary of Paul & His Letters*, InterVarsity Press: Downers Grove. p. 252.

3. Ibid, 249.

4. Marshall, I. H, (1999). A critical and exegetical commentary on the Pastoral Epistles, *International Critical Commentary*, T & T Clark: Edinburg. p.94-95.

5. Ellis, E.E., (1993). Pastoral Letters, *Dictionary of Paul and his Letters*, Ed. G.F. Hawthorne, R.P. Martin, and D.G. Reid, InterVarsity Press: Downers Grove. p. 662)

6. Ibid, 661.

7. Stott, J.R. W., (1996). The Message of 1 Timothy & Titus, *Bible Speaks Today*, InterVarsity Press: Downers Grove. p. 145.

8. Mounce, W. D. (2000). Pastoral Epistles, *Word Biblical Commentary*, Eds, Bruce M. Metzger, David A. Hubbard & Glenn W. Barker, Thomas Nelson Publishers, Nashville. See p.336

9. Ibid. 337.

10. Knight, G.E., (1992). The Pastoral Epistles, *The New International Greek Testament Commentary*, Eds., I Howard Marshall and W. Ward Gasque, William B. Eerdmans Publishing Co.: Grand Rapids. p.250.

11. Mounce, W. D. (2000). Pastoral Epistles, *Word Biblical Commentary*, Eds, Bruce M. Metzger, David A. Hubbard & Glenn W. Barker, Thomas Nelson Publishers, Nashville. p. 337

12. Stott, J.R. W., (1996). The Message of 1 Timothy & Titus, *Bible Speaks Today*, InterVarsity Press: Downers Grove. pp.146-147.

13. Mounce, W. D. (2000). Pastoral Epistles, *Word Biblical Commentary*, Eds, Bruce M. Metzger, David A. Hubbard & Glenn W. Barker, Thomas Nelson Publishers, Nashville. p. 338.

14. Knight, G.E., (1992). The Pastoral Epistles, *The New International Greek Testament Commentary*, Eds., I Howard Marshall and W. Ward Gasque, William B. Eerdmans Publishing Co.: Grand Rapids. p.251.

15. Mounce, W. D. (2000). Pastoral Epistles, *Word Biblical Commentary*, Eds, Bruce M. Metzger, David A. Hubbard & Glenn W. Barker, Thomas Nelson Publishers, Nashville. p. 338.

16. Stott, J.R. W., (1996). The Message of 1 Timothy & Titus, *Bible Speaks Today*, InterVarsity Press: Downers Grove. p.148.

17. Mounce, W. D. (2000). Pastoral Epistles, *Word Biblical Commentary*, Eds, Bruce M. Metzger, David A. Hubbard & Glenn W. Barker, Thomas Nelson Publishers, Nashville. p. 340.

18. Ibid, 340.

19. Kelly, J.N.D., (1998). The Pastoral Epistles, *Blacks New Testament Commentary*, Ed. Henry Chadwick, Hendrickson Publishers: London. p.135.

20. Stott, J.R. W., (1996). The Message of 1 Timothy & Titus, *Bible Speaks Today*, InterVarsity Press: Downers Grove. p.149.

21. Ibid, 149.

22. Ibid, 149.

23. Ibid, 149.

24. Kelly, J.N.D., (1998). The Pastoral Epistles, *Blacks New Testament Commentary*, Ed. Henry Chadwick, Hendrickson Publishers: London. p. 136.

25. Mounce, W. D. (2000). Pastoral Epistles, *Word Biblical Commentary*, Eds, Bruce M. Metzger, David A. Hubbard & Glenn W. Barker, Thomas Nelson Publishers, Nashville. p. 342.

26. Kelly, J.N.D., (1998). The Pastoral Epistles, *Blacks New Testament Commentary*, Ed. Henry Chadwick, Hendrickson Publishers: London. p. 136.

27. Ibid, 136.

28. Ibid, 136.

29. Mounce, W. D. (2000). Pastoral Epistles, *Word Biblical Commentary*, Eds, Bruce M. Metzger, David A. Hubbard & Glenn W. Barker, Thomas Nelson Publishers, Nashville. p. 343.

30. Kelly, J.N.D., (1998). The Pastoral Epistles, *Blacks New Testament Commentary*, Ed. Henry Chadwick, Hendrickson Publishers: London. p.137.

31. Ibid, 137.

32. Mounce, W. D. (2000). Pastoral Epistles, *Word Biblical Commentary*, Eds, Bruce M. Metzger, David A. Hubbard & Glenn W. Barker, Thomas Nelson Publishers, Nashville. p. 344.

33. Stott, J.R. W., (1996). The Message of 1 Timothy & Titus, *Bible Speaks Today*, InterVarsity Press: Downers Grove. p. 150.

34. Ibid, 150.

35. Ibid, 150.

36. Kelly, J.N.D., (1998). The Pastoral Epistles, *Blacks New Testament Commentary*, Ed. Henry Chadwick, Hendrickson Publishers: London. p. 137.

37. Mounce, W. D. (2000). Pastoral Epistles, *Word Biblical Commentary*, Eds, Bruce M. Metzger, David A. Hubbard & Glenn W. Barker, Thomas Nelson Publishers, Nashville. p. 344.

38. Kelly, J.N.D., (1998). The Pastoral Epistles, *Blacks New Testament Commentary*, Ed. Henry Chadwick, Hendrickson Publishers: London. p. 137.

39. Mounce, W. D. (2000). Pastoral Epistles, *Word Biblical Commentary*, Eds, Bruce M. Metzger, David A. Hubbard & Glenn W. Barker, Thomas Nelson Publishers, Nashville. p. 344.

40. Towner, P. H., (1994). 1-2 Timothy & Titus, *The IVP New Testament Commentary Series*, Ed. Grant R. Osborne, InterVarsity Press: Downers Grove, IL. p. 139.

41. Mounce, W. D. (2000). Pastoral Epistles, *Word Biblical Commentary*, Eds, Bruce M. Metzger, David A. Hubbard & Glenn W. Barker, Thomas Nelson Publishers, Nashville. p. 345.

42. Towner, P. H., (1994). 1-2 Timothy & Titus, *The IVP New Testament Commentary Series*, Ed. Grant R. Osborne, InterVarsity Press: Downers Grove, IL. p. 139.

43. Kelly, J.N.D., (1998). The Pastoral Epistles, *Blacks New Testament Commentary*, Ed. Henry Chadwick, Hendrickson Publishers: London. p. 137.

44. Ibid, 137.

45. Ibid, 138.

46. Mounce, W. D. (2000). Pastoral Epistles, *Word Biblical Commentary*, Eds, Bruce M. Metzger, David A. Hubbard & Glenn W. Barker, Thomas Nelson Publishers, Nashville. p. 346.

47. Kelly, J.N.D., (1998). The Pastoral Epistles, *Blacks New Testament Commentary*, Ed. Henry Chadwick, Hendrickson Publishers: London. p. 138.

48. Stott, J.R. W., (1996). The Message of 1 Timothy & Titus, *Bible Speaks Today*, InterVarsity Press: Downers Grove. p. 153.

49. Towner, P. H., (1994). 1-2 Timothy & Titus, *The IVP New Testament Commentary Series*, Ed. Grant R. Osborne, InterVarsity Press: Downers Grove, IL. p. 140.

50. Kelly, J.N.D., (1998). The Pastoral Epistles, *Blacks New Testament Commentary*, Ed. Henry Chadwick, Hendrickson Publishers: London. p. 138.

51. Towner, P. H., (1994). 1-2 Timothy & Titus, *The IVP New Testament Commentary Series*, Ed. Grant R. Osborne, InterVarsity Press: Downers Grove, IL. p. 140.

52. Ibid, 140.

Chapter 7

1. Our intension in this section is not to discuss the doctrine of God's judgment in detail. To do so is beyond our expertise and the scope of this course. However, we do offer this brief section to expose the necessity for believers to recognize that what we accomplish on earth, as evidence of our faith in Christ, will be subject to God's righteous judgment through Christ Jesus.

2. cf. Travis, S.H., Judgment of God, in *New Dictionary of Theology*, Ed. Sinclair B. Fergiuson, David F. Wright, and J.I. Packer, InterVarsity Press: Downers Grove, Il 1998, p.358.

3. Ibid, pp. 358-359.

4. Ibid, p. 359.

Chapter 8

NONE

Chapter 9

1. Henry, Matthew, (1935). *Gospel of Luke*, Fleming H. Revell Company: New York, vol. IV, p. 752.

2. Mathewson, Dave, L., *The Parable of the Unjust Steward (Luke 16:1-13): A Reexamination of the Traditional Views in Light of Recent Challenges*, Journal of Evangelical Theological Society, 38:1 (March 1995), pp. 29-39.

3. Henry, Matthew, (1935). *Gospel of Luke*, Fleming H. Revell Company: New York, 1935. vol. IV, p. 753-754.

4. Ibid., 754.

5. Ibid., 753.

6. Ibid., 754.

7. Martin, John A., (1983). Luke, *The Bible Knowledge Commentary*, Eds. John Walvoord and Roy Zuck, Victor Press p. 246.

8. Henry, Matthew (1935). *Gospel of Luke*, Fleming H. Revell Company: New York. vol. IV, p. 754.

9. While the timing of this parable is debatable among theological traditions, the principles gleaned from this passage about faithfulness, rewards and loss of rewards are applicable.

10. McConaughy, David, (1918) *Money the acid test; studies in stewardship,* New York : Missionary Education Movement of the United States and Canada.

Chapter 10

1. Campbell, David, (1985). Joshua, in *Bible Knowledge Commentary*, Eds. John Walvoord & Roy Zuck, Victor Books, p. 345.

Chapter 11

1. Tam, Stanley (1969) *God Owns My Business*, as told to Ken Anderson. Word Books: Waco, Texas.

Chapter 12

NONE

Chapter 13

1. According to the Federal Reserve, consumer debt including revolving and non-revolving debt in January 2006 is 2.162 trillion dollars. See federal reserve web site: http://www.federalreserve.gov/releases/g19/current/default.htm

2. From on an article by William Branigin Jan. 12, 2004 Washington Post; see www.washingtonpost.com/ac2/wp-dyn/a100112004jan12?language=printer See also Dr. Robert Manning's web site www.creditcardnation.com for other helpful sociological studies and numbers on the credit card fiasco in America.

Chapter 14

NONE

Chapter 15

1. The section on Stages of Giving based on *Fowler's Stages of Faith* was written by Dr. Wes Willmer in his book *God & Your Stuff* and was a portion of a paper presented at a President's faculty luncheon at BIOLA University on "Our Stuff Saturated Society and BIOLA University: How should we respond" by Dr. Wes Willmer and Chad Cunningham. We presented this helpful chart that enables believers to assess their own development. I have modified the content in this section for use in this text.

2. M. Scott Peck quoted from James W. Fowler's *Stages of Faith*, Harper Collins: San Francisco, CA, 1995.

3. James W. Fowler, *Stages of Faith*, Harper Collins: San Francisco, CA, 1995, p. xii.

4. Thomas Schmidt, "Rich Wisdom: New Testament Teachings on Wealth," *Christianity Today* (Cora

Stream, IC: May 12, 1989), p. 30.

5. P. H. McNamara, "What People Give Indicates Their Spiritual Health," in *More than Money: Portraits of Transformative Stewardship*, (MD Alban Institute, 1999.

6. Gary L. Thomas, The Glorious Pursuit: Embracing the Virtues of Christ, NavPress: Colorado Springs, CO, 1998, p. 108.

Chapter 16

1. The information contained in the following section has been adapted from Crown Financial Ministries' pamphlet on insurance, originally composed in 1985 by Larry Burkett, co-founder of Crown Financial Ministries and updated in 2003.

PART IV

Study Tools

APPENDIX A—WORLDVIEW COMPARISON CHART*

Money and Possessions	World	Followers of Christ
Ownership	*Personal discretion*	*Faithful steward of/for God*
Earnings	*Personal selfish gain*	*Labor for Christ, enjoy His blessing and share with others*
Giving	*Personal glory*	*To glorify God*
Saving	*Personal security*	*To adequately provide for family*
Investing	*Personal peace*	*For God's purposes*
Debt-free	*Personal freedom*	*To be a bond-servant of Christ*

*This chart has been adapted from one presented by Chuck Bentley at a Crown Financial Ministries leadership staff training event.

APPENDIX B—FAITH AND MONEY STEWARDSHIP PERSPECTIVES CHART

CONCEPT/ACTION	Poverty Perspective Asceticism mentality	Stewardship Perspective Balanced view of faith and money	Prosperity Perspective Prosperity Mentality
Money/Possessions	*An evil to avoid*	*An entrusted responsibility*	*An entitlement*
Work/Vocation	*Meet only basic needs*	*Opportunity to serve Christ*	*To become rich*
Godliness	*The poor*	*Faithfulness in any circumstance*	*The wealthy*
Giving	*An obligation*	*Opportunity to express love and gratitude, also to attain eternal rewards*	*For earthly gain*
Spending/Consumption	*Produces guilt*	*Prayerful and responsible*	*Consumptive and careless*
Leisure Time	*Is not appropriate*	*A gift to be used responsibly*	*A primary goal*

Appendix C—Faith and Money Stewardship Matrix

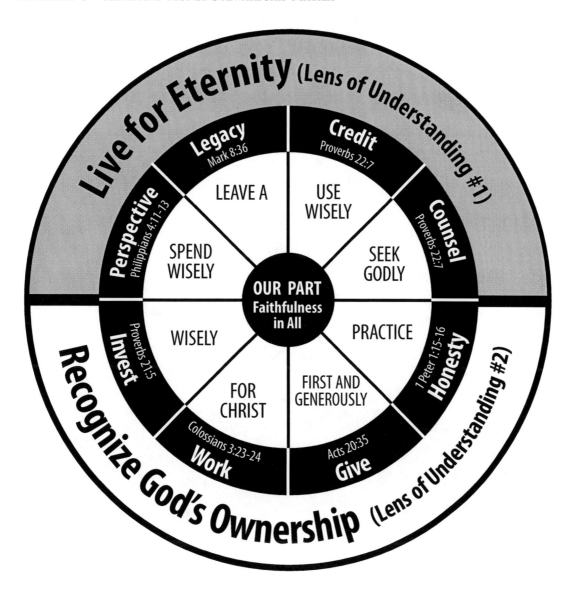

APPENDIX D—CONTENTMENT PROCESS CHART

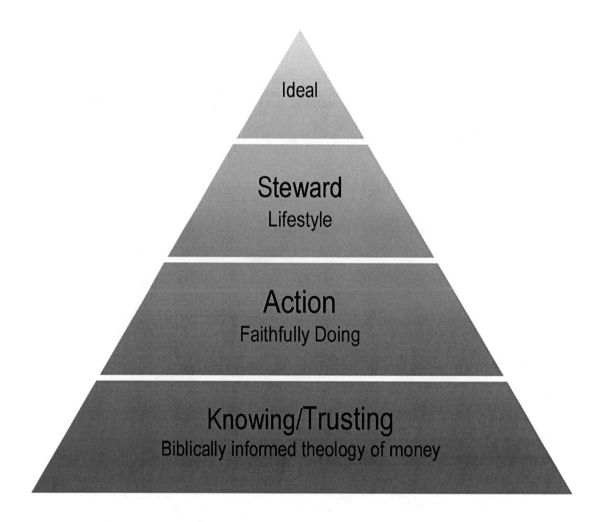

CONTENTMENT PROCESS—THE GODLY STEWARD'S JOURNEY

<u>Note:</u> Contentment is a process that grows through disciplined effort toward the ideal. Knowledge coupled with trust leads to action, faithfully doing what God desires. The right actions become a habit, the lifestyle of a steward. The steward's lifestyle leads to increasing contentment and moves in the direction of the ideal.

FAITH AND MONEY—SPENDING MATRIX

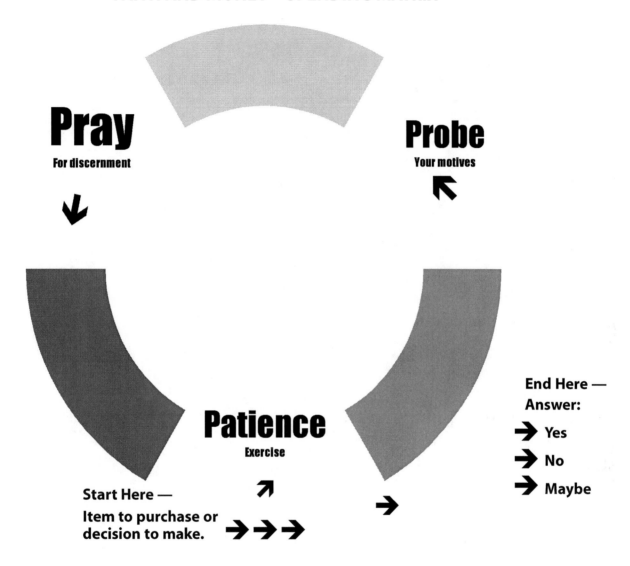

Note: Read this chart from left to right, following the arrows around the circle. The arrows indicate a cyclical process for thinking through decisions. Generally postpone purchases for 24-36 hours. For major decisions like a job, take longer—perhaps even several weeks, if possible—to make the decision. Determine a customary threshold of cost for employing this process. For example, my wife and I have a $100 limit. For every purchase over $100 we use this process together. Sometimes we use it for smaller purchases to avoid quick decisions on items that can be budget busters. We've learned that little purchases each day can add up to more than we would think.

APPENDIX F—POSITIONING MONEY THEMES CHART

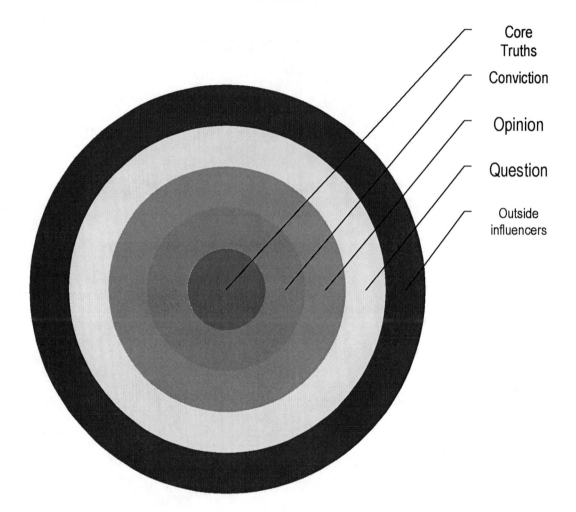

Core
Truths

Conviction

Opinion

Question

Outside
influencers

POSITIONING STEWARDSHIP ISSUES
Examples

Core Truths	Convictions	Opinions	Questions
God's/Our Part	Insurance	Mortgage	How much is enough?
Honesty/Giving	Student loans	Insurance	To whom should I give?
Counsel/Debt	Retirement	Stock Market	How much do I give?
Work/Eternity			
Perspective			

<u>Note:</u> The point of this chart is to encourage answering questions about money and faith by first appealing to core truths—the bulls eye—and then working outward. Many people work from the outside in, which is a great way to come to the wrong conclusions. Reliable core truths are gained through discovering what the Bible teaches about money. The examples listed above represent only a few of the many possibilities. *This chart is an adaptation of one used by Dr. Eric Thonnes in his theology courses at Talbot School of Theology.

APPENDIX G—HOW TO MAKE BAD CAREER DECISIONS

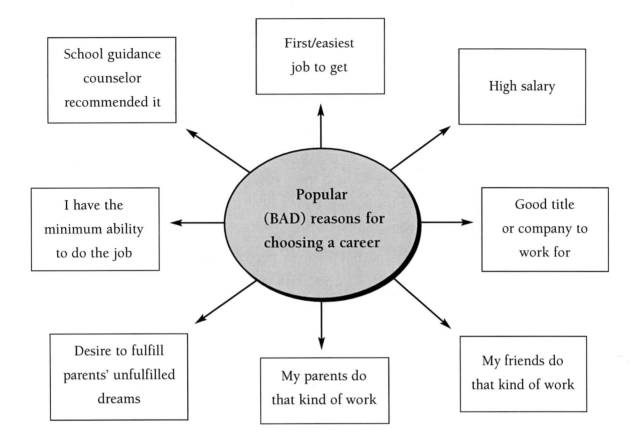

School guidance counselor recommended it

First/easiest job to get

High salary

I have the minimum ability to do the job

Popular (BAD) reasons for choosing a career

Good title or company to work for

Desire to fulfill parents' unfulfilled dreams

My parents do that kind of work

My friends do that kind of work

APPENDIX H—HOW TO MAKE GOOD CAREER DECISIONS

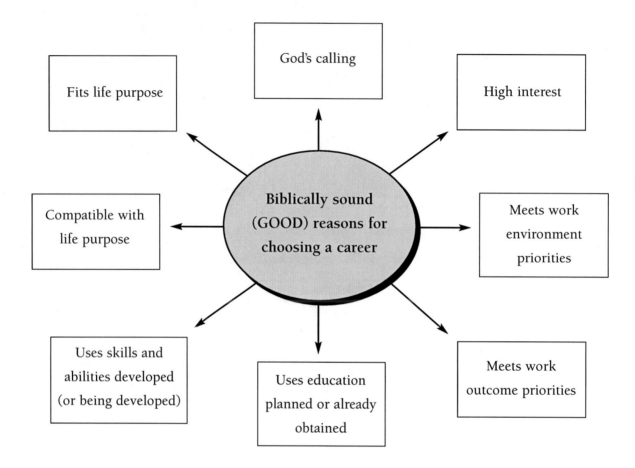

APPENDIX I—OLD TESTAMENT GIVING CHART

To Whom	Frequency/duration	Found in (text)
1. Priests	*Perpetual*	*Numbers 18:21-24*
2. Festivals	*Perpetual*	*Deuteronomy 12:17-18*
3. Poor and helpless	*Every third year*	*Deuteronomy 14:28-29*

The combined amount of giving for the Hebrew works out to approximately 23-25% annually.

Faith and Money: A Practical Theology Curriculum and Study Guides

by Chad E. Cunningham and Howard Dayton

> ### Overview
>
> *This curriculum and study guide is required for students taking the Faith and Money course for credit. We recommend it for all who use the textbook, because it broadens exposure and enriches understanding.*
>
> *We encourage you to be a good "Berean" (cf. Acts 17:10-12). We present powerful concepts that should challenge your current understanding and behavior of the subject. Although we are dedicated to studying the issue of faith and money, we are fallible and do not claim to have a corner on truth. We expect you to think critically, reflect, and study the biblical passages for yourself to mold your beliefs. There will likely be disagreements; we want them to be biblically and theologically informed disagreements rather than emotionally charged responses based on personal and social biases.*
>
> *This Curriculum and Study Guide is broken into two sections. Section One contains the two curriculum and syllabus options. Section Two contains questions that go beyond the "Think About It" sections at the end of each textbook chapter. This section provides the opportunity for a deeper personal or group study of the Scriptures relevant to each chapter.*

SECTION ONE: CURRICULUM GUIDES

This section contains two sample syllabi. Instructors may use these as guides in developing their own syllabus with appropriate dates, personal information, etc.

Syllabus A is an undergrad 15-week traditional three-credit-hour university course. Syllabus B is a seminary level three-credit-hour course in a two-week intensive class setting. The seminary syllabus requires significant pre-reading and post-class projects (see the supplemental readings section in the syllabus).

Congratulations! You are about to dig deeper into the relationship of money to faith. Stay focused. Be faithful. Finish strong!

Undergraduate Syllabus

ADVANCED BIBLICAL STUDY—FAITH and MONEY

ABC University

Instructor:

Th 3:00-5:40 Room #

Date

Syllabus

I. COURSE DESCRIPTION

As a key component of life and spiritual formation, the *Faith and Money* course explores key theological themes and biblical texts related to personal use of money and possessions with the outcome of integrating them into the students' value system and lifestyle. Attention will be placed on practical implementation of biblical financial principles in the students' life development and vocation. Topics to be covered: materialism and spirituality, eternity, honesty, work/vocation, giving and spirituality, counsel, saving, debt.

II. VALUES [WHAT WE BELIEVE IS IMPORTANT]

VALUES ⇒ ACTIONS ⇒ LIFESTYLE

1. Scripture is authoritative in all areas it speaks to and <u>is</u> the guidebook for life.

2. Integration of our faith with confidence into both corporate and individual lives.

3. Utilization of general revelation as appropriate for faith and life development.

4. Process of growth in knowledge (mind), being (character) and impact (practice) for God's glory.

5. Progressive transformation into the likeness of Christ on a daily basis.

6. Transformation of culture for Christ through the impact of our daily lives in our sphere of influence.

III. LEARNING OUTCOMES [WHAT I WANT FOR <u>YOU</u>]

GIVE 1ST ⇒ SAVE 2ND ⇒ LIVE 3RD

As a result of participating in this course, the student should achieve the following learning outcomes:

1. Think biblically and theologically *for personal application* through the identification and articulation of three key foundational themes related to Faith and Money, stating how these themes are interrelated to thinking and actions. [readings, personal Scripture study, lectures] (Cognitive)

2. Integrate scriptural truth related to the seven key areas of stewardship into your way of life (daily) and vocation (what you do). [stewardship project, journal, readings, Scripture study, practical assignments] (Cognitive/behavioral)

3. Critically discern false cultural/media ideology and impressions about money, possessions, success, worth, happiness and values from biblical truth about those themes through implementing the decision-making process (skills). [class discussions, journals, reading, Scripture study]. (Cognitive)

4. Experience personal contentment through an understanding of God's character, truth about money and realistic spending behavior (Spiritual growth). [journal, practical applications, readings] (Affective)

5. Challenge and transform assumptions about money and possessions from family upbringing, culture and experience into a more biblically and theologically informed view. [lectures/discussions, readings, Scripture study]

6. Become a responsible, disciplined consumer "not tossed by the winds of culture" through practicing financial faithfulness during and after the course; establish a lifestyle of godly stewardship: **Giving first and more ⇒ Saving more ⇒ THEN Living.** [readings, journal, practical exercises]

IV. BOOKS/READINGS

1. Alcorn, Randy *Money Possessions and Eternity*, Tyndale House: Wheaton IL rev. ed. 2003.

2. *Cunningham, Chad. E. and Dayton, Howard, Money and Faith: A Practical Theology: First Edition*, Crown Financial Ministries, Inc., Gainesville, GA © 2005.

3. Willmer, Wes, God and Your Stuff: *God and Your Stuff: The Vital Link between Your Possessions and Your Soul*, NavPress: Colorado Springs, CO, 2002.

4. Readings from the reading packet as assigned.

V. SOME INFORMATION ABOUT THE COURSE (What you should expect)

1. This course is an advanced biblical elective. I expect students to manage their course load and their time.

2. This course is not an easy alternative to harder courses. I expect a great deal from students (both personally and practically) and will treat them as responsible adults. Each student must earn the grade received. This course is not an easy "A."

3. Out of respect for my time and the time of classmates, I expect students to be present and on time in class. Only in extreme circumstances are excuses allowed (personal immediate family tragedy, accident [car wreck, broken leg, etc.] or sickness [not a checkup]). If a school event such as sports, the debate team, or SIFE event necessitates missing class, a letter from the advising professor/coach is required.

4. Cellular phones, ipods, and other gadgets (including text messaging options) are to be turned off during class time out of respect to the professor and classmates. (For every time I leave my phone on [and it rings], each student receives one point toward their overall final grade. [And, no, you cannot call my number during class.])

5. For questions about an assignment, project, or practical application, please take the time to schedule an appointment with the professor. Generally, decisions about a project or paper will not be made before or after class because I might forget what I told you unless I can focus only on your question.

VI. ACTIVE LEARNING EXERCISES (COURSEWORK REQUIREMENTS)

 A. Personal Reading (per schedule, and as assigned)   25%

  1. Alcorn, Randy, (2003). *Money, Possessions and Eternity*, Tyndale Publishers.

  2. Cunningham, Chad, E. and Dayton, Howard, (2006). *Faith and Money: A practical theology,* Crown Financial Ministries, Gainesville, GA.

  3. Willmer, Wes, (2002).*God and Your Stuff* (book analysis) Claims report on Willmer.

  4. Handouts—various reading handouts given in class as assigned by professor.

 B. Personal Practical Applications   p/f

  1. Deed (of all personal assets)

2. Track spending—through the duration of the course.

3. Financial Statement and Debt List

4. Spending Plan developed

C. Personal Discipline Assignments

1. *Personal Journal*   20%

    (neatly handwritten in a bluebook or printed out from your computer in a readable font and stapled together). The personal journal will consist of three sections: 1) **Introduction:** your introductory understanding of money and faith issues at the beginning of the course (one page). 2) **Body:** weekly (three entries <u>minimum</u>) based on "takeaways" you have learned from the study questions in your Crown course textbook and class conversations. 3) **Conclusion:** your final comments, insights, and understanding at the end of the course (one or two pages). Weekly entries should be approximately one or two paragraphs in length. No one else will have access to your journal. *The journal will be handed in twice for assessment: at mid-term and prior to finals week.*

2. *Media Analysis Assignment*   15%

    Students will submit a minimum of three pages typed in a size 12 font, double-spaced with one-inch margins. This paper should critically analyze the various *claims* and content of an appropriate (instructor-approved) media (movie, TV series program) noting what *messages* they send. *Highlight issues of discontinuity or continuity to a biblical understanding of wealth, success, happiness, or values, integrating what has been learned* from the course related to the film, program, or documentary. <u>Students must inform the professor in writing by week three of the specific media program they will be evaluating before starting the assignment. Students who do not receive written approval for their media program will be given no credit for the assignment.</u>

    Examples: watch four episodes of *Extreme Makeover Home Edition* in the semester; or watch *The Apprentice* or watch four episodes of *Three Wishes* or spend at least four hours evaluating TV advertisements. Or you may choose to watch a movie related to money: e.g., *Citizen Kane.*

3. *Stewardship project*   20%

    Using information from your pre-test questionnaire, personal journal, course reading, and lectures, synthesize the course material and creatively apply what you have learned to future life and vocation. This project is due one week prior to finals week (a project description will be handed out later in the course).

4. *Wedding analysis/parental interaction (conversations to be assigned)* 20%
Each student will research the entire cost of a wedding: ceremony, dinners, clothes and jewelry, honeymoon, etc. Determine the average cost of a wedding and calculate the cost to include interest if the costs were charged.

Additionally, students will be assigned topics (generally two) on which to communicate with their parents throughout the semester. This communication will in person or by phone (no email). Students will summarize their conversations in a word document, noting their parent's responses, interaction and what they (the students) learned in the process.

D. Participation and personal attendance
Come prepared for all class sessions.

VII. GRADING

Media Analysis Assignment	15%
Practical Applications (4)	pass/fail
Personal Journal	20%
Wedding/Parental Conversation	20%
Reading (on time completion of reading)	25%
Stewardship project	20%

**Note: assignments turned in late will receive lower grades.

GRADING STANDARDS

Plagiarism: ABC University sees any form of plagiarism as a serious problem with serious consequences. Please refer to the academic integrity statement in the Student Handbook, Academic and Behavioral Standards section.

Grading Standards for Written Work: Whereas ABC University desires to maintain the highest standards with respect to the composition of all written work, any student paper exhibiting poor grammar, spelling errors, typographical errors, or other substandard academic expression shall have the overall grade for that paper reduced accordingly. Generally, a paper will be deemed substandard and ineligible to receive an "A" grade when it averages three or more compositional errors per page. Moreover, at the discretion of the professor, the substandard paper may be returned to the student for correction and resubmission with appropriate grade penalties. Students deficient in writing skills may seek assistance at the Writing Center.

LATE ASSIGNMENTS

Assignments turned in late will receive a lower grade.

VIII. FORMAT FOR WRITTEN WORK

Write with clarity and conviction, appropriately using the system of citing with which you are most comfortable. Do not submit a paper that has not been spell-checked at least two times.

IX. INSTRUCTOR AVAILABILITY

It is generally a good idea to email a day in advance of a visit about a specific question or assignment. I am usually in during office hours, but occasionally my plans change. However, I have an open door policy, so please stop by whenever you would like to talk.

X. ANTICIPATED COURSE SCHEDULE (subject to change by the professor)

Date	Class Topics	Assignment Due
Section I. Foundations—Thinking Biblically and Theologically		
2/2	Money, meaning and significance	Personal Questionnaire (in class)
		Commence tracking spending
		Issler/Moreland article—next time
2/9	Chapters #1-4 Conceptualizing	*Alcorn: Preface, pp. 3-28*
	1. Conceptualizing: Why Is Money Important?	
	2. Impact of Money on Life	
	3. Starting off Right: The Godly Steward	
	4. Wealth Reloaded: A Christian View of Wealth	*F and M Text: 1-4*
2/16	Chapter #5 and 6	
	5. Materialism and Spirituality	*Alcorn: pp 29-74*
	6. Needs, Wants and Contentment	*F and M Text 5-6*
		Media Analysis—focus due

Section II. A Fresh view the Godly steward

2/23	Chapter #7 Refresh: Peering into Eternity	*Alcorn: pp.107-138*
		F and M Text 7
3/2	Chapter #8 Release: Let God Be God	*Alcorn: pp. 93-106*
		F and M Text: 8
		Deed
3/9	Chapter #9 Fidelity: A Fresh Glance	*F and M Text: 9*
	Topic: Faithfulness in our oversight	**Financial Statement**

Section III. Balance—Thinking Integratively and Practically

3/16	Chapter #10 Honesty: God's Mandate	*Alcorn: 139-170*
	Topic: A steward's ethic of honesty	*F and M Text 10*
		Journal (Mid-term)
3/23	Missions conference—no class	
3/30	Chapter #11 Thrive: The Blessing of Work	*Alcorn: pp. 281-304*
	Topic: Toward a renewed theology of work	*F and M Text: 11*
	Guest speaker	
4/6	Chapter #12 Plugging in: The Importance of Counsel	*F and M Text: 12*
	Topic: Foolish or wise	
4/13	Chapter #13 Credit: Danger! Use with Caution	*Alcorn: pp 305-326*
	Topic: The trap: happiness through debt	*F and M Text: 13*
		Debt list
4/20	Break—no class	
4/27	Chapter #14—Store It up: Giving's Big Picture	*Alcorn: pp. 173-194*
	Topic: Toward a theology and ethic of giving	*F and M Text: 14-15*
	Chapter #15 Growing in Faith and Giving	*Alcorn: pp.195-222*
	Topic: Where are you?	**Wedding Analysis**

5/4	Chapter #16—Using Your Head While You	
	Live by Faith	*Alcorn: pp. 327-352*
	Topic: Investing biblically	*F and M Text 13*
	Guest speaker—	**Spending Plan (Budget)**
	Investment Ethicist,	
5/11	Review	*Alcorn: pp. 381-422*
	Topic: Faithful to God's adventure for you	**Stewardship Project**
5/16	Review and Reload	*Alcorn: pp. 353-380*
	The balanced Godly steward	**Journal (Final)**
		Tracking spending (4mos.)
5/22	Finals Week	Review of Projects
		Food, film and fun/Location-TBA
		Reading report/Willmer—Claims

MONEY AND FAITH: KEY PASSAGE LIST

1. Luke 12:15   Conceptualizing: Why Is Money Important?
2. Hebrews 13:5   Impact of Money on Life
3. 1 Timothy 3:16-17   Starting off Right: The Godly Steward
4. Proverbs 30: 8b-9   Wealth Reloaded: A Christian View of Wealth
5. 1 John 2:15   Materialism and Spirituality
6. 1Timothy 6:10   Needs, Wants, and Contentment
7. Mark 8:36   Refresh: Peering into Eternity
8. 1 Chronicles 29:11-12   Release: Let God Be God
9. 1 Corinthians 4:2   Fidelity: A Fresh Glance
10. Leviticus 19:11   Honesty: God's Mandate
11. Colossians 3:23-24 Thrive: The Blessing of Work
12. Proverbs 12:15   Plugging in: The Importance of Counsel
13. Romans 13:8   Credit: Danger! Use with Caution
14. Acts 20:35   Store It up: Giving's Big Picture
15. John 15: 5   Growing in Faith and Giving
16. Proverbs 21: 5, 20 Using your Head While You Live by Faith

SUPPLEMENTAL READINGS

Novak, M., (1991). *Introduction and Theology of Democratic Capitalism*, in The Spirit of Democratic Capitalism, Madison books: New York.

Rodin, Scott, (2000) *Introduction and Docking the Ship*, in Stewards in the Kingdom: A Theology of Life in All its Fullness

Smith, Ian, (1993) *God and Economics*, in God and Culture: Essays in honor of Carl F. H. Henry, ed. D. A. Carson and John Woodbridge. Eerdmans Publishing Co.

Stackhouse, John G., (2000) *Money and Theology in American Evangelicalism*, in More Money, More Ministry: Money and Evangelicals in recent North American history. ed, Eskridge and Knoll, Eerdmans Publishing Co.

Clapp, Rodney, (1998) *The Theology of Consumption and the Consumption of Theology*, in The Consuming Passion: Christianity and the consumer culture, ed Rodney Clapp, InterVarsity Press: Downers Grove.

Myers, David, (1998) *Money and Misery*, in The Consuming Passion: Christianity and the consumer culture, ed Rodney Clapp, InterVarsity Press: Downers Grove.

Resseguie, James, (2004) *Consumption: The Spiritual Life and Possessions*, in Spiritual Landscape: Images of the Spiritual Life in the Gospel of Luke. Hendrickson Publishers: Peabody, MA.

Murchie, David, (1978) *The New Testament View of Wealth Accumulation*, Journal of Evangelical Theological Society.

Foster, Richard, (1988) *The Discipline of Simplicity*, in Celebration of Discipline: The path to spiritual growth. Harper Collins Publishers: New York.

TOPICS

Issler, K. and Moreland, J.P., (2005) Today's confusion about happiness, in *The Lost Virtue of Happiness*, NavPress: Colorado Springs.

Moreland, J.P., (1997) *Ethical Egoism and Biblical Sel-Interest*, in Westminster Theological Journal.

Packer, J.I., (1993) *Lifestyle, leisure, and pleasure*, in God and Culture: Essays in honor of Carl F. H. Henry, ed. D. A. Carson and John Woodbridge. Eerdmans Publishing.

Wuthnow, Robert, (1994) *Faith and Work*, in God and Mammon in America, The Free Press: New York.

Alcorn, Randy, (2003) *Debt: Borrowing and Lending*, in Money, Possessions and Eternity Tyndale House Publishers: Wheaton, IL.

Wuthnow, Robert, (1997) *What Clergy are saying*, in The Crisis of Churches: Spiritual Malaise, Fiscal Woe, Oxford University Press: New York

Miller, Elliot, (2005) *Tithing: Is it New Testament*, Christian Research Institute

Pryor, Austin, (1990) *A Biblical View of Retirement*, Sound Mind Investing.

Seminary Course Syllabus

PT 760 Seminar—

ABC Seminary

Money and Faith: A Practical Theology

Instructor:

Intersession two weeks

M-F 6:00pm-10:00 pm

Location:

A. Pre-reading assignments

Students are to secure a copy of the following nine books or journals from their school library (if your library does not have a particular text, use the interlibrary loan process to secure a copy) and read the appropriate chapters or sections prior to the first day of class.

On the first day of class, provide a Microsoft Word document containing three claims per section from each of the readings listed below. The form can be one large document or separate documents. Include in each section the bibliographic information at the top of the page and include page number(s) for each claim quotation (12-point font, double-spaced, with one-inch margins).

These pre-readings are designed to stimulate your thinking on the breadth and importance of faith and money. Capture the contribution of each author to the study of this topic regardless of whether you agree with their theology.

1. Novak, M., (1991). *Introduction and Theology of Democratic Capitalism*, in The Spirit of Democratic Capitalism, Madison books: New York.

2. Rodin, Scott, (2000) *Introduction and Docking the Ship*, in Stewards in the Kingdom: A Theology of Life in All its Fullness

3. Smith, Ian, (1993) *God and Economics*, in God and Culture: Essays in honor of Carl F. H. Henry, ed. D. A. Carson and John Woodbridge. Eerdmans Publishing Co.

4. Stackhouse, John G., (2000) *Money and Theology in American Evangelicalism*, in More Money, More Ministry: Money and Evangelicals in recent North American history. ed, Eskridge and Knoll, Eerdmans Publishing Co.

5. Clapp, Rodney, (1998) *The Theology of Consumption and the Consumption of Theology*, in The Consuming Passion: Christianity and the consumer culture, ed Rodney Clapp, InterVarsity Press: Downers Grove.

6. Myers, David, (1998) *Money and Misery*, in The Consuming Passion: Christianity and the consumer culture, ed Rodney Clapp, InterVarsity Press: Downers Grove.

7. Resseguie, James, (2004) *Consumption: The Spiritual Life and Possessions*, in Spiritual Landscape: Images of the Spiritual Life in the Gospel of Luke. Hendrickson Publishers: Peabody, MA.

8. Murchie, David, (1978) *The New Testament View of Wealth Accumulation*, Journal of Evangelical Theological Society.

9. Foster, Richard, (1988) *The Discipline of Simplicity*, in Celebration of Discipline: The path to spiritual growth. Harper Collins Publishers: New York.

B. Post-class project/readings

Stewardship Manifesto (see project description in syllabus; Part IV Course requirements.)

Read: Schneider, John, (2002). *The Good of Affluence: Seeking God in a Culture of Wealth*, Grand Rapids, MI, William B. Eerdmans, (219)

In a Microsoft Word document, write three claims from the author per chapter and provide a brief paragraph stating why this claim is significant to the subject. Interact with the novel concepts proposed by the author in light of what you have learned in this course.

SYLLABUS

I. COURSE DESCRIPTION

As a key component of life and spiritual formation, the *Faith and Money* course explores explore key theological themes and biblical texts related to personal use of money and possessions with the outcome of integrating them into the students' value system and lifestyle. Attention will be placed on understanding for application, at an introductory level, the biblical and theological themes of God's financial principles related to the students' personal spiritual growth, vocation or ministry context and family.

II. LEARNING OUTCOMES

As a result of participating in this course, the student should achieve the following outcomes:

COGNITIVE

1. Acquire knowledge and understanding of a biblical view of money by defining a godly steward and delineating three key perspectives of a steward. (readings, personal study questions, Manifesto)
2. Establish a thoughtful and wise financial ethic to guide personal financial decisions by articulating and defending seven key elements of the practice of stewardship. (readings, class discussion)
3. Discern two evaluative methods for countering media dogma related to consumer behavior. (readings, class discussion)
4. Develop and cultivate three key biblical attitudes related to money and possessions.

AFFECTIVE

1. Experience a deepened relationship with Christ through application of Scripture by spending more time in the Word, giving more, and serving more. (personal journal)
2. Extend a sense of community with other students through daily prayer, class work and interaction. (prayer requests, classroom interaction)
3. Internalize the importance of stewardship in relationship to character development by realizing the materialistic pull of our society and making three changes to simplify lifestyle. (Personal journal/spouse interaction conversation, class sessions)
4. Experience greater worship through a reaffirmation of God's calling by articulating three ways to worship Him through vocation.

Behavioral

1. Redirect spending habits by recognizing the three key areas for spending evaluation and adding them to the decision-making model.

2. Create and maintain an individualized spending plan appropriate to current living situation and incorporate the seven key elements of stewardship.

3. Be faithful to God with money and possessions out of love for Him in the little decisions as well as big ones by giving first, saving next and then living. (Manifesto, scriptural study)

4. Live with a balanced perspective in relation to money and possessions by being neither judgmental nor anxious about others.

III. COURSE TEXTS

Cunningham, Chad, E., (2006). *Faith and Money: A Practical Theology: Student Curriculum*, First edition, Crown Financial Ministries, Inc: Gainesville, GA.

Getz, Gene, (2004). *Rich in Every Way: Everything the Bible says about material possessions*, Howard Publishing: West Monroe, LA.

Schneider, John, (2002). *The Good of Affluence: Seeking God in a Culture of Wealth*, Grand Rapids, MI, William B. Eerdmans, (219)

Selected articles from the readings handout packet (as assigned).

IV. COURSE REQUIREMENTS

Students must complete the course requirements. (See course descriptions for details of weighting and other instructions).

1. Attendance, participation and practical applications

    Given the size of the class, a good portion of our time will be devoted to interaction and discussion of the reading materials and biblical passages. Student are required to be familiar with the assigned texts and ready to contribute to the dialogue. Three points will be deducted from the overall grade for each absence beyond the allowance in current student policies.

    Practical Applications (Pass/Fail)—a: Track spending. b: Deed. c: Financial Goals. d: Debt List. e: Spending Plan/projection. (See appendix section in the textbook.)

2. Required reading (Reading report)   25%

   To supplement the course presentations and discussions, students must read the course notes per schedule, all required texts listed above, and articles as assigned by the professor in the readings handout (5).

   Due: last day of class; Overall report, except Schneider (see below).

   Due: January_ in office— John Schneider, The Good of Affluence, claims 10%

3. Reflection Journal and Study Questions   25%

   As topics are assigned, students will provide written reflections based on their current knowledge of the subject. These may be printed or neatly handwritten in a bluebook. The personal journal will consist of three sections: 1) **Introduction:** your introductory understanding of money and faith issues at the beginning of the course (one page). 2) **Body:** weekly (three entries <u>minimum)</u> journal entries based on takeaways you have learned from the study questions, readings and class conversations. 3) **Conclusion:** your final comments, insights, and understanding at the end of the course (one or two pages). Weekly/daily entries should be approximately one or two paragraphs in length. No one else will have access to your journal. *The journal will be handed in twice for assessment: at mid-term and prior to finals week.*

   *Study questions will be assigned by the professor throughout the course; see study guide section of Faith and Money textbook.

   Due: Friday_, 200_ (before break) and Thursday _, 200_ (to be handed back on Friday).

4. Topical Paper or Theological Dictionary Article   15%

   Each student will choose a theological topic, issue, or construct related to money and possessions. Consult the appropriate theological dictionaries (five minimum—cf. Glynn, John *Commentary and Reference Survey* for appropriate tools), and write an article worthy of submission for publication (six pages maximum). **Get approval for your topic or issue from the professor prior to conducting research.** Provide a one-page outline for making an eight-minute presentation to the class.

   Due: Friday, 20th, 200_

5. Personal Manifesto for Renewal of Stewardship in local Church/life   25%

   Synthesize the course material and creatively apply it to future vocation or ministry, using information from #2, 3 and 4 to develop the final manifesto. Submit one double-spaced, typewritten paper (10 pages maximum) that reflects your philosophy of stewardship with an implementation plan for the project (see assignment descriptions for directions). Provide outline of paper, claims, and a works-consulted page—not to be counted in overall paper. Use appropriate citation methods.

Due: one week after class

<u>100%</u>

<u>Plagiarism:</u> ABC Seminary sees any form of plagiarism as a serious problem with serious consequences. Please refer to the academic integrity statement and article on plagiarism in the Talbot Graduate Student Handbook.

<u>Grading Standards for Written Work</u>: Whereas ABC Seminary desires to maintain the highest standards with respect to the composition of all written work, any student paper exhibiting poor grammar, spelling errors, typographical errors, or other substandard academic expression shall have the overall grade for that paper reduced accordingly. Generally, a paper will be deemed substandard and ineligible to receive an "A" grade when it averages three or more compositional errors per page. Moreover, at the discretion of the professor, the substandard paper may be returned to the student for correction and resubmission with appropriate grade penalties. Graduate papers are expected to demonstrate a higher level of academic expression than undergraduate papers. Students deficient in writing skills may seek assistance at the Writing Center.

V. COURSE SCHEDULE and ASSIGNMENTS (SUBJECT TO CHANGE)

Week One:

MONDAY: Money, money, money…and faith?
            Setting the Stage/ Explanation of Themes

TUESDAY: Conceptualizing: Why Is Money Important?
Getz—Front section and appendix (pp. xiii—11)
Cunningham— Front Section and Part #1 (Chapters 1-6)
            1. Conceptualizing: Why Is Money Important?
            2. Impact of Money on Life
            3. Starting off Right: The Godly Steward

4. Wealth Reloaded: A Christian View of Wealth

5. Materialism and Spirituality

6. Needs, Wants and Contentment

Handout booklet—

WEDNESDAY: Perspective of the Godly Steward: Lenses of Understanding

Reading due:

Getz—Part 1

Cunningham— Part #II, Chapters 7-8

7. Refresh: Peering into Eternity

8. Release: Let God Be God

Handout booklet—

THURSDAY: Perspective of The Godly Steward: Key Issues Related to Money and Faith

Reading due:

Getz—Part 2

Cunningham—Part #II, Chapter 9

9. Fidelity: A Fresh Glance

Handout booklet—

FRIDAY: Perspective of The Godly Steward: Continued

Reading due:

Getz—Part 3

Handout booklet—

****Journal 1st review due**

Week Two:

MONDAY: Off/Practice of the Godly Steward

Read and work on your projects

Getz—Part 4 and 5

Cunningham—Part III, Chapters 10-11

10. Honesty: God's Mandate

11. Thrive: The Blessing of Work

Handout booklet—

TUESDAY: Practice of the Godly Steward

Getz—Part 6

Cunningham—Part III, chapter 12-13

           12. Plugging in: The Importance of Counsel

           13. Credit: Danger! Use with Caution

Handout booklet—

WEDNESDAY: Eternal Perspective and Rewards of the Godly Steward

Work Due:

Reading due:

Getz—Part 7

Cunningham—Part III, Chapters 14-15

           14. Store It up: Giving's Big Picture

           15. Growing in Faith and Giving

Handout booklet—

THURSDAY: Eternal Perspective and Rewards of the Godly Steward

Work Due:

Getz—Part 8 and 9

Cunningham—Part III, Chapter 16

           16. Using Your Head While You Live by Faith

Handout booklet—

Journals due

FRIDAY: Wrap up

Work Due:

Papers due—discussions

Post-Questionnaire

Reading report due

VI. READING REPORT

Books

____% of reading complete on time; ____% of reading complete

1. Cunningham, C. E., and Dayton, H., (2006). *Money and Faith: A Practical Theology, first edition*, Crown Financial Ministries, Inc. – Notebook. Due: per schedule.

2. Getz, G., (2004). *Rich in Every Way: Everything the Bible Says About Material Possessions*, Howard Publishing: West Monroe, LA. Per schedule.

3. Schneider, J., (2002). *The Good of Affluence: Seeking God in a Culture of Wealth*, Grand Rapids, MI, William B. Eerdmans.

   Due: per schedule

SUPPLEMENTAL READINGS HANDOUT PACKET

Novak, M., (1991). *Introduction and Theology of Democratic Capitalism*, in The Spirit of Democratic Capitalism, Madison books: New York.

Rodin, Scott, (2000) *Introduction and Docking the Ship*, in Stewards in the Kingdom: A Theology of Life in All its Fullness

Smith, Ian, (1993) *God and Economics*, in God and Culture: Essays in honor of Carl F. H. Henry, ed. D. A. Carson and John Woodbridge. Eerdmans Publishing Co.

Stackhouse, John G., (2000) *Money and Theology in American Evangelicalism*, in More Money, More Ministry: Money and Evangelicals in recent North American history. ed, Eskridge and Knoll, Eerdmans Publishing Co.

Clapp, Rodney, (1998) *The Theology of Consumption and the Consumption of Theology*, in The Consuming Passion: Christianity and the consumer culture, ed Rodney Clapp, InterVarsity Press: Downers Grove.

Myers, David, (1998) *Money and Misery*, in The Consuming Passion: Christianity and the consumer culture, ed Rodney Clapp, InterVarsity Press: Downers Grove.

Resseguie, James, (2004) *Consumption: The Spiritual Life and Possessions*, in Spiritual Landscape: Images of the Spiritual Life in the Gospel of Luke. Hendrickson Publishers: Peabody, MA.

Murchie, David, (1978) *The New Testament View of Wealth Accumulation*, Journal of Evangelical Theological Society.

Foster, Richard, (1988) *The Discipline of Simplicity*, in Celebration of Discipline: The path to spiritual growth. Harper Collins Publishers: New York.

TOPICS

Issler, K. and Moreland, J.P., (2005) Today's confusion about happiness, in *The Lost Virtue of Happiness*, NavPress: Colorado Springs.

Moreland, J.P., (1997) *Ethical Egoism and Biblical Sel-Interest*, in Westminster Theological Journal.

Packer, J.I., (1993) *Lifestyle, leisure, and pleasure*, in God and Culture: Essays in honor of Carl F. H. Henry, ed. D. A. Carson and John Woodbridge. Eerdmans Publishing.

Wuthnow, Robert, (1994) *Faith and Work*, in God and Mammon in America, The Free Press: New York.

Alcorn, Randy, (2003) *Debt: Borrowing and Lending*, in Money, Possessions and Eternity Tyndale House Publishers: Wheaton, IL.

Wuthnow, Robert, (1997) *What Clergy are saying*, in The Crisis of Churches: Spiritual Malaise, Fiscal Woe, Oxford University Press: New York

Miller, Elliot, (2005) *Tithing: Is it New Testament*, Christian Research Institute

Pryor, Austin, (1990) *A Biblical View of Retirement*, Sound Mind Investing.

SECTION TWO: STUDY GUIDE

This section contains study questions that go beyond the "Think About It" sections at the end of each chapter. Your answers to these questions will help you journal what you are learning as they provide a deeper personal or group study of the Scriptures relevant to each chapter.

Chapter 1—Conceptualization: Why Is Money Important?

❑ Key Verse: Luke 12:15 *"Then he said to them, 'watch out! Be on your guard against all forms of greed; a man's life does not consist in the abundance of his possessions.'"*

In what ways do you live as though your life consists only of stuff (example: music, ipods, cars)?

❑ Read and reflect on Luke 12:15 in context.

Isaiah 55:8-9

1. Based on this passage, what can we learn from God's nature that should guide our thinking on the topic of money and possessions?

Luke 16:1-11

2. What do these verses communicate about the importance of managing possessions? What could the New Testament believer understand about Jesus' teaching? Explain.

3. Based on the previous texts, how does handling money affect our fellowship with the Lord?

2 Timothy 3:16-17

1. How does this passage affect your understanding of what you will learn about money in Scripture?

Chapter 2—Impact of Money on Life

❏ Key Verse: Hebrews 13:5 *"Let your character be free from the love of money, being content with what you have; for He Himself has said 'I will never leave you nor forsake you'"* (NAS).

❏ Read, reflect on and respond to the following questions.

Read Hebrews 13:5.

1. What does this not say about money?

2. What do you learn from this passage about the character of God related to our needs?

3. In what way have you allowed money to influence your character?

4. Describe how money has affected your family both positively and negatively.

Read Romans 12:1-2.

1. With the topic of Faith and Money in mind, what is Paul saying about the world and its ways in this passage?

2. In what way are you renewing your mind against our culture's values and perspectives related to money?

3. What practical steps will you take to combat worldly thinking about money?

Chapter 3—Starting off Right: The Godly Steward

❑ Key Verse: 2 Timothy 3:16-17 *"All Scripture is inspired by God and profitable for teaching, for reproof, for correction, for training in righteousness; so that the man of God may be adequate, equipped for every good work"* (NAS).
❑ Read, reflect on and respond to the following questions.

1. Have you considered that Scripture speaks clearly and authoritatively in the area of faith and money? Why or why not?

2. Spend the next 15-30 minutes reflecting on your family background and cultural background in relation to money. How have they influenced your perspectives either positively or negatively in relation to faith and money?

   Family background

   Cultural background

3. List the events, circumstances or training in your life that have shaped your current understanding of money.

4. What, if anything, has hindered your use of Scripture in handling money?

5. What is your current understanding of the term "steward"?

6. How has your thinking changed in light of the definition offered?

7. Theologian Scott Rodin was quoted in the text as saying people make false starts when addressing the issue of faith and money by moving directly to the "how to." Do you agree or disagree? Why?

8. Describe the difficulty of focusing on the "being" versus the "doing" related to faith and money.

9. What quotation was the most meaningful to you? Why?

Chapter 4—Wealth Reloaded: A Christian View of Wealth

❑ Key Verse: *Proverbs 30: 8b-9 "Give me neither poverty nor riches; Feed me with the food that is my portion, That I not be full and deny You and say, 'Who is the Lord?' Or that I not be in want and steal, and profane the name of my God"* (NAS).

❑ Read, reflect on and respond to the following questions.

1. Would you describe your current understanding of money as being good or evil? List at least three reasons for your conclusions.

2. What perspective of faith and money do the authors present in this chapter?

Read Proverbs 30:8b-9.

3. What principles can you glean from this passage?

4. How has this passage influenced your understanding of money's place in your life?

Read Psalm 112.

5. List as many observations about faith and money from this passage as you can.

6. What does the Psalmist say is the key element in prosperity?

7. What principles can be gleaned from this Psalm in relation to faith and money?

8. How can we avoid taking an unbalanced perspective about wealth from this passage?

Read Psalm 49.

9. List your observations from this Psalm in relation to faith and money.

10. Describe the fate of those who place their trust in wealth.

11. Describe what happens to material possessions.

Chapter 5—Materialism and Spirituality

❑ Key Verse: 1 John 2:15 *"Do not love the world nor the things in the world. If anyone loves the world, the love of the Father is not in him"* (NAS).
❑ Read, reflect on and answer the following questions

Read 1 John 2:15-17.

1. What does the text say about the world related to materialism? What does this Scripture say about our devotion?

Read James 4:1-4.

2. What does James say is the reason behind conflict among believers? What can we learn from James about our wants?

Read Colossians 3:1-8.

3. What is Paul saying about earthly things? On what are we to focus? Since we are raised in Christ from our former ways, from what are we to rid ourselves?

Read I Timothy 6:9-10, 17; 2 Timothy 2:4.

4. What do these passages teach us about riches? What happens to those who focus on getting rich?

5. How does money and stuff hinder your response to Christ's will?

Re-read 1 Timothy 6:3-10 and answer the following questions.

6. What is Paul saying about our needs and wants in this passage?

7. What should we strive to gain?

8. What dangers are associated with the desire to get rich?

Chapter 6—Needs, Wants and Contentment

❑ Key verse: 1 Timothy 6:10 *"For the love of money is a root of all sorts of evil, and some by longing for it have wandered away from the faith, and pierced themselves with many a pang"* (NAS).

❑ Read, reflect on and answer the following questions.

Read the entire chapter of 1 Timothy 6 in at least three different Bible translations: NAS, NIV, NET. Spend at least 30 minutes meditating on the chapter, asking God to teach you and open your heart to it.

1. What was your previous understanding of this passage in relation to money?

2. What differences are there in the translations?

3. In about 30 minutes, make as many observations from the text as you can (look for common themes and, terms. Who is the audience? What was Paul's purpose in this section?

4. When you first read the passage, what three observations impressed you the most?

5. What is the connection between false teachers and money?

6. List at least three practical applications for life from this passage.

Chapter 7—Refresh: Peering into Eternity

❏ Key Verse: Mark 8:36 *"For what does it profit a man to gain the whole world and forfeit his soul?"* (NAS)

❏ In light of the brevity of life, read and reflect on the following passages and answer the questions.

1 Chronicles 29:15

1. In what way might being a sojourner influence the accumulation of more things and money?

2. What challenges do you have that hinder you from living like a sojourner on earth?

3. Identify at least three strategies you will implement to minimize accumulating more baggage (possessions) while on earth.

Psalm 39:4-7; Psalm 103:13-16; Psalm 90:10, 12

4. Occasionally people live as if there is no tomorrow. Given these passages, how might you reorient yourself to the fact that life is short in comparison to eternity?

5. List at least three specific strategies.

Ecclesiastes 12:13-14

While it is clear from the discussion in Chapter 7 that those who have accepted Jesus Christ as their Savior will spend eternity with God, our earthly works will still be judged.

7. How might this fact translate into a renewed perspective on how you use God's money? List several examples that apply to you personally.

Our Test: *1 Corinthians 3:11-15 and 2 Corinthians 5:9-10*

These two passages identify the quality of what a person has done on earth; what we do on earth will be tested for its ultimate value. Take time now to assess how well you are doing on this test.

8. What have you learned from your assessment?

Our Hope: *2 Corinthians 4:18 and 2 Peter 3:10-13*

9. Knowing that what exists today in the material world will not remain, and that what is important are things "not seen" which are "eternal," describe what this hope means to the believer.

10. Think about the "new heaven" and "new earth." What hope does this fact bring you?

11. Follow up on Peter's rhetorical question in verse 2 Peter 3:11, "what sort of people ought you to be in holy conduct and godliness?" Describe how the believer should act.

Our Citizenship: *Philippians 3:20 and 1 Peter 2:11*

12. Being a citizen of the United States of America is a popular topic recently. The Christian's citizenship, however, is really heaven. As a citizen of heaven, how should one live in relation to money and things?

13. What steps can be made to exemplify your eternal citizenship regarding how you use God's resources?

Chapter 8—Release: Let God Be God

❑ Key Verse: 1 Chronicles 29:11-12 *"Everything in the heavens and earth is yours, O Lord, and this is your kingdom. We adore you as being in control of everything. Riches and honor come from you alone and you are the ruler of all mankind. Your hand controls power and might and it is at your discretion that men are made great and given strength"* (TLB).

❑ **Read and reflect** on your attitude of ownership toward your possessions.

Psalm 24:1 and 1 Corinthians 10:26

1. What do these passages teach about the ownership of your possessions?

2. Do you consistently recognize the true owner of those possessions? Give two practical suggestions to help recognize God's ownership.

1 Chronicles 29:11-12 and *Psalm 135:6*

3. What do these verses say about the Lord's control of circumstances?

Proverbs 21:1

4. What do these passages tell you about the Lord's control of people?

Genesis 45:4-8:

5. Why is it important to realize that God controls and uses even difficult circumstances for good in the life of a godly person?

6. How does this perspective affect you today?

Philippians 4

7. What has the Lord promised about meeting your needs?

8. Give an example from the Bible of the Lord providing for someone's needs in a supernatural way.

Application: Taking your previous answers into consideration, answer these two questions:

9. How does this apply to you today? Be specific and practical.

10. How will you incorporate this perspective in your ministry? Be specific and practical.

Chapter 9—Fidelity: A Fresh Glance

❏ **Key Verse:** 1 Corinthians 4:2 *"Moreover, it is required of stewards that one be found trustworthy"* (NAS).
❏ Read and reflect on the passages below and answer the following questions.

Genesis 1:26; Psalm 8:4-6; 1 Corinthians 4:2
1. Based on these passages, define a steward in your own terms.

2. Regardless of what is entrusted, what is required of a steward?

Matthew 6:19-34 (Read in context.)
3. What theme is addressed in this passage?

4. What principles can be learned about handling our finances and life from this passage?

Luke 12:13-21

5. How does verse 15 affect the average Christian today?

6. Why did Jesus call the young man a fool?

Luke 16:1-13

7. Why did the master remove the steward in this passage?

8. What principle can be observed in verse 10?

9. How would you apply the principles in this passage to your life today?

10. In your own words, contrast your life with eternity.

Chapter 10—Honesty: God's Mandate

❏ Key Verse: Leviticus 19:11 *"You shall not steal, nor deal falsely, nor lie to one another"* (NAS).
❏ Read and interact with the following verses.

1. What can be learned from these individual passages related to honesty?
    a. *Deuteronomy 25:13-16*

    b. *Leviticus 19:11-13*

    c. *Ephesians 4:25*

    d. *1 Peter 1:15-16*

2. Are you consistently honest in the smallest detail? If not, how do you propose to change?

3. What are two factors that motivate or influence us to act dishonestly?

4. How do these principles apply to you?

Proverbs 14:2 and Proverbs 26:28
5. What do you learn about honesty from these passages?

Romans 13:9-10
6. What does this passage tell us about honesty?

Read Exodus 18:21-22, Psalm 15:1-5, Proverbs 12:22 and 20:7, Isaiah 33:15-16, Ephesians 3:9, and 1 Thessalonians 4:7.

7. What can we learn about honesty from these passages?

8. Why is honesty so overlooked as an indication of spiritual health in our culture?

Chapter 11—Thrive: The Blessing of Work

❏ Key Verse: Colossians 3:23-24 *"Whatever you do, do your work heartily, as for the Lord rather than for men. . . . It is the Lord Christ whom you serve"* (NAS).
❏ Read and interact with the following verses.

Genesis 2:15.

1. Why is it important to recognize that the Lord created work before sin entered the world?

Genesis 3:17-19.

2. What was the consequence of sin on work?

2 Thessalonians 3:10-12.

3. What do these passages say to you about work?

Genesis 39:2-5, Exodus 35:30-35, Exodus 36:1-2, and Psalm 75:6-7.

4. What do these verses tell us about the Lord's involvement in our work?

Genesis 39:2-5—

Exodus 35:30-35—

Exodus 36:1-2—

Psalm 75:6-7—

5. How do these truths differ from the way most people view work? How will this perspective affect your work?

Ephesians 6:5-9, Colossians 3:22-25, and *1 Peter 2:18.*

6. What responsibilities do the employer and employee have according to these verses?

Employee responsibilities:

Employer responsibilities:

7. For whom do you really work? How will this understanding change your work performance?

Proverbs 6:6-11, Proverbs 18:9, and *2 Thessalonians 3:7-9*

8. What does the Lord say about working hard?

9. Do you work hard? If not, describe what steps you will take to improve your work habits.

2 Corinthians 6:14-18

10. Can you give some examples from the Bible of people who retired?

11. How does retirement, as it is practiced in our culture, differ from what is communicated in Scripture?

Chapter 12—Plugging in: The Importance of Counsel

❑ Key Verse: *"The way of a fool is right in his own eyes, but a wise man is he who listens to counsel"* (Proverbs 12:15, NAS).
❑ Read, reflect on and answer the questions below.

Exodus 18:17-27 and Joshua 9
1. What principles about seeking counsel can be observed in these passages?

Psalm 16:7, 32:8, 119:98-100, Proverbs 1:1-3, 8-9, 11:14, 12:15, Ecclesiastes 4:9-12, 2 Timothy 3:16-17, Hebrews 4:12
2. What do we learn about counsel from these passages?

Proverbs 12:15, 13:10, and 15:22
3. What hinders you from seeking counsel?

Psalm 16:7 and 32:8

4. Does the Lord actively counsel His children? How?

Psalm 106:13-15

5. Have you ever suffered for not seeking the Lord's counsel? If so, describe what happened.

Psalm 119:24 and 105, **2 Timothy 3:16-17,** and *Hebrews 4:12*

6. Should the Bible also serve as your counselor? Why?

7. What prevents your consistency in studying the Bible for counsel in life?

Proverbs 1:8-9

8. Who should be among your counselors?

Psalm 1:1-3, Proverbs 12:5

9. Whom should you avoid as a counselor? What is your definition of a wicked person?

10. In what circumstance(s) would seeking the input of a person who does not know Christ be appropriate?

Chapter 13—Credit: Danger! Use with Caution

❑ Key Verse: Romans 13:8 *"Owe nothing to anyone except to love one another"* (NAS).

❑ Read, reflect on and answer the questions below.

Identify principles that deal with debt.

New Testament

Matthew 6:24, Luke 16:10-12, Romans 12:1-2, 1 John 2:15-17

Romans 13:7-8

1 Corinthians 7:23

1. What can be gleaned from these passages regarding debt?

Identify principles that deal with debt.

Old Testament

Proverbs 1:13-15, 3:27-28

Exodus 22:25

Leviticus 25:36-38

Deuteronomy 15:1-13; 28:12

Psalm 37:21

2. What do these verses say about debt repayment?

2 Kings 4:1-7

3. What principles regarding getting out of debt can you identify from this passage?

4. Can you apply any of these principles to your present situation? How?

Proverbs 22:26-27 and Proverbs 17:18

5. What does the Bible say about cosigning (striking hands, surety)?

Proverbs 22:26-27—

Proverbs 17:18—

Proverbs 6:1-5

6. If someone has cosigned, what should he or she attempt to do?

Chapter 14—Store It up: Giving's Big Picture

❏ **Key Verse:** Acts 20:35 *"Remember the words of the Lord Jesus, that He Himself said, 'It is more blessed to give than to receive'"* (NAS).

❏ Read, reflect on and answer the questions below:

Matthew 23:23, 1 Corinthians 13:3, and 2 Corinthians 9:7

1. What do these passages communicate about the importance of the proper attitude in giving?

Matthew 23:23—

1 Corinthians 13:3—

2 Corinthians 9:7—

2. How can a person develop the proper attitude in giving?

3. Describe your attitude in giving.

Acts 20:35

4. How does this principle from God's perspective differ from the way most people view giving?

5. List the benefits for the giver that are found in each of the following passages:

Proverbs 11:24-25—

Matthew 6:20—

Luke 12:34—

1 Timothy 6:18-19—

Malachi 3:8-10

6. What did Malachi say about the tithe in this passage?

2 Corinthians 8:1-5

7. Identify three principles from this passage that should influence how much you give.

8. What timeless truth can be applied from the New Testament's teaching regarding the tithe and giving?

9. Prayerfully (with your spouse if you are married) seek the Lord's guidance to determine how much you should give. You will not be asked to disclose the amount.

Numbers 18:8-10, 24, **Galatians 6:6, and** *1 Timothy 5:17-18*

10. What do these verses communicate about financially supporting your church and those who teach the Scriptures?

Numbers 18:8-10, 24—

Galatians 6:6—

1 Timothy 5:17-18—

Galatians 2:9-10

11. What does this passage communicate about giving to the poor?

12. Are you currently giving to the needy? If not, what is hindering you?

Chapter 16—Using Your Head While You Live by Faith

❑ Key Verse: Proverbs 21:20 *"The wise man saves for the future, but the foolish man spends whatever he gets"* (TLB).

❑ Read, reflect on and answer the questions below.

Genesis 41:34-36, **Proverbs 21:20, and** *Proverbs 30:24-25*

1. What do these passages say about savings?

2. If you are not yet saving, how do you propose to begin?

Luke 12:16-21, 34

3. Why did the Lord call the rich man a fool?

4. According to this parable, why is it scripturally permissible to save only when you are also giving?

1 Timothy 5:8

5. What is a scripturally acceptable goal for saving?

1 Timothy 6:9

6. What is a scripturally unacceptable reason for saving?

1 Timothy 6:9-10

7. According to this verse, why is it dangerous to want to get rich? Do you have a desire to get rich?

1 Timothy 6:11

8. What should you do if you have the desire to get rich?

Proverbs 21:5, Proverbs 24:27, Proverbs 27:23-24, Ecclesiastes 3:1, Ecclesiastes 11:2, and Isaiah 48:17-18

9. What investment principle(s) can be learned from each of these verses, and how will you apply each principle to your life?

Genesis 24:35-36, Proverbs 13:22, and *2 Corinthians 12:14*

10. Should parents attempt to leave a material inheritance to their children?

11. How do you plan to implement this principle?

Proverbs 20:21 and *Galatians 4:1-2*

12. What caution should a parent exercise?

Gambling is defined as *betting and playing games of chance for money.* Some of today's most common forms of gambling are casino wagering, betting on sporting events, horse and dog races, and state-run lotteries.

13. What are some of the motivations for gambling?

14. Do these motives please the Lord? Why?

Proverbs 28:20, 22

15. How does gambling contradict the scriptural principles of working diligently and being a faithful steward of the Lord's possessions?

Summary Questions

❏ Key Verse: James 1: 22 *"But prove yourselves as doers of the word, and not merely hearers who delude themselves"* (NAS).

❏ Read, reflect on and answer the questions below.

Deuteronomy 30:15-16, Joshua 1:8, and *Hebrews 11:36-4.*

1. What does each of these passages communicate about financial prosperity for the believer?

Deuteronomy 30:15-16—

Joshua 1:8—

Hebrews 11:36-40—

Reflect on the life of Job in Job chapter 1, Joseph in Genesis Chapters 37-47, and Paul in Philippians 4.

2. Did they experience periods of financial abundance as well as periods of financial poverty?

3. Was their poverty a result of sin or lack of faith?

4. Should all Christians expect to always prosper financially? Why?

Psalm 73:1-20

5. What does this passage say about the prosperity of the wicked?

Philippians 4:11-13 and 1 Timothy 6:6-8

6. What do these passages say about contentment?

Philippians 4:11-13 —

1 Timothy 6:6-8 —

7. How does our culture discourage contentment?

8. How do you propose to practice contentment?

Matthew 22:17-21 and Romans 13:1-7

9. Does the Lord require us to pay taxes to the government? Why?

James 2:1-9

10. What does Scripture say about partiality (showing favoritism)?

11. Are you guilty of partiality based on a person's financial, educational, or social status?

Romans 12:16 and Philippians 2:3

12. How do you plan to overcome partiality?

Acts 4:32-37 and 1 Thessalonians 4:11-12

13. What do these passages communicate about lifestyle?

14. How do the following factors influence your present spending and lifestyle?

Comparing your lifestyle with that of friends and other people —

Television, magazines, catalogs, and other advertisements—

Your study of the Bible—

Your commitment to Christ and to things important to Him—

15. Do you sense that the Lord would have you change spending habits or your standard of living?

If so, in what way?

Deuteronomy 6:6-7, Proverbs 22:6, **and** *Ephesians 6:4*

16. According to these passages, who is responsible for teaching children how to handle money from a biblical perspective?

17. Stop and reflect for a few minutes. Describe how well you were prepared to manage money when you first left home as a young person.

18. Describe how you would train children to budget, give, save and spend wisely.

Summary continued: Next step questions

19. State three practical steps you will take to implement what you have learned in this course over the next year.

20. List the people who will provide moral and spiritual support regarding your goals.

    a.

    b.

    c.

21. Describe below the top three principles you gained from this course and what you will do to maintain them.

22. Describe two ways your relationship with Jesus Christ has become more intimate since you have taken this course.

23. List three ways you will seek to influence your peers with what you have learned and experienced while taking this course.

PRACTICAL APPLICATIONS

Monthly Spending Plan - A

Month _____ Year _____

CATEGORY	INCOME	TITHE/GIVING	TAXES	HOUSING	FOOD	TRANSPORTATION	INSURANCE
Allocated Amount	$	$	$	$	$	$	$
Date							
1							
2							
3							
4							
5							
6							
7							
8							
9							
10							
11							
12							
13							
14							
15							
This Month Subtotal	$	$	$	$	$	$	$
16							
17							
18							
19							
20							
21							
22							
23							
24							
25							
26							
27							
28							
29							
30							
31							
This Month Total	$	$	$	$	$	$	$
This Month Surplus/Deficit	$	$	$	$	$	$	$
Year to Date Spending Plan	$	$	$	$	$	$	$
Year to Date Total	$	$	$	$	$	$	$
Year to Date Surplus/Deficit	$	$	$	$	$	$	$

PLAN SUMMARY

This Month		Previous Month/Year to Date		Year to Date
Total Income $_____		Total Income $_____		Total Income $_____
Minus Total Expenses $_____	**+**	Minus Total Expenses $_____	**=**	Minus Total Expenses $_____
Equals Surplus/Deficit $_____		Equals Surplus/Deficit $_____		Equals Surplus/Deficit $_____

Monthly Spending Plan - B

Month _____ Year _____

CATEGORY	DEBTS	ENT/REC	CLOTHING	SAVINGS	MEDICAL/DENTAL	MISCELLANEOUS	INVESTMENTS	SCHOOL/CHILD CARE
Allocated Amount	$	$	$	$	$	$	$	$
Date								
1								
2								
3								
4								
5								
6								
7								
8								
9								
10								
11								
12								
13								
14								
15								
This Month Subtotal	$	$	$	$	$	$	$	$
16								
17								
18								
19								
20								
21								
22								
23								
24								
25								
26								
27								
28								
29								
30								
31								
This Month Total	$	$	$	$	$	$	$	$
This Month Surplus/Deficit	$	$	$	$	$	$	$	$
Year to Date Spending Plan	$	$	$	$	$	$	$	$
Year to Date Total	$	$	$	$	$	$	$	$
Year to Date Surplus/Deficit	$	$	$	$	$	$	$	$

Quit Claim Deed

This Quit Claim Deed, Made the _____ day of _____

From: _____

To: The Lord

I (we) hereby transfer to the Lord the ownership of the following:

Witnesses who hold me (us) accountable
in the recognition of the Lord's ownership:

_____

_____

_____

Stewards of the possessions above:

_____

_____

This instrument is not a binding legal document and cannot be used to transfer property.

Personal Financial Statement

Date _____

Assets (Present market value)

Cash on hand/Checking account	$ _____
Savings	_____
Stocks and bonds	_____
Cash value of life insurance	_____
Coins	_____
Home	_____
Other real estate	_____
Mortgages/Notes receivable	_____
Business valuation	_____
Automobiles	_____
Furniture	_____
Jewelry	_____
Other personal property	_____
Pension/Retirement	_____
Other Assets	_____

Total Assets $ _____

Liabilities (Current amount owed)

Credit card debt	$ _____
Automobile loans	_____
Home mortgages	_____
Personal debt to relatives	_____
Business loans	_____
Educational loans	_____
Medical/Other past due bills	_____
Life insurance loans	_____
Bank loans	_____
Other debts and loans	_____

Total Liabilities $ _____

Net Worth (Total assets minus total liabilities) $ _____

Life Goals - A

Date _____

Giving Goals

Would like to give _____ percent of my income.

Would like to increase my giving by _____ percent each year.

Other giving goals: _____

_____

Debt Repayment Goals

Would like to pay off the following debts first:

Creditor	Amount
_____	_____
_____	_____
_____	_____

Educational Goals

Would like to fund the following education:

Person	School	Annual cost	Total cost
_____	_____	_____	_____
_____	_____	_____	_____
_____	_____	_____	_____
_____	_____	_____	_____

Other educational goals: _____

Lifestyle Goals

Would like to make these major purchases: (home, automobile, travel, appliances)

Item	Amount
_____	_____
_____	_____
_____	_____
_____	_____

Would like to achieve the following annual income: _____

Life Goals - B

Date _____

Savings and Investment Goals

Would like to save _____ percent of my income.

Other savings goals: _____

_____

Would like to make the following investments: Amount

_____   _____

_____   _____

_____   _____

_____   _____

Would like to provide my/our heirs with the following: _____

_____

Starting a Business

Would like to invest in or begin my/our own business: _____

_____

_____

Describe your standard of living that you sense would please the Lord.

_____

_____

_____

_____

_____

_____

_____

_____

_____

_____

277

Debt List

Date _____

Creditor	Describe What Was Purchased	Monthly Payments	Balance Due	Scheduled Pay-Off Date	Interest Rate	Payments Past Due
Wells Fargo	Student loan	n/a	24,000	n/a	7.9%	—
"	"	n/a	24,000	n/a	7.9%	—
Wells Fargo	credit card	$50.00	$3,238.62	3 yrs	12%	—
Totals						

Auto Loans	Monthly Payments	Balance Due	Scheduled Pay-Off Date	Interest Rate	Payments Past Due
Totals					

Home Mortgages	Monthly Payments	Balance Due	Scheduled Pay-Off Date	Interest Rate	Payments Past Due
Totals					

Business/Investment Debt	Monthly Payments	Balance Due	Scheduled Pay-Off Date	Interest Rate	Payments Past Due
Totals					

Biggers / Smalls Analysis:

When dealing with a purchase rather than an existing loan, the analysis of the Biggers and Smalls reveals another way to move more quickly toward financial freedom. The question is whether to buy your dream house as soon as possible, or buy something less expensive and move into the dream house later.

This analysis involves two couples, the Biggers and the Smalls. The Biggers are the typical homebuyers who get the biggest house they can afford right away. The Smalls are disciplined home buyers who decide they can live in a smaller home for a few years to save a significant sum of money. Both couples have $60,000 to spend as a down payment. They both desire to own a house that costs $300,000.

Biggers / Smalls

The Biggers go ahead and buy their $300,000 house with a 6 percent, 30-year mortgage. Their monthly payment is $1,439 and at the end of their mortgage they will have paid a total of $578,012 for the house.	The Smalls decide that they can live in a smaller home for a while in a less expensive neighborhood. They buy a house for $180,000 with a 5 percent, 7-year mortgage. Their monthly payment is $1,696 and at the end of this mortgage, they will have paid a total of $202,470 for this house.

Note that the Smalls get a lower interest rate on their mortgage because the term is shorter. The shorter term will require extra discipline in their budget to pay the extra $257 per month versus the Biggers, but the Smalls have a goal and are working toward it. A longer-term mortgage will have a higher interest rate, but it can still be treated like a seven-year loan by making large enough payments each month—as illustrated in the House Pay-down example. There is also some additional safety with a longer-term mortgage in the event of lean times, since the extra principal payments each month would be optional rather than required.

At the end of the first 7 years, the Biggers are still making payments on their 30-year mortgage.	At the end of the first 7 years, the Smalls sell their newly debt-free house and buy the house next door to the Biggers. They apply the total value of the old house ($180,000) as a down payment on their new one ($300,000). Once again, they do a 7-year loan at 5 percent and their payments are still $1,696.

We understand that interest rates and house prices change during a span of seven years. However, they could change in favor of the Smalls. In addition, the savings illustrated here are so large that the changes in house prices and interest rates are likely to be insignificant compared to the savings.

Continued on next page

At the end of the 14 years, the Biggers are still making payments on their 30-year mortgage. In fact, they are just now making reasonable principal payments. The 169th payment (the first payment in the 15th year of their loan) is comprised of $552 of principal and $887 of interest).

The Smalls now have a debt-free home which cost them $344,940 overall. However, the good news doesn't stop there. They are so used to making payments of $1,696, that they start making those payments into an investment earning 4 percent. When the Biggers pay off their house (16 years later), the Smalls have over $455,000 in the bank.

Overall, both families have the debt-free home of their dreams, but the Smalls got there sooner and have a significant amount of money in the bank from their efforts.

Percentage Guide

GROSS INCOME	$25,000	35,000	45,000	55,000	85,000	115,000
1. Tithe/Giving	10%	10%	10%	10%	10%	10%
2. Taxes[1]	*2.7%	11.2%	14.8%	17.2%	23.5	26.3%
NET SPENDABLE	**$21,825**	**27,580**	**33,840**	**40,040**	**58,475**	**73,255**
3. Housing	39%	36%	32%	30%	30%	29%
4. Food	15%	12%	13%	12%	11%	11%
5. Transportation	15%	12%	13%	14%	13%	13%
6. Insurance	5%	5%	5%	5%	5%	5%
7. Debts	5%	5%	5%	5%	5%	5%
8. Entertainment/ Recreation	3%	5%	5%	7%	7%	8%
9. Clothing	4%	5%	5%	6%	7%	7%
10. Savings	5%	5%	5%	5%	5%	5%
11. Medical / Dental	5%	6%	6%	5%	5%	5%
12. Miscellaneous	4%	4%	6%	6%	7%	7%
13. Investments[2]	—	5%	5%	5%	5%	5%
If you have school/child care expenses, these percentages must be deducted from other categories.						
14. School/Child Care[3]	8%	6%	5%	5%	5%	5%

[1] Guideline percentages for tax category include taxes for Social Security, federal, and a small estimated amount for state, based on 2002 rates. The tax code changes regularly. Please be sure to insert your actual tax into this category.

[2] This category is used for long-term investment planning, such as college education or retirement.

[3] This category is added as a guide only. If you have this expense, the percentage shown must be deducted from other budget categories.

* In some cases earned income credit will apply. It may be possible to increase the number of deductions to lessen the amount of tax paid per month. Review the last tax return for specific information.

Note: The Percentage Guide is based on a married couple with two children.

Single adults should adjust the Percentage Guide as follows: Food 10-14%, Transportation 12-15%, Insurance 4%, Debts 5%, Entertainment/Recreation 6-8%, Clothing 5-7%, Savings 5-7%, Medical/Dental 5%, Miscellaneous 4-7%, Investments 5%, and School 0-7%.

Housing remains the same unless you have roommates. If you have roommates, reduce Housing to 25% and add the Housing surplus to the other categories.

Single parents should adjust the Percentage Guide as follows: Food 12-14%, Transportation 12-14%, Insurance 3-4%, Entertainment/Recreation 3-4%, Clothing 5-6%, and Miscellaneous 3-4%. The Percentage Guides for the other categories will remain the same.

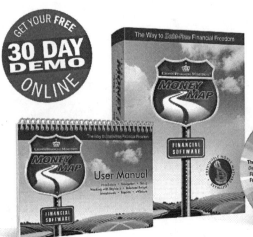